WRITING BLACKNESS

WRITING
BLACKNESS

John Edgar Wideman's Art
and Experimentation

JAMES W. COLEMAN

LOUISIANA STATE UNIVERSITY PRESS
BATON ROUGE

Published by Louisiana State University Press
Copyright © 2010 by Louisiana State University Press
All rights reserved
Manufactured in the United States of America
First printing

Designer: Michelle A. Neustrom
Typeface: Whitman, text
Printer: McNaughton & Gunn, Inc.
Binder: John H. Dekker & Sons

Library of Congress Cataloging-in-Publication Data

Coleman, James W. (James Wilmouth), 1946–
  Writing blackness : John Edgar Wideman's art and experimentation /
James W. Coleman.
     p. cm.
  Includes bibliographical references and index.
  ISBN 978-0-8071-3644-7 (cloth : alk. paper) 1. Wideman, John Edgar—
Criticism and interpretation. 2. African Americans in literature. I. Title.
  PS3573.I26Z625 2010
  813'.54—dc22
                                                    2009049831

The paper in this book meets the guidelines for permanence and
durability of the Committee on Production Guidelines for Book
Longevity of the Council on Library Resources. ⊗

Once again, for my sons, Jay and Lee Coleman

CONTENTS

PREFACE

One of the most shocking and frustrating things that I have ever heard in the classroom is the recent statement by a graduate student that John Edgar Wideman's *The Cattle Killing* (1996) is "amateurish." The student's evaluation was apparently based on the overall difficulty of the densely structured work. Similarly, a fellow professor who started but did not finish reading this same Wideman novel commented, "I don't understand what he is doing." It was interesting that the professor, who seemed to blame Wideman for this lack of understanding, gave up the attempt to understand instead of accepting the challenge of continuing to read the novel. Far too few advanced academics read Wideman's works, all of which are difficult, although not all are as difficult as *The Cattle Killing.* Among my undergraduate students, almost no one raises a hand when I ask, "Who has read anything by John Edgar Wideman?" Obviously, Wideman enjoys critical acclaim because of a dedicated group of scholars who study his work and others who appreciate very good, unconventional writing, but he does not attract anything close to the number of serious readers that he deserves. I want this study to bring more readers to Wideman. Although it may not be realistic to expect to reach a broad audience of general readers, I hope this straightforward analysis of the structures and themes of Wideman's writing will make it more accessible to graduate students, professors, and the small number of general readers interested in engaging Wideman's always experimental, difficult, very rich works.

Along these lines, I have organized my analysis around related interpretations of individual texts that connect each one to the overall development of the body of work. By tracing a thematic and formal evolution throughout Wideman's works, I try to make them more readable and understandable, hopefully opening the writing up to readers so that they can interpret it in additional ways.

* * *

John Edgar Wideman was born in Washington, D.C., on June 16, 1941, but grew up in Pittsburgh, living first in the economically impoverished black Homewood community and then in the predominantly white, upper-middle-class Shadyside area, where he attended Peabody High School. At Peabody, it started to become clear that Wideman was a remarkable person. He showed almost equal talent in athletics and academics, becoming captain of the basketball team and class valedictorian. In 1959, he was awarded a scholarship to attend the University of Pennsylvania, where he achieved all–Ivy League status in basketball and Phi Beta Kappa membership. Then, in 1963, he and J. Stanley Sanders of Whittier College in Whittier, California, won Rhodes scholarships and went to Oxford University. Along with Sanders, Wideman became one of the first three blacks to win this most prestigious of prizes, the only black Rhodes scholar before that time being Alain Locke in 1905. Wideman returned from Oxford to teach at the University of Pennsylvania and to found and direct its Afro-American Studies program. He later taught at the University of Wyoming and the University of Massachusetts, Amherst, and now teaches at Brown University. Wideman published his first novel in 1967, and has since published nine additional novels, four collections of short stories, and four books that I call "auto/biographies" because, as I show in chapter 1, they combine two genres. He has won the PEN/Faulkner Award twice, has been nominated twice for the National Book Award, and has received the MacArthur Fellowship.

Wideman has ruminated about the more complex aspects of his personal life in interviews and other public media and, in greater depth, in fiction related to his life and in his auto/biographies. Wideman's later fiction and his auto/biographies concern endeavors and occurrences that are largely factual. Among these, the most prominent are his struggle to become a writer who puts African American culture, history, and perspective in the foreground; the personal attempt to return to his black roots that accompanied his artistic struggle; and his experiences of personal tragedy. In his first three novels, European and American white writers are his main influences. African American life, while very much a part of this early fiction, is in many ways secondary to white culture, white experience, and themes and writing techniques taken from white writers.

Starting in about 1973, however, Wideman began an effort to make African American life and culture central to his work as he attempted to renew ties both to his family and to Homewood, his childhood community in Pittsburgh. In 1976, his brother Robert was sentenced to life in prison for robbery and murder, and in 1986, his youngest son, Jacob, also confessed to murder and received a life sentence. Wideman has talked about these tragedies and written about them in his auto/biographies and fiction.

Writing about the personal has become a primary aspect of Wideman's quest to center black reality in his work and of his overall development as an experimental writer. About his use of the personal and intimate in his fiction and auto/biographies, Wideman said: "I write about the most intimate, the most personal events in my life, but the fun or the privilege of the artist is that through transformation, through the use of a medium, like language, everything becomes coded, and the reader no matter how astute or how familiar with the writer or the writer's life, can't really decode the real life from the fictional life" (Rowell 97–98). The auto/biographies allow Wideman to examine and analyze his life in a fictionalized form that protects his privacy and that of his family and friends. Because he always mixes fiction with the factual in the auto/biographies as well as the novels and short stories, readers cannot expect to get a clear sense from his writing of what really happened. Readers can know only the stories, not the truth or the reality.

As the analyses of chapter 1 demonstrate, Wideman uses similar techniques whether writing fiction or auto/biography. When asked if he has noted any difference between the fictional and the auto/biographical accounts of his personal life, he responded: "I don't think there is much difference. Any reality, any creative reality depends upon a lot of arbitrary assumptions and stylizations and some frame, some ideological frame that a person imposes on their experience" (Silverblatt, "John Edgar Wideman" 120). This means that, in Wideman's writing, real life receives fictional shaping in auto/biography, and that both his fiction and his auto/biographies are artistic productions of the creative imagination. In the first two auto/biographies, *Brothers and Keepers* (1984) and *Fatheralong: A Meditation on Fathers and Sons, Race and Society* (1994), the characters and events may seem more grounded in reality than in the fictive space of the novels—and they are, in fact, based more on real life. In the novels, the reality of Wideman's life is integrated into the fiction, thus making reality indistinguishable from fiction. But while the first two auto/biographies seem more clearly fact-based, it is difficult to make any distinctions between the novels and *Hoop Roots* (2001), the third auto/biography, as far as fictional content is concerned, since *Hoop Roots* depends upon and emphasizes fictional technique as well. The fourth auto/biography, *The Island: Martinique* (2003), is apparently in part a travel journal that records daily activities, but overall its content and technique are still highly fictional. *Hoop Roots* and *The Island: Martinique* evolve toward a greater representation of the very complex fictional techniques and structural practices of the writer/character in the auto/biographies, John Wideman. Just as important, as is true in much of the fiction, writing and storytelling relating to the concept of race and to racism in the lives of John, his family, and African Americans generally are always themes in the auto/biographies.

Wideman has a large body of experimental work. In addition to the auto/biographies, he has written the novels *A Glance Away* (1967), *Hurry Home* (1970), *The Lynchers* (1973), *Hiding Place* (1981), *Sent for You Yesterday* (1983), *Reuben* (1987), *Philadelphia Fire* (1990), *The Cattle Killing* (1996), *Two Cities* (1998), and *Fanon* (2008). His collections of short stories are *Damballah* (1981), *Fever* (1989), *The Stories of John Edgar Wideman* (1992), and *God's Gym* (2005). In the first chapter of this study, I analyze the overall formal and thematic development of Wideman's auto/biographies. In the four chapters that follow, I turn to the development of most of the fiction.

WRITING BLACKNESS

Brothers and Keepers, Fatheralong, Hoop Roots, and The Island: Martinique

THE FICTIONALIZED AUTO/BIOGRAPHIES

The voice of the narrator, John Wideman, in *Brothers and Keepers* (1984) is personal and private as he portrays a cast of real-life characters from his family and community in the process of telling the tragic story of the incarceration of his brother Robert and their estrangement.[1] Wideman does not make a clear distinction between fiction and auto/biography,[2] and, although *Brothers and Keepers* is fictionalized like the other auto/biographies, the central story of the incarceration of Robert Wideman is true. The text is an "auto/biography" because, like the other three works I include under this rubric, Wideman focuses as much on the stories of other people in the past and the present, particularly family and community people, as he does on his own.

I am indebted to Heather Andrade for her use of the term "auto/biographical" with regard to Wideman's works. In describing what happens in *Brothers and Keepers*, she helps to make my point: "[I]t is not enough for Wideman to simply listen to [his brother as he tells his story] . . . . Wideman must also recognize that through [listening to his brother] he can find his own story. He lives [within his brother's story] inasmuch as [his brother] lives within his own. . . . [T]he story is no longer simply [the brother's], or Wideman's, or anyone's—the story belongs to the community" ("Mosaic Memory" 361). *Brothers and Keepers* purports to be a biography of Wideman's brother Robby more clearly than the other three auto/biographies purport to be biographical, but what Andrade says applies to all four. Wideman's own reflections on this subject in fiction, auto/biography, and interviews show that he would concur with Andrade; he is always writing the story of his own life, which is inseparable from the story of family and community in the past and present. This may be implicitly true for anyone writing an autobiography, but the difference in Wideman's works is that this conception of auto/biography is a consciously integral part of his creed.

Brothers and Keepers tries to find the complex truth that underlies the brothers' apparently intrinsic differences and their divergent lives, one being a very successful professor and writer and the other a felon. It is useful, when examining the structure of this work, to recall what Wideman said about using fictional techniques in auto/biography to fictionalize real people and events. *Brothers and Keepers* consists of fragmented scenes that shift rapidly and a fragmented voice that jumps from one thing to another as in a Wideman novel. The structure represents the complex, nonlinear, multidimensional reality encompassing Wideman, his brother, their family, and the community that has brought them to where they are. By the end, John gives the voice and formal construction of the story to Robby to tell it and write it from his perspective, symbolically making him the author. Through this narrative device, structure conflates with theme as the brothers, the family, and the community come together with Robby by accepting his version of the story as the central one that is sympathetically shared by all, freeing him from alienation, if not jail.

One can trace how this conflation of theme and structure develops from early in the first section, entitled "Visits," where John, exploring the reasons for the book and the narrative process, writes: "I continued to feel caged by my bewilderment, by my inability to see clearly, accurately, not only the last visit with my brother, but the whole long skein of our lives together and apart. So this book. This attempt to break out, to knock down the walls" (18). Being a writer, John naturally chooses to write a book to help him understand.[3] He also contemplates the story of Robby, himself, and the community as a complex, nonlinear, multidimensional reality:

> You never know exactly when something begins. The more you delve and backtrack and think, the more it becomes clear that nothing has a discrete, independent history; people and events take shape not in orderly, chronological sequence but in relation to other forces and events, tangled skeins of necessity and interdependence and chance that after all could have produced only one result: what is. The intertwining strands of DNA that determine a creature's genetic predispositions might serve as model for this complexity, but the double helix, bristling with myriad possibilities,

is not mysterious enough. The usual notion of time, of one thing happening first and opening the way for another and another, becomes useless pretty quickly when I try to isolate the shape of your life from the rest of us, when I try to retrace your steps and discover precisely where and when you started to go bad. (19)

He implies that he must write a story with "multiple shifts in narration, movement between past/present/future . . . [and] multiple beginnings" (Andrade, "Mosaic Memory" 364).

Given the "whole long skein" of relevant personal experience, family background, and community history, the narrator realizes that he should focus on and deal honestly with himself before he can determine where Robby "started to go bad." He begins by asking himself what happened and how he changed when he left Robby and the community. Apparently, adapting to the white world beyond Homewood forced the narrator to turn into a chameleon that no one could know, which would certainly alienate him from Robby and others: "My motives remain suspect. A potential for treachery remains deep inside the core. I can blend with my surroundings, become invisible" (34). This honest critique of the self is only a start.

While interrogating himself, the narrator realizes that he cannot trust his use of words alone to establish a truly strong relationship with his brother, but at the same time, words are all he has as a writer. The words of his self-indictment are words and words alone: "[W]ords like 'insight' and 'altered perspective' are bullshit. They don't tell you what you need to know. Am I willing to go all the way? Be with you? Share the weight? Go down with you wherever you have to go? No way to know beforehand. Words can't do that. Words may help me find you. Then we'll have to see" (34). This notwithstanding, John will go to Robby figuratively and symbolically by using words to portray the journey. In the rest of "Visits," the narrator's words give an in-depth physical and emotional description of the family members going from Homewood to Western Penitentiary and a description of the route and journey. The trip ends with them successfully crossing the space of the waiting room and beginning the visit, but the "room roars behind our backs" (54). They have gotten there, but the ominous last words of "Visits" are a reminder that they have a long way to go. Words are still the key, but the text will reveal that the narrator's words and the story's figuration are insufficient if he does not share them, and thus share telling the story, with Robby.

The next section, "Our Time," seems to break totally from the first part and start in a different direction, but this is only one of the shifts in narrative focus that are necessary to capture the complex reality the narrator has been describing and to move toward sharing the storytelling. Discussing "Our Time" and the last section, "Doing Time," Eugene Philip Page writes that "[o]ften shifting without notice from paragraph to paragraph, the text oscillates among a variety of points of view. There are brief passages of John's first-person narration . . . But [also] there are many passages in Robby's first-person oral style" (7). Further, "[t]hese shifting points of view and styles have many implications. Besides illustrating the theme of John's learning how to listen to Robby, they literally widen the role of writer to include Robby—his notes, his poems, his speech, and his letter. By alternating between John's and Robby's consciousnesses, they also enact Wideman's pervasive emphasis on the necessity of a close, supportive, intersubjective web of human relationships" (7–8). In this context of shared storytelling, John starts telling the story of Robby's friend Garth in his own voice that is inflected by Robby's voice and perspective. Initially, this story is perplexing because it is hard to see how it is relevant. By the end, however, the narrator makes it clear that by telling it he is picking up on what Robby gave him: Robby "began the story of his troubles with Garth's death" (76). Their mother had told the narrator the same story six years earlier, but he had not listened closely enough to realize, as he does now, that the story showed "how desperate and dangerous Homewood had become." Homewood was a place controlled by racist powers where, because he was a young black man, Garth suffered from an illness that the health clinic ignored unil it was too late to help him. Robby is also a young black man affected by racism, and although he certainly cannot be excused for committing a crime, the environment was a great influence, one to which many, including John, might have fallen victim.

As "Our Time" develops, the narrator makes attempts to stop telling Robby's story for him, thus making it the narrator's story, and to give the voice of the story over to Robby. Continuing his self-analysis, the narrator repeatedly emphasizes the point that he is not capable of listening to his brother long enough to stop writing fiction that is about him, the narrator, and of writing Robby's story from his point of view. It is a question of whether the narrator—and not his brother, the supposed criminal—is trustworthy: "Do I write to escape, to make a fiction of my life? If I can't be trusted with the story of my own life, how could I ask my brother to trust me with his?" (78). He realizes that he "had to depend on [his] brother's instincts, his generosity. I had to listen, listen" (80).

The narrator increasingly gives the voice of the story to Robby in the remainder of "Our Time": In the rest of part 1, he lets Robby talk a lot, with his own voice intruding only briefly. Except in one fragment, only Robby speaks in part 2; and in part 3, Robby talks after the narrator makes a short comment at the beginning. What the narrator hears and sympathizes with is an account of Robby inadvertently falling into the role of family rebel, thus finding himself isolated in that way, and also being trapped in Homewood by the racist forces that killed Garth and that were the real object of his rebellion. This is largely the cause of Robby's problems. Robby does have character flaws that make him very susceptible to falling into the trap of dope, crime, and murder, but the narrator clearly implies that the same thing might have happened to him if he had stayed in Homewood. The last thing Robby says is that he was ready to "[p]arty hearty" even right after he and his friends committed the crime (166). In the context of everything he has said, though, Robby comes across as a genuinely good person who is very talented, like his brother, but who fell into the trap of environment.

In spite of this, John still knows that *Brothers and Keepers* is his book and the property of the outside world while Robby remains in jail, and he has not symbolically addressed this in the narrative by including Robby as a writer engaged in the narrative process. The preface to "Doing Time," the last section, foreshadows Robby's inclusion in the narrative process through sporadic references to Robby trying to write to John: *"I've decided to write notes to you"* (169). *"It's ten days or so since I wrote last"*; *"I haven't written or done anything in two weeks. . . . I'll write again soon"* (170).

"Doing Time" progresses toward Robby's inclusion. First, in his own voice, Robby describes the pain of drug addiction and fear of running after his crime, and then, in part 2, "Summer 1982," the narrator immerses himself in Robby's perspective through the vehicle of his own narrative description. He portrays another journey to the prison alone by a new route that takes away the familiar, distracting landmarks and anticipated steps of the trip that had prepared John and the family for the prison. The description opens John up to the full shock of the prison's horror, and he makes the following assessment: "The keepers run prisons with little or no regard for prisoners' rights because license to exercise absolute power has been granted by those who rule society" (187). He portrays himself as seeing the world as Robby must see it and having a better sense of "doing time" than he ever has: "[Robby] sees in me what I see in him. The knowledge that this place is bad, worse than bad" (190). He thus further breaks down his privileged position as writer and gives Robby voice in the narrative.

Important concerns in "Doing Time"—part of a revision after the initial draft of *Brothers and Keepers* failed (199)—are making it bring everything together and the impact of the finished book on the realities of John the writer and Robby the prisoner.

> The book would end with this section. Since I was writing the book, one way or another I'd be on center stage. Not only would the prison section have to pull together many loose ends, but new material had to surface and be resolved. Aside from logical and aesthetic considerations, finishing the book as object, completing the performance, there was the business of both rendering and closing down the special relationship between my brother and myself that writing the book had precipitated. All the questions I'd decided to finesse or sidestep or just shrug off in order to get on with writing would now return, some in the form of issues to be addressed in concluding the book, some as practical dilemmas in the world outside the book, the world that had continued to chug along while I wrote.
>
> Robby was still a prisoner. He was inside and I was outside. Success, fame, ten million readers wouldn't change that. The book, whether it flopped or became a best-seller, would belong to the world beyond the prison walls. Ironically, it would validate the power of the walls, confirm the distance between what transpired inside and outside. Robby's story would be "out there," but he'd still be locked up. Despite my attempts to identify with my brother, to reach him and share his troubles, the fact was, I remained on the outside. With the book. Though I never intended to steal

his story, to appropriate it or exploit it, in a sense that's what would happen once the book was published. (199–200)

The most important point about the overall significance of the book is implied and not stated: Robby can in a sense free himself by projecting his story outside the prison walls with the book if he becomes an author. In turn, he will abrogate John's theft of his story.

The evolving draft of the book and particularly "Doing Time" has already helped John; he continues to show additional ways that the writing has given him insight into himself. He characterizes himself and Robby as equals by taking a different look at their lives and what they have done in crucial life situations. John admits that he would not have the strength his brother has to face the reality of prison life, which leads him to compare "what I'd accomplished outside the walls with what he'd managed inside" (202), and to conclude that "maybe my brother has done more with his life than I've done with mine." He also confesses to the crime of cheating on his wife, Judy, which he deems worse than Robby's offense of letting his new girlfriend that he has met in prison continue to believe a lie that assuages her pain presently but will hurt her eventually: "My betrayal was worse than my brother's because I initiated the deceit, the lies. I didn't get trapped by somebody else's lie." They are both "[d]amned if [they] do. Damned if [they] don't" (215). However, while John sees some virtue in Robby's deception, he describes himself as simply weak and dishonest.

Writing "Doing Time" also makes the narrator see that going back to deal with Robby in prison is like going back to the past of the Homewood community: "When you're in the prison visiting lounge, you never know who you might run into. It's like returning to Homewood. I've been away from my old neighborhood over twenty years, beginning in 1959 when I left Pittsburgh to play basketball at the University of Pennsylvania in Philadelphia. Since then Homewood has been a place to visit, with visits sometimes separated by years" (222). As is true of his connection with his brother, he is very much related to and a part of—and not superior to—the community that produced him and his brother. Making sense of the Homewood past that he has not dealt with adequately is also bonding with his brother.

The end of "Doing Time" shows Robby beginning to contribute to the book. He talks constantly about writing, takes steps to become a writer, and even writes something.[4] Robby has spoken in a black vernacular voice throughout *Brothers and Keepers*, but to be a writer he must also master his own writer's voice that incorporates Standard English into the vernacular. Presented verbatim, the graduation speech he gives when he gets his associate degree in jail shows that he has learned to use a standard, educated voice (240–42). The postscript is a note that Robby has written to John that explains the progress he has made toward becoming a writer; in it, his voice blends the vernacular with Standard English, demonstrating that he is becoming one: "I tried to write the road story [about being on the run from the law] but I haven't gotten very far. I dunno, I guess everything looks so bleak it's hard to get interested in anything. But anyway, as far as my case is concerned, I put in a habeas corpus in the Federal Court 3rd Circuit. They denied it and I really don't know what else to do. I've run out of ideas. Everything seems against me. I don't mean to sound too pessimistic but things are bleaker than they've ever been. . . . I'm going to start writing the road story again. I really do want it told so I must work if I want rewards. Be cool, Bro" (243). He is still only talking about trying to write his book instead of writing it. However, he realizes the hard work that a writer must do, and even at this stage of writing a note, he is telling his own story in a writer's voice.

Robby's graduation speech and the accompanying note, the last words, make him an author along with his brother, and portray a humanity that transcends his supposed criminality and that is a quality shared with his brother and Homewood. His words about himself stand above his brother's words about him, and are the ultimate key that frees him in the book. The book is the symbol of his freedom that goes outside the prison walls.

The central problem in *Fatheralong* (1994) is that the concept of race has subtly and indirectly, but very powerfully, alienated John Wideman from his father and John's sons from him. Race is not the same as color or culture; John, the narrator of the book, calls it a "paradigm." In the preface entitled "Common Ground," which envisions a world where black people can come together outside the dictates of race, John defines his terms: "The word *race* evokes a paradigm, a systematic network or pattern of assumptions, relationships, a model of reality, of history and causation as complete, closed, and pervasive as a religion. Race is not a set of qualities inhering in some 'other,' it's the license to ascribe such qualities allied with the power to make them stick" (xv). Race is not so much scientific or real as it is a set of beliefs and attitudes attributed to those who are supposedly black or white. This ultimately means that one is inferior because of any acknowledged or imputed trace of African ancestry, color or culture notwithstanding, or superior because of an imagined pure white ancestry derived from Europe. This is only the simple foundation of the paradigm of race; it often works in more complex ways that reveal a range of prejudices based on skin color. However, its basis is white superiority and black inferiority, and it always supports and perpetuates white political and social power. The paradigm of race defines black men as inferior to white men, and the imposition of this stigma results in a highly negative and destructive silence between black fathers and sons. The narrator says that the "paradigm of race works to create distance between sons and fathers. One of the worst aspects of this distance is the unwitting complicity of the victims perpetuating it. Because we don't talk or can't talk father to son, son to father, each generation approaches the task of becoming men as if no work has been accomplished before" (71). Silence caused by the paradigm of race prevents black fathers and sons from sharing the stories that would break down walls of alienation, unite them, and provide a foundation for black fathers and sons who will follow them.

There are similarities and differences between *Brothers and Keepers* and *Fatheralong*. The narrator describes a creation story from Chinua Achebe's *Things Fall Apart:* "Told countless times, countless ways, in each recounting [an event] happens again, not in the past, but alive and present in Great Time, the always present tense of narrative where every alternative is possible . . . where all stories are true" (62). [5] *Fatheralong's* "chronological manipulation," "convoluted circularity," and "event shuffling" (Julien 19–20) represent alternative narrative possibilities and multiple stories that are possibly true. The structure is characterized by narrative shifts, different beginnings, and movements back and forth in time that resemble the devices used in *Brothers and Keepers* to allow John to connect to his brother. In *Fatheralong*, John is a writer who tries to structure a similar narrative process that creates familial bonds and cuts through silence—in this case, that of fathers and sons. John also places a thematic emphasis on storytelling and writing to bring him closer to his father and sons, which is reminiscent of the use of the theme of storytelling and writing to unite black brothers in *Brothers and Keepers*. However, "*Fatheralong*'s six sections unfold in three movements: after demonstrating on an abstract level the invalidity of a common ground (a place free from the racial paradigm), the book shifts to the personal level and then concludes that the racial factor is here to stay—a capping stone rather than an epiphanic gesture, as that basic truth informs the book from beginning to end" (Julien 18). In this context, sometimes John briefly feels close to his father when he listens to his story, but he never gives long stretches of the narrative over to his father, which would confirm bonding and sharing as in *Brothers and Keepers*. By the end, John does not come together with his father through storytelling and writing as he does with Robby. Although structure and theme unite as in *Brothers and Keepers*, no overall, conclusive narrative process of storytelling and writing liberates in *Fatheralong*; although storytelling and writing, in all of their complexity, address the paradigm of race, they do not eliminate its effects.

Separated by open spaces in the text, multiple parts and beginnings of the story "Promised Land" subtly move back and forth in time as John tries to recall a substantive memory of his father in an attempt to write a story about him:[6] "About three years ago my father was driving me to the Greater Pittsburgh Airport" (3). "Going to Pittsburgh meant staying in my mother's house. . . . Meant including my father when possible, when there was no necessity and little likelihood of my parents being thrown together too intimately" (6). "His car's running poorly, doesn't always start right up, but my father thinks it will make it to the airport and back" (9). "Two years ago on the way to the airport I asked my father if he'd like to take a trip to South Carolina sometime" (15). "After flying into Pittsburgh early on October 15 I spend the afternoon and evening at my mother's house, then pick up my father next morning from the Leroy Irvis Towers, a state-subsidized high-rise for the elderly in the Hill District" (21). "My father, suitcase in hand, is out of the tightly secured Irvis Towers before I can ring the front doorbell to get in" (30). John indicates further that the parts of the story indistinguishably merge as he tries to portray his father: "The morning three years ago blends with others, before and since . . . [with] me wondering each time . . . what it meant to see so little of him each trip" (10). Generally, his approach represents the complexity of writing a story, but along the way he mostly documents how brief encounters when he is arriving or leaving make him feel distant from his father. And even his trip to Promised Land, South Carolina, when he is alone with his father for over seven hours, only leaves him with a question that reveals estrangement: "Why had it been impossible all these years to believe in this man's actual life?" (34). At the end, the facts he remembers have no substance. This story is a largely failed attempt to deal with alienation.

"Fatheralong," another story in which John tries to engage his father, reveals that he is closer to his mother and sure of her love. Near the end, he describes that while his mother is integral to the process of successful storytelling, his father is the antithesis: "When I found myself in novel situations, I often tried to translate what I was experiencing into a story I might tell her. Whether or not I actually narrated the tale to her or anyone else, I wound up explaining things to myself by explaining them to her. She was *there*, like the internal words and rhythm of consciousness are there. A closeness and intimacy the opposite of oppressive, since her presence freed me, helped me grow and expand" (84–85). He says further, "My father, present or not, evoked boundaries." His mother is inseparable from the story that affirms his deepest self; she *is* the story, if he tells it or if it transpires in consciousness. His father is a barrier outside the nexus of the story. The figures of speech portraying connection with the mother and separation from the father are emblematic of what happens in storytelling and writing in "Fatheralong" and throughout the text.

It may appear that "Littleman" marks a high point in which storytelling comes to fruition, but one has to examine this conclusion closely. "Littleman" portrays a different version of the trip to Promised Land from the one in the story of that title. It centers on the family relative from Promised Land named Littleman. John constructs most of the story, which has the typical structure of multiple beginnings and movement back and forth in time, but at one point after the prefatory phrase "my father said," he puts the story in the words of his father, Edgar, for several pages (117–20). The recording of Edgar's story about his manliness gives the appearance that John is listening to him to a much greater extent than anywhere else in the text. However, Edgar's story abruptly stops, and John starts an account of him, Littleman, and Edgar in a bar in Promised Land. Part of what John imagines is that he and his father are connected and fighting the white men in the bar: "My dad and I, back to back, turning the joint out. Pow. Pow. Blam. Dudes falling out, carried out. How you doing, old man? I'm fine, how you? Blam" (125). John describes the story's impact: "[T]he danger I'd placed us in spiced the evening for me. . . . Along with the silliness, something rich and good about being with men of my family. Another kind of spice, a mellow, simple contentment arising from this meal together. . . . Knowing we were connected" (125–26). John's characterization of Littleman begins in the third sentence, where the latter is telling connecting family stories, and at the end, he also recounts Littleman's story, linking them to unknown ancestors whose graves they will visit the following day. Further, he confirms the importance of ancestor stories like Littleman's and the ones he can write: "Like the vital fluid of our blood, the stories of our fathers and mothers were gifts. A chance, an opportunity to create life" (126). But some of the "spice"—"Pow. Pow. Blam. Dudes falling out, carried out. . . . Blam"—of his story after he listens to Edgar's sounds ironic, and no other part of the story shows storytelling bonding them. This raises questions about the seemingly positive story in which Littleman is the central, positive character. (The story supposedly portrays a connection between men, and one can perhaps also ask questions about its title and the moniker Littleman, James Harris).

The next story, "Picking up My Father at the Springfield Station," belies a bond between father and son. It switches back and forth to different places and times that are physical and psychological, among which are: Pittsburgh, where family members have inexplicably left Edgar behind when traveling to the narrator's oldest son's wedding; Amherst, Massachusetts, the place of the wedding; a road outside the Arizona State Prison where the narrator's other son is, where he remembers another road in Promised Land near the Wideman home; Promised Land itself, where the narrator traveled earlier; Columbia, South Carolina, site of a historical exhibit of African American family portraits; places of the mind, such as the one where the writer invites the reader to "[i]magine yourself making me up, being me, freeing yourself" (145), or where he contemplates various historical instances of black oppression; and the Springfield, Massachusetts, train station where the narrator picks up Edgar. Like the encounters in "Promised Land," the short portrayal of the actual meeting and car ride to Amherst emphasizes the characters' great distance from each other through their superficial banter and the narrator's thinly veiled negative tone: "During the ride we chatted like old friends who hadn't seen each other for a very long while. Little stuff, newsy stuff flowed easily, buoyed the conversation, preparing us for the big stuff we'd get around to sooner or later. If we ever did" (167). Father and son will continue to fail to listen and talk to each other substantively. The narrator's story still does not bond him with Edgar; in spite of its multiple narratives, it first and foremost highlights Edgar's fostering of alienation and the family's reinforcement of it.

The narrator is still John but also another person because of his markedly different, seamy characterization.[7] He reveals this most strikingly through the story of his visit to a strip club, the Mardi Gras, near the train station while he is waiting for his father. He wonders: "Would I be embarrassed to ask my father to join me. . . . If we went together, would it spoil the little rush I might enjoy going alone? What would he think? Of the idea, of the two of us strolling in to check out women's bodies" (160–61). John calls the Mardi Gras his "secret" world that he cannot acknowledge to his father and others (161). His life alone in this world is self-alienating, showing that he has in a sense become his father: "Edgar deserted his family; John likes to sneak into the Springfield Mardi Gras striptease show" (Julien 21). John's self-alienation presents further negative implications for him as a writer trying to engage in a substantive narrative process.

John concludes the book by trying to invent a narrative world in which he can connect to and save his incarcerated son, and also come together with his father and other male ancestors. In the creation myth that begins "Father Stories," the earth takes the shape of the stories of the storytellers making it up, but it is "*a world also unfinished because all the stories had not been told*" (178). Maybe death and evil became real because some did not speak; or the world would be worse if all stories were told; or there are no more stories; or untold stories are the only ones with value, and people are lost when their stories are; or "*the storytelling never stops and this is one more story and the earth always lies under its blanket of mist being born.*" In the final analysis, the myth articulates the wide-open possibilities and never-ending process of storytelling that is the essence of human reality.

The myth is hopefully the introduction to a new, successful story. After this, the first of the writer's usual comments about storytelling and writing sounds positive: John wants to "begin again because I don't want it to end. All these father stories that take us back, that bring us here, where you are, where I am, needing to make sense, to go on if we can and should." At various junctures, though, he intersperses musings that apparently undercut his narrative project. "I'm remembering these things in no order, with no plan. These father stories. Because that's all they are" (184). "Everything happens only once, then everything changes. The notion of duration, of continuity, the possibility of making sense, no more or less than a fragile survival strategy. A hedge against chaos. Nice work if we can get it. The idea that time unfolds linearly in seconds, minutes, hours, years, the terms we've constructed to tame it, feels utterly unconvincing" (186). At the end, however, John asserts that he and his incarcerated son must "speak [the] stories to one another" (197) that will break down "wall[s] between my grandfathers and myself, my father and me, between the two of us, father and son, son and father." Perhaps this can happen in spite of comments that sound contrary.

John in this piece also tells several stories that express his love for his son. The first one is a surrogate story that he attributes to his wife. He recounts his wife's story of connection to the son intertwined in her connection to her father and the place in Maine that he left her, but it nevertheless ends with fear and concern for the son that is evoked in the image of the upheaval of her world, "[t]he very ground she loved be[coming] undeniable evidence of loss and pain" after his tragedy (180). The other stories are John's disparate fatherly memories of the son from an early age to the incident that led to his incarceration. All the stories show fierce longing for the son that is tantamount to love. Importantly, the stories lead to the last bonding, connecting word, "Love" (197). More than anywhere else, there is the possibility of telling stories that bring John and his sons and John and Edgar together.

This does not mean that there is an overall narrative process in *Fatheralong* that liberates, though. All the stories except the last one confirm John's alienation from Edgar without significantly mediating it. Further, one cannot clearly say that "Father Stories" changes the book's thematic trajectory. Even with the story's relative optimism, John never tells/writes it face-to-face with the son, and the son does not speak for himself. The continuing existence of the paradigm of race is behind all of this. Even as he raises hope, John says that "[t]he powers and principalities that originally restricted our access to the life free people naturally enjoy still rise" (197). American institutions and practices from slavery onward have perpetuated racism, and the paradigm of race still maintains alienating silence among black men by preventing them from telling each other liberating stories.

The stories John tells are useful, nevertheless. From a positive perspective, even stories that emphasize alienation are a way of encountering and dealing with it and at least making the problem clear, and perhaps the alienated one more familiar. This could open the way to a future when, hopefully, black fathers and sons will be able to move beyond the silence enforced by the paradigm of race, and their stories will be spoken freely to each other instead of in isolation like John's. This will then make it possible to tell different kinds of stories that will effectively bond and connect.

Hoop Roots (2001) moves beyond the thematic and structural patterns of the first two auto/biographies, but writing/storytelling is still the beginning. John Wideman, the narrator/writer, loves writing and also writes about love—the love of playground basketball, family, and community—and about love's ambiguity, mystery, and heartbreaking failure.[8] He writes about race because it affects writing, love, and everything he loves and that is important. In turn, he writes about how family and community rituals, basketball, and music symbolically address race, just as his writing does. Reminiscent of the first two auto/biographies, the writing implies the oral voice of storytelling, and structure and theme conflate through experimental narrative forms that convey the connection of topics and represent writing/storytelling. The focus in *Hoop Roots,* however, is the individual writer's attempt to capture his own life through experimental techniques of writing/storytelling, making its narrative quest different from that of the first two auto/biographies, and also making this work more thematically and structurally complex. The narrator/writer portrays an inextricable nexus of writing/storytelling, race, love, basketball, family, and community, in the process showing that there is very little, if any, difference between fictional creation in the auto/biographies and in the fiction.

The first piece, "More," makes the point that the process of telling a story has greater importance than the meaning, just as playing the game of basketball is more important than the outcome. Each moment of telling the story is like each moment of taking a shot, whether it goes in or not. It is a "moment of power" that "lets you feel as if fate's in your hands, lets you decide with a flick of your wrist whether something grand or devastating will befall you" (21).

By the end, "More" has set the tone for the rest of the book: The narrator is not nearly as concerned with a realistic description of basketball players and play on the court as he is with writing/storytelling. He mainly weaves play in the game of basketball into his conceptualization of storytelling and into the structure of his stories, which often have long paragraphs consisting of a flow of thought and ideas and unconventional punctuation. He sees a representation of playground basketball in the structure of his stories. Structurally, a story continuously embodies the same open-ended, improvised creative "moment of power" that he finds in play on the playground.

The narrator in "First Shot" emphasizes that he is creating a story from his imagination instead of portraying reality. After an opening section that is descriptive of real people and events from his past, he makes it clear that, although the people were real and the events did happen, this writing is his imaginative recollection. It is not a duplication of what actually happened and what people actually did. In the rest of "First Shot," the narrator makes many of the same thematic connections between basketball and storytelling that he makes in "More." Generally, playground basketball is improvisation like writing; it is "the unfolding narrative, told and retold, backward, forward, sideways, inside out, of who you would turn out to be" (56). It is an improvised, continuously moving narrative of life told through play.

The first two stories are similar structurally, just as they focus on storytelling and connect basketball and storytelling similarly, and "First Shot" is probably the least experimental and difficult story in the book because of its structure. It does not rely as much on long, drawn-out sentences and paragraphs that represent the movement of play on the basketball court. Overall, the story focuses more on recognizable daily life from the past of the Homewood community and on people there, particularly family members, whom Wideman has written about previously. One of the clear points it makes is that playing basketball on the Homewood playground was a way of developing a place in a community of men. Besides this, it presents analyses of the exploitation of the black male image in sports and the destruction of black men in youth gangs. These discussions are interesting and relatively easy to follow because readers are familiar with both topics. However, "Learning to Play" is very experimental and difficult because the narrator structures it with Great Time specifically in mind.

In interviews and often in his recent writing, Wideman says that life exists in "Great Time."[9] Great Time does not move in a day-to-day, linear fashion according to clocks and calendars; instead, it constantly moves backward and forward and in all directions at once, making all time the present time and all things happen simultaneously. Stories are hard to follow because all events interrelate in time.

Characterization, setting, narration, and overall narrative structure fit into this pattern of connectedness. In very ambiguous chronologies, many episodes of plot run together and assume a bizarre, dreamlike quality; it is hard to tell where something is taking place and if it is taking place for the first time. The identities of separate characters often become one as multiple, composite people sometimes speak in the third-person and sometimes merge into the first. In a context of shifting narrative perspectives and roles, a narrator can tell a story and interact with a listener, but can also listen to the story he is telling and the stories of others, all of which are concurrent.[10] Narrators explain how Great Time works and use narrative devices to convey it within the overall complexity of narrative structure that represents its movement. However, a narrator's story can reflect Great Time, but cannot specify every event and every person in every story. Besides what he cannot hear, see, or know because there is just too much to encompass in the conglomeration of life, there are details, emotions, and relationships in his own life that are vague and hard to sort out, articulate, or explain because so much has happened and is happening in many places. A lot remains unclear for any narrator telling a story, just as it is for those with whom he interacts and for the reader. Specificity is not important, though. It is important that a narrative encompass everything that is there, although it cannot articulate or show it explicitly. Great Time is always open-ended, ongoing, and shrouded in mystery, but it is no less meaningful for this.[11]

Early in "Learning to Play," the narrator is imagining the past. He is creating from memory the story of his life of forty years ago when his grandmother was dying and he was first learning to play basketball: "I am lost now in the universe of wondering what thought I would have been thinking as I entered [my grandmother's] little room at the top of the stairs in the house on Finance Street" (71). The piece starts with a long, italicized paragraph about a strange, anonymous woman the narrator loved and lost thirty years ago who is somehow reincarnate in another very attractive woman in the present (67–68). After this, it seems at the outset that the narrator is straightforwardly telling the story of being torn between love for his grandmother and love for basketball in his distant past (68–82). One hint of the complexity of his feelings later and the accompanying complexity of the story is the unsettling smell of his grandmother, the source of which he cannot specify (69–70).

The italicized passage in which someone is dangerously *"[c]limbing [a] pyramid"* (87) is a good example of the nonrealistic narrative structure and ambiguous, composite characterization that represent Great Time. The place and time are not clear: *"Where am I. Where am I"* (91). However, in several instances, the speaker refers to the Mayan culture of Mexico. At one point, he talks about *"flying here to research the roots of hoop for my book, your film. The wonderful synthesis of both we intended to create"* (91). This seems to identify him, at this moment at least, as the writer John Wideman, who is in Mexico working on a joint book/film project of *Hoop Roots* with the girlfriend vaguely characterized later. They supposedly go there to research because *"the Mayans used to play* [an ancient version of] *b-ball"* (90). Overall, though, the speaker has a surreal existence that is much more than Wideman's. In line with this, a speaker in a later section of "Learning to Play" asks where he is, what is happening, who he is with, and finally, "who am I" (113). The speaker in "Learning to Play" is a synthesis of speakers, somewhat like the synthesis of book and film he mentions, talking all at once from an amalgam of places in Great Time.

The presence of the unknown female lover from thirty years ago is another important indicator of Great Time in the story; references to the woman intrude to fragment the story and break the illusion of a straight-forward development. It turns out that the speaker cannot separate the anonymous woman he cannot locate, but who lives vividly somewhere in the story, from his current lover or his wife, whom he was married to and left after more than thirty years. He seems to have an overall sense of inadequacy and failure with regard to love.

The part of the narrator's story in what is supposed to be the knowable present ironically fragments into an almost unintelligible plot. He and his current lover tell each other stories to become better acquainted (113–27). As the "stories bleed in" (126) with each other, the narrator becomes aware of part of his story that he has tried the hardest not to visualize and to tell. This is the image of him looking, in spite of himself, at his grandmother's soapy nakedness in the bathtub, in which he was not supposed to be interested because filial love forbade sexual awareness (126). He suffers a "confusion of filial and sexual love" (Jahn 63) and "struggle[s] to distinguish filial from erotic love" (66). This disrupted idea of filial love merges with the other painful and fearful images of his love connections with women.

The narrator must accept his entire story that plays out against a bizarre, dreamlike background of Great Time and move forward. He seems to doubt that everything can ever be "restored, renewed, [and] lovers united" in the storytelling process, and realizes that "each fragment bear[s] memories of ancient crimes, ancient pain and loss" (134). In this context, he has to confront the feelings that he deems inappropriate about his grandmother, which are inseparable from his great love, and confront all the memories about relationships with women that make him uncomfortable. He has to take into account his feelings about basketball as well. He loved playing basketball as much as he loved the women, including his grandmother, and playing was as important as any of the relationships with them.[12] He cannot deny the full range of his feelings or break down the complexity of his life, but through the story he can come to terms with a more realistic view of who he is. "I must learn to tell myself old stories I really don't want to hear. Face my heart's truth in them, in the words I'm telling now, this attempt to sort through the past, prepare for what's next" (130–31). Overall, the process of telling stories means surviving and going on.

Parts of "Who Invented the Jump Shot (A Fable)" represent Great Time also; however, the narrator's main intention is to write a fabulous story, "A Fable," that brings attention to the idea that racial superiority is constructed through and embedded in language and unconsciously accepted as true. The narrator implies his own narrative theory as he prepares to write his experimental story: "Treacherously, the conqueror's narrative [of white superiority] insinuates itself. . . . Once you learn to speak a language, does it speak for you" (141–42). The implied answer to the question is "yes." The white "conqueror" dominates, and the belief that he is superior in all aspects of human encounter and endeavor "treacherously [insinuates]" itself in his dominant "[language/] narrative." The speaker's conscious intentions notwithstanding, the "conqueror" "speaks" his superiority through the speaker when he "speaks" the language. The narrator's query about language sounds like the words of the postcolonial theorist Frantz Fanon, who helps to make the point: "A man who has a language consequently possesses the world expressed and implied by that language" (*Black Skin* 18).[13] Possessing the language may be a way to share the "conqueror's" power, but it is also an acceptance, conscious or unconscious, of his beliefs about himself, his world, and values. This is especially important for oppressed people of color, to whom the narrator and Fanon are talking.

The story highlights the fabulous on one level, and on another subtly reveals the fabulous that goes on all around us hidden in language. As far as "inventing" is concerned, the jump shot is not a tool or machine normally thought of as an invention. However, it is the same as an invention because it is the equivalent of ingenious business technology. There is a simple but acutely perceptive idea behind the jump shot that makes it the mainstay that revolutionized modern basketball, contributing greatly to turning the sport into a large corporation that produces vast wealth. According to the narrator's theory, the "conqueror's [language/] narrative" of his superiority is a centralized societal story that is already in the words before each individual tells his own story; storytellers do not have to think consciously that white people are skilful, intelligent inventors prior to characterizing them as such in their stories because "white" *means* invention. If speakers were to tell stories about who "invented the jump shot," they would have to name someone white. The phrase juxtaposes the incongruous to prepare for the story's portrayal of the fabulous that is both clear and concealed in language. The fabulous that is concealed is white superiority's voracious pretense of owning everything important, even things that one would not normally think of, and does not have to think of consciously, like the jump shot.

Writing against the white story that hides its fabulousness and sounds true, the narrator tries to break the web of deceit ironically with a purposefully fabulous story with black and white characters. It is not a question of telling a story that definitively decides the truth: The truth is more complex than the neat white story would suggest and too complex for the narrator to portray definitively. However, his story is in fact *more honest* because it does not give the illusion of reality while hiding its complexity. More significantly, it raises and examines issues of race and class that the white story obfuscates, making it possible for readers to think about and discover the truth for themselves.

At the same time that the narrator theorizes his narrative, he reminds himself that he is under the power of the white story and must try to break free. Alluding to black people and other ethnic minorities that he will portray, he says: "*Howling. Savages.* Where did those words come from. Who invented them. . . . Certain words attract us, their sound, their weight. It's easy to stray. Say the words as if you believe them. Lost again. Found again. *Savages. Howling.* . . . [T]he mystery, the temptation of being other than I am disciplines me. Playing the role of a character I would not choose in most circumstances to be renders me hyperalert. Pumps me up and maybe I'm most myself" (141–42). The words come from the white story whose language he must speak and that in fact "speaks for him," and refers to the very characters he wants to portray, admittedly giving him an aversion to them. He must make the characters "most [himself]" through his own fabulous story, which will somehow disrupt the white story and liberate him from it. Apparently part of the "mystery" and "discipline" of "[p]laying the role of a character" that he already mentioned, the narrator can only further describe this subversion as a process of "struggling for other words, my own words . . . my words are words I've earned, words if they fail me, I'm bound to fall on like a sword—in other words, I already understand what it's like to be one of the dark passengers [in the car that he will create] (142). The "mystery" remains, but liberation from the white story somehow resides in the process of using words—a hazardous one, by the narrator's account—to create characters and construct the unconventional, fabulous story.

This story is different in form, structure, plot, characterization, and thematic development and conclusion from any story that one would anticipate. A highly arbitrary summary fits its intentionally fabulous construction.[14] The setting is first an academic conference about the invention of the jump shot. Then the narrator changes it to 1927, with a white man driving a group of black basketball players who later became the Globetrotters to Hinckley, Illinois, to play. Hinckley is a town of a mostly white "hicks" who at one point kill or run off all the black residents except one, Rastas. The story's setting shifts to an earlier time in Hinckley when "gillies [transport] the Globies into town," and "Hinckley hicks line up for miles at these canvas-topped depots" (152–53). In this setting, Rastas is also killed on the night when, after being denied admission to see the Globetrotters, a Hinckley white mob mistakenly thinks he is kissing an injured white girl whom he is helping. Near the end, the story is back in 1927. The white driver of the car full of Globetrotters is "also a minority" (158). "[A]ppalled by the raw deal Rastas received," the narrator reflects that in the near future "some clever, evil motherfucker will say, Sew stars on their sleeves. It'll work like color. We'll be able to tell who's who. Keep them apart. Mongrels. Gypsies. Globetrotters. Constantly coming and going. Sneaking in and out of our cities. Peddling dangerous wares. Parasites. Criminals. Devils" (159). The last paragraph returns to the setting in the present at the conference: "So *who* invented the jump shot. Don't despair. All the panelists have taken their seats at the table facing the audience. The emcee taps a microphone and a hush fills the cavernous hall. We're about to be told."

The narrator's experimental story only gives disparate, fragmented images of racism and class exploitation centered around the spectacle of blackness in America and American sports, but through the images it successfully portrays a dangerous, deadly history spawned by ideas of racial superiority, also hidden in the story of someone white inventing the jump shot. Symbolically, the writer's story has challenged and reopened the story in which whiteness is grand and good and has produced a great history so that it can have a different ending. At the beginning, whites at the conference have already rewritten history (137) and claimed owner-ship of the jump shot, but when the story goes back to the conference at the conclusion, the inventor is still to be named.

In "The Village," the narrator/writer develops a narrative showing that playground basketball's spontaneity, improvisation, and creativity and his experimental writing are responses to societal oppression just as analytical writing is. The story evolves from the analytical toward the experimental form represented in the free-flowing structure of words and radical structuring of ideas through disparate comparisons; the experimental form parallels the black cultural response of the basketball court.

The story starts with a clear comparison and takes surprising comparative turns. Playground basketball opposes mainstream racial domination; NBA basketball supports it. The latter "functions to embody racist fantasies, to prove and perpetuate 'essential' differences between blacks and whites, to justify the idea of white supremacy and rationalize an unfair balance of power, maintained by violence, lies, and terror, between blacks and whites" (167). Later, to make the point that playground basketball is where mainstream racist white definitions get challenged by more democratic ideas about humanity, the writer makes the unexpected comparison between the playground and American blackface minstrel shows of the nineteenth century. Whites in blackface putting on minstrel shows and whites watching them were stereotyping and making fun of blackness, but they were also trying to copy the way black people acted, thus revealing their fascination with and attraction to blackness. "Why did the crowds keep returning. What did they really see" (170). The writer does not answer these questions. However, he makes it clear that along with everything else, the mimicry of black culture conveyed black styles to the whites that included ways of resisting and acting freely in an oppressive world—"[s]tyles of self-representation and self-presentation honed in a hostile world, styles designed surreptitiously to alter imbalances of power" (170–71). These lessons learned from blackness were especially important for immigrant whites in the nineteenth century. For them, blackface minstrelsy "mirror[ed] in a curiously affecting fashion what it means to be white, poor, and underclass, subject to a version of reality dictated by white people, a ruling elite imagining itself above you" (171). Here, "The Village" goes beyond the issue of race to allude to how the white ruling class oppressed lower-class whites and set them against black people at the same time, reinforcing some of the implications of race and class in "Who Invented the Jump Shot (A Fable)."

The writer concludes his comparisons and closes his argument. He says that "[p]layground hoop is partially a response to the mainstream's long, determined habit of stipulating blackness as inferiority, as a category for discarding people, letting people crash and burn, keeping them outsiders" (173). Further along, he acknowledges that the argument for playground basketball may not be as clear-cut as he has made it. There are connections among the different types of basketball: "Obviously professional basketball, school ball, amateur leagues, pickup ball, playground hoop are deeply intertwined and always have been" (178). In this context, he has not documented basketball's history well enough to substantiate the distinction that he has made between playground basketball and other forms. In spite of this, he rests his argument on a point similar to ones he has already made about playground basketball, when all is said and done, still representing democratic ideals (179).

This brings the writer to a transition in the story where he begins to find and clarify his true direction in line with the overall goal of the experimental writing in *Hoop Roots*: "Has it taken me this long to figure out again that the deepest, simplest subject of this hoop book is pleasure, the freeing, outlaw pleasure of play in a society, a world that's on your case to shape up, line up, shut up" (179). He is talking about remembering his objective of replicating the play of basketball in the "play" of his writing. In other words, he has to remind himself not to concentrate so hard on *analyzing* the significance of basketball in American society that he forgets that the most important aspect of his writing is "play."[15] He wants to change his focus from analysis to "play" by putting more emphasis on highly experimental writing centered on the topic of playground basketball and on the playing of the game itself. This means making writing a more highly spontaneous, open-ended creative process that has very flexible rules and that follows no rigidly set plan. The comparison between playground basketball and blackface minstrelsy before the writer consciously reminded himself to "play" is a spontaneous act that is experimentation, too. The difference is that he has now changed the story's direction, and "play" is now the conscious objective.

Later, the writer does not find it easy to break away from analysis, though. Going back to describing what he sees on the basketball court that he and his girlfriend Catherine are passing, he becomes caught up again in analyzing what the players' ways of playing the game mean in terms of supporting or rebelling against mainstream culture. He concludes that one player has "the kind of refined skills and rare natural gifts and flair for expressing them that's showcased by NBA ads to sell its product. . . . [Y]ou could argue it all fosters a pay-trumps-play, cartoon version of basketball ultimately destructive for players and the game" (182). He soon realizes that he must back off this "critique" or analysis and observe the court to see what the play of the men expresses about their lives.[16]

This observation inspires the writer to focus on experimentation again. He is looking at the court before him, but starts talking about what he remembers about the styles of dress on the court years ago when he, a retired player now, played the game. He then suddenly starts talking about playground basketball as "Carnival as it's been practiced from the sixteenth century on, all over this 'New World' hemisphere anywhere significant populations of African-descended immigrants have settled" (184). The court turns into what he remembers from the past, and then, in a wild, spontaneous comparison, it turns into Carnival.

In the rest of the story, the writer continues his emphasis on experimental "play" that takes priority over analysis. Near the end, he says: "To resist being ripped off and redirected, to escape being kidnapped and whitewashed by the mainstream, playground hoop like all cultural practices at the margins engages in a constant struggle to reinvent itself, pump out new vibrations, new media and messages of yea-saying, saying loudly, clearly, *Yes.* We're here, still here, and we're human, we're beautiful" (189). The fluid structure of writing that violates grammatical rules makes the point that playground basketball is spontaneous expression that defies the mainstream and defines the lives of players. "The Village" ends with language that is less analytical and more fully and clearly "play." "*Next. Who got next*" (190). "Not today, good brother. Not today on this Village court. But I'll be back." The writing repeats the words spoken on the playground court that symbolize the court's expressive physical play. The writing, the words from the basketball court, and the play on the court symbolized by the words become one to bring the story to culmination. Moving from "next" to "next" and coming "back" symbolizes freedom that defies main-stream control.

The narrator of "Naming the Playground" definitely engages in the intricacies of writing/storytelling, but his concentration on recognizable characters and events in the analysis of social issues makes the story more accessible. An early section of "Naming the Playground" is a definition of a story explaining its great power to create reality that accrues from the relationship of structure and theme (194–95), and the narrator writes this story to conform to his definition. However, although he abstractly conceives storytelling and sometimes "plays" as in "The Village," he still portrays the problematic lives of recognizable characters, and clearly presents a basic point about the importance of black men playing basketball and telling stories to document their lives.

Tragedy inseparable from racism encompassed the lives of the two apparently different men who are the story's focus, Maurice Stokes and Eldon Lawson, but similarly the shaping of playground basketball and the portrayal of "Naming the Playground" are integral parts of their survival in the face of tragedy. The two lives, played out on the court and in the narrator's story, are the "[o]ne in the many. Many in one" (215); they connect all the African American men like them who have played on the Westinghouse playground in Homewood. The narrator would rename the playground "*The Maurice Big Mo Stokes/Eldon L. D. Lawson Memorial Playground*" to symbolize the reality of all their lives, also symbolized in their play and his story. Playing basketball and telling stories about those who played have not stopped racism from destroying black men, but have been ways to oppose it by giving expressive shape to lives and to reality.

In the last story, "One More Time," the narrator's experimental form moves around in a free association of things, people, and events that makes storytelling an incantation to bring back the love of his dead grandmother Freeda, the main character. Primarily depicting the same summer as "Learning to Play" when Freeda got sick and he was watching her as well as sneaking off to play basketball, the narrator explores love by focusing on art and his own artistic imagination. In the middle of the story, he introduces a photograph of Freeda (228) and, in an imaginative description, defines it as folk art. The photograph of her youth inspires many different spontaneous interpretations that he writes down, including loving reveries of her and the family and a history of basketball. As in "Learning to Play," he cannot separate his love of basketball, expressed here in the imaginative history he is writing, from his love of Freeda. However, he puts love at a distance by placing the photograph of the loved one in a context of folk art. Also, expressing the kind of love he has for basketball begins to take him away from the direct articulation of emotion to a representation of the imaginative approach that basketball and writing have in common.

Looking at the photograph, the narrator improvises to create a story about a whole range of incongruous things that are inextricably connected, including another more purely imagined history of basketball that is improvisatory like both writing and playing the game. He imagines that Freeda goes along with him as he imagines the history. At "the beginning," basketball is "about the shuffle, the dance, the space, the drive to excel, to fly" (237, 239). Basketball is thus like many other things ancient and modern that are emblematic of black culture, from ancient African ring dances symbolizing freedom to the rituals for the same purpose in the streets and churches of Homewood. By the end of "One More Time," Freeda, love, and basketball during this summer come together in the improvised description that the story becomes. Moving away from the emotional stance that he took at the beginning, the narrator is displaying creative imagination much more than he is concentrating on emotional love.

"One More Time" is like the rest of *Hoop Roots*. Love is inseparable from basketball, family, community, race, and music, and they are all inseparable from writing/storytelling. However, John Wideman, the narrator/writer, wants first and foremost to define and bring attention to an experimental creative, imaginative process of writing/storytelling that is his life.

The fourth auto/biography, *The Island: Martinique* (2003), is supposedly a travel narrative about Martinique written for *National Geographic*. *National Geographic* "offered the opportunity to go anywhere in the world and write about it" (xx); Wideman chose Martinique. However, beneath this very transparent guise, the auto/biography exhibits the importance of writing and a process of writing/storytelling like the other auto/biographies. Not maintaining the pretense of an actual travel narrative for long, the narrator turns in the introduction to the real subject: "All writers of fiction and poetry (maybe all writers period), no matter the conventions or illusions we employ, no matter how well we deploy them, are ghost writers, necromancers evoking and revitalizing the past through imagined beings, conversations, events, because our subject, what we write about, is 'not present,' long gone. Our labor transforms us, too, into born-again imaginary creatures, the *I, she, they, he, we, it* voices of the author's invented second-selves materializing as the reader reads and becomes, by reading and entering into a dynamic exchange, part of the imaginary also" (xxiv–xxv).

The book is "fiction" that interrogates a historical past, particularly but not solely Martinique's, to show its relationship to the present. Its main focus is history's sad, painful, bitter legacy of white oppression, insidiously hidden in the present, that the narrator/writer imagines and the readers imagine with him through the process of his writing/storytelling as he becomes the "*I, she, they, he, we, it*" of the past and present. A parallel focus is the narrator/writer's personal life and ongoing quest to find love, both of which are deeply infected by self-reproach, which has engendered emotions similar to those spawned by history's legacy. Like *Hoop Roots, The Island: Martinique* is the individual writer's attempt to deal with his personal life through writing/storytelling; it adds to the previous work a grim meditation on history's influence on both writer and reader, symbolizing liberation from personal and historical oppression through the writer's experimentation.

The narrator calls his experimentation "creolization," and at various places defines or reveals what he does with it. Creolization is experimental writing conveying unconventional, free-flowing, open-ended, extemporized linguistic structures, thematic formations, and images: "[T]he reader should expect improvisation, spontaneity, play, breaking rules to rule here" (xxv). Through its ongoing experimentation, creolization brings to the surface history's hidden truth, which is unpleasant, unsettling, and disruptive, and which changes the meaning of the present and ultimately heals: "Creolization is an ongoing process of renaming. Like good poetry it perpetuates between words and meaning, sound and sense a state of tension, unease, competition, dissonance, irony. Keeps old wounds alive, not because suffering ennobles, but because wounds hurt and creolization wants to insure wounds don't close before healing's complete" (48–49).

Creolized writing shows the superficiality of an oppressive concept of race—what Wideman calls, in *Fatheralong* and elsewhere, the "paradigm of race"—and symbolizes the importance of an opposing idea of hybridity: "Is the only choice for Martinique either/or—French or West Indian. Why remain trapped within a racialized paradigm of essentialist oppositions—black or white, European or African"; "[m]ust 'hybrids' be 'disembodied' and 'unsure.' Doesn't creolization embody the certainty of uncertainty and improvise rootedness with spontaneous performance" (97).

The writer also reveals what creolization does more specifically for him and the reader. As far as he is concerned, creolization is improvisation that breaks him down and articulates his subject's present reality and history through him, thus changing who he is: Creolization "lets the subject, in this case Martinique, breathe, plant its flag, articulate its claim, inhabit the writer's territory" (xxvi); it allows the writer "to be invaded, to live in other skins, to assume risks. Encourage the island to problematize, call into question who I am and who I'm not." Further, through creolization, the writer articulates what love is and expresses it, and since for him love can heal, he thus potentially heals himself and his lover, and the readers too, through the discovery of love. In this context, creolization potentially allows the writer to ameliorate his pervasive negative tone in *The Island: Martinique*. Creolized writing helps the reader to visualize the complex reality of oppression and "to be invaded" like the writer by the underlying truth about its complicity in the present: It employs "the strategies of Creole speech—imitation, parody, eclectic sampling, recycling the old, spontaneously improvising the new, layering meanings (multiple rhythms) to speak simultaneously to different layers of an audience. . . . [S]o [the oppression hidden] beneath is problematized, recontextualized, accrues new meanings, stimulates an alternative vision that rescues the viewer from the usual unexamined scenery dutifully absorbed" (41). By exposing it through creolization, the writer tries to mediate history's legacy and to create the chance for political and personal change.[17] Everything considered, creolization is experimentation that generates a liberating connection among writer, reader, and the book's themes that involves the writer and reader on the political and personal levels.[18]

Near the end of chapter 1, "Journal," the narrator defines the basic concepts "tour" and "tourists" that underlie his exploration, and explains the concomitant web of oppression linking them. The "packaged tour sells clients access to difference. The scam works because it's part of a totalizing system that dispossesses. Guided tours, slavery, the urge toward conformity arise from the ruins: One order subdues and plunders another. Sells stolen goods back to the victim" (93–94). The tour is a profitable economic enterprise based on people experiencing exotic racial "difference," true human diversity being, as the narrator will show, much larger. Tourism ironically "plunders" the slavery system and enslaves the tourist with a comforting, limiting experience of "difference" that slavery's ideology had prescribed in the first place. The victims historically also wrongly perceive "difference" in the tourist, which reexploits and enslaves them again. Because of this, the reenslaved historical victim has a similarity to the tourist: The "slave's vision of freedom perpetuates slavery by locating the key to freedom in the wrong hands [in whiteness]. Like the tour locates difference in the wrong place *elsewhere,* in someone not the tourist" (94). In reality, then, both the enslaver/tourist and the historically enslaved, now the object of tourism, are victims.[19] However, in spite of the complexities and conceptual mergence inherent in "tour/tourists," there is no question that the categories are separate: "[S]laves and tourists [are] at opposite poles of the scale of privilege and freedom."

In this context, the narrator questions his role as writer/tourist, but cannot determine whether the writer can invade the space of others without claiming his ownership of it or right to it as the tourist does. In "29 December 2000," he struggles with the feeling that he is a trespasser on a funeral scene, and tries to console himself with the idea that what he writes about it as touring writer opens up liberating perspectives and that he leaves without claiming he belongs or owns anything there. "Does the traveling writer liberate space by not claiming it. Authentic touring. Passing through and asserting no prerogative, acknowledging by one's departure that one doesn't belong, never expected to be anything other than observer or passerby. Isn't it okay then to stop and join the mourners. . . . Why should anybody be offended by a stranger who brings nothing, takes away nothing. But is the author really so innocent. How does she or he differ from any other rude, crude trespasser on grief's privacy" (30). His role may be inseparable from the privilege of tourism, which leaves the writer with uneasiness that he never fully resolves; however, he maintains the process of creolized writing, implying that he can successfully confront his culpability and that of his readers.

The last seventeen pages of *The Island: Martinique*, which consist of one sentence of ideas spontaneously and very skillfully structured together, stand out as the best examples of creolization's experimentation, but the narrator starts in a creolized style at the beginning of "Journal." He and his girlfriend arrive on Martinique on "25 December 2000" immersed in past tradition: "This trip to an island begins—as if it's a story or a dream—on Christmas Day, a day, a time of year overbearingly fraught with symbolism, with memories and images no matter how familiar, obvious, and drained of meaning, that still wash over us, immerse us, drown us in sentimentality and nostalgia and regret" (3). The structure of this first sentence already indicates the "improvisation, spontaneity, play, breaking rules" (xxv) that is creolization. By the end, when the sentence concludes with "regret," its tone has moved toward the pervasive negativity that creolized writing contests.

After bitterly exploding the oppressive myth of Christianity and further registering the text's pervasive bitterness, the narrator links the privileges that he enjoys as a tourist on Martinique with the historical past of slavery:

> What is Africa to me.
> I'm free at last to enjoy the spoils. Cook in the tropical heat day after day, get blacker till I split one afternoon, like a raisin in the sun. Prodigal son returned. High John the Conqueroo with his lady, be she black or white or some green-eyed, beige in-betweener—no one seems to give a flying fuck as long as my credit card computes, the numbers rising into the azure void of the heavens almost as fast as the speed of light, networking, interfacing, alchemizing from the nothingness of that empty blue empyrean miracles of instant gratification, wine, water, music, clothes, meals, shelter, sex on demand if the numbers are willing, if they climb fast and far, almost as fast as the dreams of old Africans who, clambering out of the boiling surf, continuing their ancient journey, disembarking daily on these shores, chained, greased, half-starved, puking, chanting, willing themselves instantly elsewhere, Africans shape-shifting, escaping the whips, the searing blue of their captors' eyes. (8–9)

In the last long, improvised sentence, the narrator directs sarcasm toward himself, and then makes it obvious that the economic privilege enjoyed by tourists like him is tied to and a manifestation of slavery's past. The implication is also obvious that this should be a major source of sadness, bitterness, and pain for the touring reader.

In "3 January 2001," the writing unveils new visions of complicity with the past and consequent human vulnerabilities of the narrator and others. It takes a surprising course from the narrator's brief mention of returning home to a newly elected southern U.S. president (George Bush), to an associated critique of Thomas Jefferson, whose life is celebrated by tours of Monticello reminiscent of the tours on Martinique, to the narrator's improbable connection to Jefferson, the historical figure of oppression. It moves toward a conclusion: "Jefferson's estate, the Martinican plantation owner, me, you propped up by the lies, brutal violence, and selfishness of an ideology (capitalism's pseudo-Darwinian survival of the fittest) calling down to those who serve our needs, whose backs support the pulpit upon which we stand and shout, 'Hey, I got mine! Nobody's fault but your own, my friend, if you don't get busy and grab yours!'" (71). The problematic contradiction of Jefferson as enlightened leader and slave owner is historical and present as shown in tours of Monticello. As a contradictory black man who perpetuates his oppressive past, the narrator is at least broadly similar to Jefferson. He is talking primarily about himself, but also clearly indicts "you," the reader.

He further uncovers the reality that a wide range of Americans, from the average to the famous, are complicit in the lie that hides and extends the oppressive past. "We're all Americans in this soup together, aren't we, as united as the fingers of a hand in a fist when fists are necessary, as separate and different as those same fingers when it comes to what each receives as a fair share of bounties and privileges. Rich and poor, colored and white, master and slave, all the hip-hopping, Puffed-up Daddies and Don King Trumps and Madonnas and Michaels and Britneys and Rocke-fellers and J. Los and Jane Does and just plain Joes coexisting, equally in-separable, separately unequal, one big happy us against the world" (72). Average and famous black and white people in the present are all like slaves such as Booker T. Washington, implied by the improvisation on his fingers/hand metaphor, because they comply with the tour by supporting its far-reaching economy and thus its oppression that reaches forward from the past.

In "26 December 2000" and "27 December 2000," the feeling about political oppression merges into emotions that come from failures in past and present personal relationships. The narrator/writer, John, will be sixty years old on his next birthday (74), and is "far too old to consider siring more children" (10). His French girlfriend, Katrine, who is younger but beyond the usual age of childbearing, has a miscarriage the day they arrive on the island. Katrine's miscarriage fits John's longer history that includes the responsibility for the breakup of his long marriage. When he meets Katrine, it is a "hectic period in [his] life, the sad aftermath of a thirty-year marriage, remorse, guilt, hassling with lawyers and endless depressing details, little sleep, bumbling around in a kind of fog seeping from scattered pieces of lives no longer fitting together, a sense that I failed one good woman and thereby probably disqualified myself for any other, yet still a strong desire to see Katrine again" (15). John feels that fathering the child who miscarries is another sad failure of judgment in a relationship by a man who is now old.

John conflates the political with the personal by symbolizing himself and his lovers as "islands." Paralleling the book's broad political focus on islands and tourists, he is a personal "island" that forces his lovers to engage him as "tourists," and he turns them into "islands" that he relates to as a "tourist." He has been a "tourist" touring their "islands," and has made each one a "tourist" touring his "island." According to this symbolism, their relationship embodies the same opposition as tour/Martinique. John and Katrine are a "racialized paradigm of essentialist oppositions" (97) like "[t]he island's persistent either/or, black or white" (12). The creolized writing thematically and structurally represents the opposition in the relationship that parallels tour/Martinique's "essentialist oppositions": "The island called John. The island called Katrine. Called John. Called Katrine. John/Katrine. Katrine/John" (13). Just as "white" tourists and "black" islanders do, John and Katrine, a "black" man and "white" woman, look for "difference" according to "essentialist oppositions" when they should start by looking beyond the definitions of race to the true diversity within each human being. John does not say whether Katrine understands the problem; his main emphasis is his personal responsibility because of his long life as an "island/tourist." He has failed because he has been a personal "island" of "difference" interacting accordingly with his lovers.

The "[s]eparate islands" John/Katrine have the potential to come together in love by "[f]loating [and] [m]erging" (13). John thinks of the miscarried child as "the wish to be better we stake in love" (22), and imagines the chances for love as "the sound of a small boat inching through the night sea toward paradise." "Of course the bouncing, skimpy, drunken little boat doesn't make it." The plight of love and the loss of the child are inseparable from the oppressive legacy entailed in the island's history, John's tourism on the island, and his past and present personal relationships in which he has been an "island" and a "tourist" to his lovers.[20]

In "8 January 2001," the practice of creolized writing evokes the experience through which John and Katrine can achieve love greater than a relationship of "islands." Their "bodies [are] the key to the story" (83); sensing nature on the island leads to a sensual experience of bodies that makes love possible when they give themselves to each other.

> A long day in the sun can turn you into [lush ripened fruit] . . . to be consumed, to be taken by a hand or mouth imagining you are its last sweet, salty supper even as you imagine yourself, will yourself to reach out for the mouth eating you and forget you're the fruit and tired and you sprout new digits, a mouth, a hunger of your own recovered, renewed, and try to gobble up the other whose lips are closing round you, whose teeth pierce you like the sunlight piercing in a thousand places the orange sarong wrapping Katrine on the walk to the beach, the other beside you in bed infiltrating the veil of your skin, both of you feasting, gliding through gauzy transparencies of difference, wearing and stripping them, blending skin, flesh, your separate dreamings, love's crowded, shared space, a single garment you both wear at the same time. (84–85)

They move beyond the superficiality of race to true, inherent human difference or diversity and, potentially, love.[21]

John deals mostly with the political instead of the personal in the rest of "Journal" after "8 January 2001"; the last entry, "11 January 2001," implies that political change that reverses the perpetuation of past oppression is possible. A nondescript white man meets a down-and-out but still hard to describe black man in front of the Library Schoelcher, "a monument to eclectic excess" (99) named for Victor Schoelcher, French advocate of abolition of slavery on Martinique. The reference to Schoelcher at the end—"Martinique's Abe Lincoln, Great Emancipator of slaves" (100)—sounds ironic and ambiguous. However, the entire scene is "eclectic" in a way that challenges the kind of packaged, superficial display of definitive racial "difference" that the tour of Martinique is supposed to present. The last sentence is: "What might [Victor Schoelcher] have thought about the exchange we've witnessed in the almost deserted morning streets of Fort-de-France." This suggests that the encounter symbolizes the breakdown of the racial prescription of the past to allow people to engage each other differently.

Chapter 2, "Père Labat," continues the strong political focus on historical oppression. In the introduction, the narrator talks about Labat and his intentions in chapter 2: "Ironically, in a delicious creolized twist, Père Labat—an actual historical figure from Martinique's past—became embedded in the island's folk history as a bogeyman and hobgoblin. Because of his reputation for cruelty and evil caprice [toward slaves], Père Labat's name was invoked by parents to scare misbehaving children. 'Mi! Moin ké fai Pé Labatt vini pouend ou—oui! (I'll make Père Labat come and take you away!)' After discovering the many ways Labat left his imprint—from establishment hero in the economic development of the island to spectral villain in the counterculture of Creole memory—I couldn't resist a brief foray . . . into the priest's mind" (xxvii–xxviii).

Chapter 2 is perhaps the best example of the improvisation of creolized writing, with its own "delicious creolized twist[s]" similar to the folk culture's, displaying the oppressive past pushing into the present and bringing a sad, painful, bitter political legacy. In the first part of the story, the Dominican priest Labat is half awake and half dreaming in a tavern in La Rochelle, France, before he sails for Martinique in 1693 (xxvii) to become its governor. The second part portrays the cruelties inflicted on African slaves by Labat, who believed that Africans were inferior and whites were God's people of destiny. The story takes a leap at the end after "Labat recalls buying his first pair of Nikes" (111) and looks on a scene of "brown, black and mongrel faces" at a mall in the present. The scene in the mall disturbs but does not threaten Labat, because he realizes that he still has power to control the people there and the entire setting because of the oppressive historical legacy he helped to establish (112–13). In spite of the brutal acts he will commit against Africans, Labat sardonically describes fellow white oppressors as "saviors launch[ing] themselves—speckled, flaking leper's flesh hidden under brown or black or white habits, voyaging to paradise they say, seeking islands where the blood is not yet spoiled they say, to rescue the heathen they say, to wash their feet with [their] filthy hands, to baptize them with wine pissed from [their] bloated bellies" (106). This is also the third-person narrator implying the legacy engendered by the brutal political past that invades the present.

In the last paragraph, one very long creolized sentence, time simultaneously traverses past and present to represent a main theme. Labat prepares to cross the sea from the mall to Martinique with Nike shoes in his possession. He conquered the sea for oppressive economic commerce; when he goes home with the Nikes, he is maintaining the past's oppressive tenure in the present.

In "Fanon," chapter 3, the legacy of slavery creates the problem of negotiating "racial prejudice, segregation, and oppression," and slavery's dictates make the characters "islands" of "antagonistic oppositions" (xxviii): "Europe and Africa, white and black, male and female, rich and poor, tourist and dispossessed." Combining the political and personal, the chapter examines the relationship between a black man and white woman named Paul and Chantal, who represent a "virtual couple" in place of John and Katrine. They fail when facing the same problems dictated by racial ideology that John and Katrine faced as lovers and survived "generally intact." Paul and Chantal's portrayal reveals "the real odds against [love] abounding on any Martinique," in any "society bearing slavery's scars." The narrator, John, concludes that readers "may have [their] guesses" about why he created Paul and Chantal, but says further that their portrayal was a "negative talisman to ward off [his] ancient fear of losing [love]."

The last section of chapter 3 is entitled *"Revenants,"* and Fanon is a *"revenant"* in the chapter. *"Revenants* . . . signifies ghosts—the spirits who return from the dead to haunt people and places, spirits who roam past, present, and future, linking and unsettling these rigid categories of time, destabilizing our too-easy reification of impermeable boundaries between living and dead" (xxiv). The writings and image of Frantz Fanon (1925–

1961), black philosopher, psychiatrist, writer, and revolutionary born in Martinique, are revolutionary symbols from the past that stand for the breakdown of its lies and the present's that would deny their oppressive ties. Fanon is also the symbol that represents the past overcoming the present in a positive way that is the opposite of oppression's imposition from the past. Fanon implies the possibility of breaking down racial ideology and allowing the outcome of John and Katrine's relationship to replace Paul and Chantal's. Thus, accounts from the *revenant* Fanon's life and tragic death and quotations from him intersperse the chapter; in one section, his spray-painted face intrudes confusingly but poignantly on Paul and Chantal, and in one instance, Paul recalls the face and surmises that Fanon's death is the key to their failure in love.

The conception of race separates Paul and Chantal as black man/white woman, and clearly for Paul, whose inner life is revealed more than Chantal's, makes sex a possessive, oppositional racial conquest that generates jealousy and impedes love. Paul's narratives in the section show his political awareness that should allow him to undercut racial ideology and defuse jealousy and, ironically, also his jealousy spurred by racial ideology that political awareness fails to counter. This implies the great destructive power of superficial racial concepts and the need constantly to be aware of this power. The idea of race has such power and grave implications politically and personally because it has a foundation in the past that maintains it as part of everything in the present. It works unconsciously and insidiously alongside political awareness to negate it.

Paul, a writer like John, several times expresses political awareness and sensitivity. For example, he contemplates his own racial indoctrination that created a stereotypical view of Africans and embarrassment about what to him were their strange-sounding names (119). After this, he links the murder of Patrice Lumumba in 1961 and the death of Fanon the same year, and thinks about his own quest for a Euro-centered education in 1961 that "[erased] information and knowledge" about the two men (120). He started the account of his political consciousness with a general assessment: "Today I'm much older than these dead men lived to be, these fallen heroes once old enough to be my fathers. How could this be. Everything and nothing changing."

Although Paul speaks clearly and analytically about the effects of racial oppression that indoctrinates, ultimately he cannot apply the clarity of his thinking to his relationship with Chantal. At one point, he seems able to escape racial indoctrination. Anticipating John's experience of the "plentitude" of human diversity represented in the celebration of bodies at the end, he vaguely senses the significance of Chantal's "naked body in bright sunlight. . . . your body's simple ease" (127). He reflects back on the same scene when a white man started looking at Chantal's naked body on the beach: "I thought I might have slain my demons that day watching another man's eyes on you, a white guy no less. I believed I was free of jealousy that day and maybe in the days to come if I stayed lucky, stayed clear about what belonged to you, belonged to me, what could or couldn't be stolen from us, what couldn't be owned or possessed" (128). However, in the recent past racial jealousy has overwhelmed him to the extent that he hardly sounded like the same person who had analyzed his response to Africans as a young man and his jealousy and possessiveness influenced by racial conception. He responds angrily, "[s]o what if it was some other goddamn island" (136), when Chantal tries to tell him that her relationship with a white man named Antoine was from "[a] different time, different place. . . . Not our island." Paul's attitude dooms the relationship.

It is unclear whether Paul can maintain the level of mature reflection that always produces clear analyses of the political and clear thinking in relationships. The next-to-last piece in this chapter, one of several entitled "Chantal," ends with the image of Paul standing over Chantal "wanting to hurt, to rip, shaking her till she submits, her head flopping side to side as he looms over her, shaking, shaking, shaking whiteness out and blackness in or blackness in and whiteness out, she remembers thinking some crazy true thought like that just before she stopped thinking and let her body have its way, shaken, sinking" (143–44). However, maybe the last section, "Revenants," with its epigraphic quotation from Fanon, *Today I believe in the possibility of love,* suggests hope.

"*Revenants*" implies that it is the narrative of Paul the mature writer analyzing himself and the political reality of the past and present like John and John Edgar Wideman would. The narrative perspective shifts throughout the book from the introduction and chapter 1 to the last three chapters. In "*Revenants*" and chapter 4, both Paul and John, respectively, are narrators and writers trying to make *The Island: Martinique*'s point very much like John Edgar Wideman, who is most clearly implied in the introduction, and John the narrator of "Journal," who is very close to John Edgar Wideman.

"*Revenants*" is a surprising, creolized ending. Sounding like Paul talking about Fanon and Lumumba earlier, the narrator links the deaths of the two men, and adds to this the images of the desecration of their bodies. The unexpected is the connection between the deaths of Fanon and American icon Marilyn Monroe and between the desecrations of their bodies. In the second paragraph, the narrative goes back further into history to connect Marilyn Monroe and Fanon as slaves on a ship forced to dance on deck for their captors. Marilyn Monroe tells Fanon that he will finish his book and that she will read it all. He ventures that "[m]aybe we won't die. Maybe there's hope. Hope for the ones not born yet" (145). She tells him that their oppression is only the "nasty dreaming" (146) of their captors, and she and he will "[s]oon . . . wake up in another dream. Everything will be different."

Through the radically extemporized, incongruous creolized image of Marilyn Monroe and Fanon together, the past bursts into the present with revolutionary potential for change that opposes its oppressive perpetuation in the usual ways. Perhaps the significance of Marilyn Monroe is that she brings the oppression of women into the book's political perspective and makes it broader and more inclusive. Also, her substantive political tie with Fanon positively overarches John and Paul's personal relationships with Katrine and Chantal.[22] However, more than any specific significance or meaning, the image of Marilyn Monroe and Fanon disrupts expectation about slavery and oppression, and "stimulates an alternative vision that rescues the viewer from the usual unexamined scenery dutifully absorbed" (41). The writer highlights the past through the image, and then recasts it from a hopeful perspective. Hypothetically, the disruption of the past allows the possibility of a present vision in which "[e]verything will be different." Readers can now think about oppression and how it affects us in new ways, and maybe they can create a new world where oppression's hold is broken. This changed world will also be one where racial ideology will not preclude love.

The narrative process concludes positively as John describes the experience with Katrine that frees him from jealousy generated by the racial paradigm and from slavery. The last seventeen pages of chapter 4, "The Island," consist of one creolized sentence portraying John and Katrine touring Martinique and John evoking its past history as he goes. The sense of slavery's oppression becomes stronger as the chapter progresses. It culminates in the depiction of the past life of Habitation Latouche, the seventeenth-century mansion they are visiting, where John feels the presence of "Africans whose muteness, tonguelessness overcomes me, sits me down on a stone bench and keeps me sitting still, still so I can listen, interrogate the silence with my own, attend the muted spirits, summon them, beg them to forgive me for appalling distance, appalling ignorance, forgive me for not avenging their terror, their captivity, their immolation in *béké* ovens whose fires they tended and fed with the fuel of their own dark bodies, my body, my lost brethren" (160–61). At the end when they reach the sea, the writing symbolically undercuts oppression's intersection with the present through its evocation. A natural environment free of its commerce in African slaves, the sea washes over Katrine's body, making John as he watches realize that he can escape the legacy of the past by denying jealousy based on racial ideology. He wants to "mingle" his body with Katrine's, "not to possess but share the plentitude, share my fullness because there's so much, too much to squander or hoard just for myself, just for a day, so I want to share, I'm brimming with the story of the day, the pleasure and need to tell it" (166). The realization of human diversity or true difference, the "plentitude," can lead to love and also to the breakdown of oppression generally.

Gerald V. Bergevin well sums up *The Island: Martinique*'s mediation of the political and personal. About the ending, he writes: "Wideman has called forth the ghosts who inhabit the contentious boundary between love—which individuals seek to give meaning to their lives—and politics, the collective effort that is our only hope for a transformed society of the future" (Bergevin 88). At the end, John is "brimming with the story of the day, the pleasure and need to tell it" (*The Island: Martinique* 166). Here and throughout the text, the story is an experimental, creolized process that focuses on the mind and imagination to change reality, which is reminiscent of the power of Marilyn Monroe's positive "dream" (146).[23] Through the story's process, maybe he (and perhaps John Edgar Wideman) can discover the possibility of love, release guilt and self-accusation about his complicity in oppression, and move beyond sadness, pain, and bitterness about his personal life and related political reality. He gives readers the opportunity to engage oppression politically and personally by participating in the process too.[24] Everything considered, the treatment of oppression with its deep resonance in the narrator's personal life is compelling and enthralling, making this perhaps Wideman's most interesting auto/biography.

2

A Glance Away, *Hurry Home*, and *The Lynchers*

MODERNIST EXPERIMENTATION AND THE EARLY NOVELS

ohn Edgar Wideman's first three novels, *A Glance Away* (1967), *Hurry Home* (1970), and *The Lynchers* (1973), are products of an apprentice-ship period in his career. Wideman would not find the true focus of his writing, which would set the course of its development, until his publication of *Hiding Place* in 1981. At that point, he began to write about his own personal life and development and the life of the Homewood community where he grew up, emphasizing African American cultural and literary perspectives for the first time.[1]

Thematically and formally, the white modernist literary tradition heavily influences *A Glance Away*, *Hurry Home*, and *The Lynchers*. Modernism was a twentieth-century artistic movement between World Wars I and II during which literary modernists emphasized the theme of alienation and structural and stylistic experimentation. Modernist writers often created characters who projected feelings of alienation originating within the self into the outside world; in many instances, though, one cannot separate internal and external alienation. Implicitly, readers also are not in touch with their true selves and the reality of the world around them, and, like the fictional characters, suffer social, moral, and spiritual alienation. Experimentation further implies the goal of shaking readers out of complacency by giving them different and unfamiliar literary experiences, and getting them to change by looking freshly at their similar conditions. As Wideman has said many times in interviews, he has been an experimental writer throughout his career; experimentalists T. S. Eliot and William Faulkner are among several modernists who influenced his early work.[2]

Experimentation makes *Hurry Home* and *The Lynchers* challenging, but overall the three early novels are no more difficult than the auto/biographies. It may seem intuitive that fiction would be more difficult than auto/

biography since the latter supposedly deals with real life. However, as we saw in chapter 1, Wideman uses essentially the same techniques in the auto/biographies and in the novels and short stories to fictionalize life events. Therefore, while fiction and auto/biography pose equal challenges for the reader in the different phases of Wideman's writing, both the later fiction and the auto/biographies, which he began to publish after he had found the focus of his career, reveal his growth. As his career develops, he uses increasingly complex experimental fictional approaches and techniques in both genres. Wideman's move toward the postmodern allowed him to give his writing a much more clearly political focus, to theorize about the politics and the political potential of writing, and to write more self-consciously about his process of writing and the shaping of reality through words and stories.[3] Beginning in 1981, Wideman increasingly used these postmodern techniques in his treatment of issues related to being a black writer and to the African American community overall.

Many of the characters and places in the first three novels are the same as those in the fiction and auto/biographies published in 1981 and after, but in the early novels, Wideman does not specify place and people as he does later. For example, several characters in *A Glance Away* appear in works after the early novels as the same people with the same first names; as similar people with different names; or as different family members with the same name. Lawson is the name of the paternal side of Wideman's family, and although the details of their lives are different, Eddie Lawson in *A Glance Away* has come back home to accommodate to family and community after having alienated himself like the character John Wideman in later works. Portrayed similarly, DaddyGene is clearly John French, the maternal grandfather in the later writing, and Freeda is Freeda French, the grandmother. Brother Small is virtually the same as Brother Tate in *Sent for You Yesterday* (1983), and Brother's sister Alice is very much like his sister Lucy in the 1983 novel. Also, Martha, Eddie's mother, is the name of Wideman's mother's sister in the works that follow. Eddie's sister is Bette, which is what Wideman calls his mother, Lizabeth, a major character in the later writing. This is not repetition; Wideman has taken the same people and setting and made different imaginative and creative uses of them.

* * *

A Glance Away shows the influence of a Euro-centered education that emphasized the importance of the complex, experimental work of white modernist intellectuals and writers. Wideman, too, experiments in complex ways in his first novel, but he does not try to replicate the themes, techniques, and cultural milieu of white modernist writers. Instead, in *A Glance Away,* Wideman uses modernism in his own unique experimental effort to penetrate into the depths of everyday black life and authenticate it in the context of what his education influenced him to view as a great literary and intellectual tradition.

The prologue of *A Glance Away* establishes its modernist theme and experimental modernist technique of storytelling. Thematically, it portrays the past, giving an account of the birth of Eddie Lawson's brother, Eugene, and of the early life of Eddie. The general focus is the alienation of the male characters and their resulting pessimism. In spite of the characters' good intentions, something in them that they cannot articulate contributes to a disturbing milieu of estrangement. Daddygene is lovable but often at odds with his wife, Freeda, primarily because of his wine drinking and actions when he drinks. Clarence, Eddie's father, loves his wife, Martha, but becomes estranged from her as well as from his two sons. Daddygene's funeral pessimistically concludes the prologue as Freeda, Martha, and Clarence, a "triptych of sorrow" (18), stand at his grave.

Wideman augments the modernist tone through irony and fragments of popular and typically modernist mythological allusions. The narrative alludes to gospel songs in ironic contexts—"on that great gettn' up morning there will be some who have never fallen asleep" (19)—and also to playful rhythmic syllables associated with song and song jingles—"Fa la la, fa la, fa la" (20) and *"Froggy went a courting."*[4] (Daddygene used to sing the words of the latter song to Eddie.) He adds references to Greek mythology: "Goats nibbling at the blossoms . . . damn the scavenging goats, beards waterdipped and brown" (20). The goats are reminiscent of the mythic, goatlike satyr, often a figure fond of revelry, which is another instance of irony in this context. The irony, which blends with the narrator's caustic attitude, adds pessimistic coloring. Wideman constructs the rest of the novel through similar thematic formulations, which are also aspects of experimental linguistic structure.

The narrative presents the perspectives of all the characters, as illustrated in this description from the prologue of the graveside scene:

Freeda flanked by Martha and her son-in-law, Clarence. In black a compact group, the two younger people obviously supporting pale, veiled woman who stared with precarious dignity outward, eyes fixed, reflecting gray of overcast sky dim like shadow of pride and fear so familiar when for years she had watched Gene go. So close the three yet each frozen in some vague distant posture as if the secret core of each being had moved out from the soul's recesses to circumscribe and isolate the figures, catching a pose, a gesture, an inevitable attitude or expression which made escape or penetration impossible, touching like stone figures twisted into some baroque fantasy, but distinct because the stone is unfeeling, cold, dead. Freeda felt herself sink into the soft earth, each shovel full of dirt landing heavily in the hole seemed to lower her deeper and deeper, sucked down into the vacuum of the earth's bowels. Little Martha skinny, trembling in an invisible wind, a sound of someone crying deep inside her floating up to her throat, pouring out as a sigh or sob each time she relaxed the pressure on her tightly drawn, bloodless lips.

Fall day, day falling to death rattle of dirt clods on wooden box, drum roll Clarence listened to oddly aware of black silk thrust through his arm, Freeda's weight rigid, stone cold like flesh not at all; black silk on a stone mannequin who when he moved would topple into the mud. House that Gene built small now, thought he, doubly awkward in the face of love and death. Returned he had to manless women, to their sorrow, to Daddygene's wine-rotten death in the bathtub and his own slow dying in mirror eyes of woman he loved. To his sons already strangers, already were Eugene and Eddie straight limbed and silent. (18–19)

In the tradition of modernist experimentation, the writing is cryptic, elliptical, convoluted, linguistically inverted, and allusive rather than specific and clear.[5] Its rendition of the characters' minds has the overall ambiguity and complexity of William Faulkner's modernist stream-of-consciousness writing in *The Sound and the Fury* (1929). However, Wideman's narrative is different because it is predominantly third person—sometimes moving briefly into the first person—and mainly describes, comments on, and analyzes the characters to a limited extent from the third-person viewpoint. Faulkner's first-person stream of consciousness, as well as most other stream-of-consciousness portrayals, does not provide this kind of interpretive help. Regardless of the influence, Wideman's approach fits generally into the tradition of modernist experimentation in which writers develop their own complex styles and approaches to convey meaning and tone. As the novel develops, it concentrates more on in-depth portrayals of Eddie and the other main characters, but it continues to experiment with telling all the characters' stories in the way that the prologue does, adding a few variations along the way, a noteworthy one coming at the end.

In part 1, Wideman changes the focus to the drug-ridden life of the grown-up Eddie, just back from rehabilitation, and connects the novel to the modernist tradition more strongly by the inclusion of a white main character, Robert Thurley. Thurley is a professor of comparative literature who ruminates about a range of European and white American artists and their work—Sophocles, Raphael, Rabelais, Stendhal, Flaubert, Chopin, Mozart, and T. S. Eliot among them—and he also knows something about black artists and culture, as shown by a reference to Miles Davis and one of his jazz pieces (43). However, Thurley, a homosexual with a proclivity for black men, is primarily a white modernist character, and the main model for his characterization is J. Alfred Prufrock, the effete modernist figure from Eliot's poem "The Love Song of J. Alfred Prufrock."[6] Thurley is ineffectual like Prufrock, and broods over words from Eliot's poem that characterize Prufrock—the query "how should I presume?" for example —and connect him to Thurley. A major indication of Thurley's sad modernist life is the episode in which his former wife, Eleanor, forced him to participate in a love threesome in which he had to lie beside them in bed while she had sex with his best friend, Al. Part 1 gives details of a strained relationship among Thurley, Brother, and Eddie, and ends with an angst-ridden account of the love threesome.

Part 2 deepens the despair by highlighting literal and imagined death. Nothing about Eddie's present or past, including his drug rehabilitation, during which his roommate committed suicide, seems good or even satisfying. Talking to his sister, Eddie concludes that "[t]here's nothing here for me. I'm dead, Bette, the plain fact of the matter is that Eddie's dead"

(128). Their mother, Martha, overhears their conversation, in which he also tries to get Bette to go away with him and leave her, and falls down the steps dead. Traumatized, Eddie, for the first time since his childhood, goes to church on this Easter Sunday to try to find "something to drive away fear and death from the darkness" (140); he finds nothing. The last several pages of part 2 portray Thurley and Al, both drunk, going to the chapel futilely looking for refuge and hope on Easter also. After having rushed from the chapel to vomit (144) before a hopeful "message of rain in a cool draft" (145) is lost in "general darkness" at the end of part 2, Thurley sees a vision of himself dead: "He saw faces looking down on him, grief-stricken, pitying faces obscured by veils. Thurley was stiff and unmoving; the faces passed in procession peering down from a tremendous height, each one tendering only a brief pathetic glance, as if afraid a longer look would draw them into the pit where Thurley was stretched cold, unmoving as stone." Obviously, the potential for salvation in part 2 is uncertain, whether death is literal or imagined.

Wideman also uses experimental techniques probably inspired by Irish modernist James Joyce throughout part 1. Structurally, part 1 briefly experiments with a dramatic form in which characters speak their parts after their names and parenthetical expressions describe the characters and the action (49–51), which seems like parts of Joyce's *Ulysses*, and dashes precede the spoken words of characters instead of quotation marks, as in *A Portrait of the Artist as a Young Man* and *Ulysses*. Wideman's experimental techniques in this section are obvious, but fit into a generally experimental narrative and do not substantively change its overall flow, shape, or movement.

At the end of part 3, the technique changes when the narrative represents the unbroken flow of thought in the first person in Brother's mind, and then the thoughts of Eddie, Thurley, and Brother conflate. The first-person narrator briefly intrudes to refer to the conflation: "Their thoughts twist in the darkness" (178). Immediately following, thoughts become almost indistinguishable: "The fire, the fire"; "I've made many mistakes"; "Burning . . ."; "I am sick"; "Turn to the sound of crickets in the grass"; "Death is so close my flesh angers the bones"; "The fire." After this, the characters' thoughts alternate, still barely distinguishable. The novel ends with Brother's thoughts symbolizing a bond:

I wonder how far away [the sky] is somebody should know somebody should find out and tell people cause I'm sure they want to know look at them both closer to my fire now and both looking at the flames I wonder what it feels like to burn if it always hurts once your hand is in it deep and if it pops and sparks like wood and if the color is the same and if it hurts and where does it go if you keep it in smoke rises through the trees to the sky towards the black roof where the sun will come if the sun comes tomorrow does it hurt or smell and how high up the smoke kids do it stick their hands right in you gotta keep them away or they'll do it like bugs who get too close and burn up I see why they try once why they want to touch I can see it in Eddie's eyes in the white man's eyes that stare at the flame they want to touch to put them in and see if it keeps hurting I can understand why kids do it cause I want to touch myself just like one I want to put my hand in I want to go to smoke and see how high. . . . (186)

As stated, the narrative often sounds and looks similar to Faulkner's stream of consciousness, but from Brother's narration to the end (170–86), it is even more like Faulkner's writing than the rest of the novel.[7] It is almost solely an unpunctuated or irregularly punctuated first-person point of view that approximates the flow of thought without the intervention of the third person. This part of the narrative is thus more ambiguous and complex than what has preceded it. Still, it is not an attempt to replicate Faulkner directly because it evolves into the conflation of thought in three characters' minds in the first person instead of one.

Indicative of the influence of white modernists on Wideman's work, Thurley, the character derived from another white modernist figure, becomes the one among the three who creates at least a glimmer of optimism. In the bar Harry's Place where Eddie used to buy drugs, the drug dealer uses Thurley, since he is Brother's friend, to pass along a threat to Eddie to stay away after rehabilitation. The situation inspires Thurley to help the grieving Eddie, and thus to make a positive change in his own life also. Brother's thoughts encompass the three at the end, but it is Thurley who can perhaps give the emotional support to get Eddie through the night, and if Eddie can make it, maybe he can survive and the three can. The ending by no means reverses the novel's pessimism, but suggests hope like the ending of Eliot's "The Waste Land."

* * *

Cecil Braithwaite in *Hurry Home* suffers from a profound feeling of alienation. Like Thurley in *A Glance Away*, the educated Cecil contemplates words and scenes from Eliot's "The Love Song of J. Alfred Prufrock" and "The Waste Land" that support his alienation. However, also like *A Glance Away*, Eliot and Faulkner are not the only modernist influences on *Hurry Home*. James Joyce is an influence too, as Kermit Frazier points out: "The most significant references to Joyce come in *Hurry Home*, perhaps the most experimental of the three [early] novels in terms of language. And the aura of Joyce manifests itself through the use of words. Cecil, somewhat like Stephen Dedalus, is interested in language, and the extent to which it can identify things" (30). Frazier gives examples of *Hurry Home*'s Joycean language, and shows that Cecil is sometimes conscious of using Joyce.

The entire novel portrays Cecil trying, with uncertain success, to come to terms with himself; his wife, Esther; the memory of his dead son, Simon; and his community. The novel consists of several different formal structures used experimentally, including journals and letters. Generally, it is a fragmented, convoluted, elliptical narrative that is vivid and haunting because it is so elusive. *Hurry Home* is much more experimental and, if anything, more deeply enshrouds its characters in a modernist environment than *A Glance Away*. And, while Wideman's experimental approach in both novels utilizes modernist-influenced techniques, themes, and ideas to explore black reality, in *Hurry Home* Wideman uses this approach to access the deeper, hidden, abstract dimensions of blackness.

The novel is about Cecil's construction of his identity or personal history —part of a broader history of Africans, African Americans, and humankind—through dream, imagination, fantasy, and myth, which are essentially the same, as much as from objective evidence. Wideman says:

> I hope that the reader sees that what was specifically Cecil's experience becomes conflated with the whole collective history of his race, that there is a thin line between individual and collective experience which permits one to flow into the other. It has to do with imagination. Cecil can suffer because somebody centuries ago suffered on a slave ship. In the novel this happens through an imaginary voyage, but I feel very strongly that people have this capacity to move over time and space in just such an empathetic way. It's almost silly to talk about whether it's a fantasy or whether it's hap-

pening because all of our experience has that same collapsible quality. It's a question of trying to blur that line between dream and reality. (O'Brien 10)

Group history is similarly dream, imagination, fantasy, and myth:

> To go back into one's past is in fact dreaming. What is history except people's imaginary recreation? . . . You have Christians writing history, you have Muslims writing history, you have blacks writing history. Each will create a myth. And so too if you're asking about somebody's life. You will find various versions, you will get various dreamers. It's appropriate to look at Cecil's attempt to go back into his past and to create an identity as also an attempt to create a dream. There is an arbitrariness in meaning that is somehow close to the logic of dreams. The line between Cecil's actual past and his dream past—what is it? Where is it? (O'Brien 10)

Wideman implies that Cecil's imaginative, fantastic, mythic, dream journeys in which he creates individual identity are like group histories, like the creation of all identity and history, whether ostensibly based on the objective or on dreams, because historians shape the objective in a larger mythic context that is much greater than any objective foundation. In fact, the myth becomes so great that the factual sources of its foundation are almost totally obscured, leaving largely the myth.[8]

Archetypal stories and symbolic art color the tone of dream, imagination, fantasy, and myth that constitute the story. Wideman talks about some of the contributing motifs:

> Cecil's passage through the black section of town on his way to get a haircut . . . more or less parallels the Passion, and he is in fact crucified by his own people just as Christ was crucified by the Jews. That archetype is there. The shoeshine boy [who incites the people against Cecil] corresponds to a specific character in the Biblical story; there is a crowd there and the whole episode is structured around Saint John's version of the Passion. . . . When Cecil goes back to Africa his Uncle Otis tells him the story about Roderic and the Visigoths and the Moors. All that is based upon an actual story. Otis also repeats the story of Tarik, the Moorish warrior who led the invasion of Spain. (O'Brien 12)

The painting of Hieronymus Bosch is also important. "I used Bosch for tone, exaggeration, and the surrealistic manner that I sometimes employed. But also for specific details. Under [the Bosch painting *The Garden of Delights*] is where two of the characters meet, and the pretext for going to Europe is to see the real thing. The picture is used again outside The Prado where Cecil meets a friend and they talk about Bosch" (O'Brien 12). The Bosch painting adds to the novel's surrealism, particularly for readers who have seen it, and Cecil talks about it and makes it explicitly an aspect of plot and theme. There are other influences such as the music of Heinrich Schütz that impact the story subtly, but the archetypal stories of the Passion and the Moors in Spain stand out along with the symbolism of the Bosch painting.

The scene in which Cecil goes to get a haircut that is informed by the Passion concludes part 1, and is indicative of the novel's overall narrative texture. At the beginning of part 1, the phrase "Why did you do that," first spoken by a white woman when Cecil drops a crushed can down a stairwell, is a motif that will be repeated. It refers to Cecil's lack of understanding about his identity or history. He does not know why he dropped the can or why he does anything, and does not know who he is or what his past is. The question is the impetus for his dream journeys to find his identity in the rest of the book. However, Cecil searches for the answer even as he has sex with the woman who asks it, before he takes a journey to Spain in part 2. Although it seems that the affair with the woman actually happens, it is unclear whether it does: "He fantasizes a sexual encounter with one of the women in the building in enough graphic detail to lead readers to question whether the event actually occurs" (Byerman, "Queering Blackness" 100). Like a dream, the episode flows together with Cecil's preoccupation with his wife and dead son: "As my son died her red hair keeps falling. It is sand through my fingers. Here I lie with this strange white woman and Esther [his wife] downstairs and Simon [his son] dead. She asks *why did you do it*" (24–25). This question is also implied as the people in his community abuse him at the end of part 1. Cecil, the subject of ridicule because he has educated himself and gotten a law degree, really does not know why he got the degree or how he ended up the source of mockery and abuse. He inexplicably reacts like Christ in the biblical setting that is the model for the scene: "It is done; I am delivered"

(36). This apparently does happen, but reality is inseparable from dream.

In part 2, Cecil imagines that he is a part of a Bosch painting: "The 'Garden of Delights.' I am a horseman in the enchanted circle. Others ride beasts magically corresponding to their species of damnation. Leopards, lions, camels, oxen, bears, hogs, deer, unnamable eclectic mounts, haunches of bloodhound, head, chest, and forelegs of an eagle, pelicans on a goat's narrow back, mounts and mounted leisurely around a charmed circle in whose center a still pool with naked women standing thigh deep in dark liquid. . . . Men and beasts in an arbitrary hierarchy, even an arbitrary stability of form amuse themselves as best they can within the closed circle of the sensual dream" (51).

Along with the other thematic and formal elements of modernist experimentation, the tone generated from Cecil's viewing of Bosch's dream-like work colors the portrayal of his relationship with two white characters. Charles Webb is a writer whom Cecil meets while he is standing in front of a Bosch painting. He has an illegitimate black son of whom Cecil reminds him, and he pays Cecil's way to the Prado Museum "[t]hree thousand miles away" to see another version of the painting (44). Cecil feels contradictorily attracted to and repulsed by Webb because both of them are dreaming their past: "I dread enough the mystery of my own past without entangling those longings and memories with another man's dream of himself" (51). Webb sometimes dreams himself as a Prufrock figure: "Webb walked along the beach dreaming a Prufrock dream of himself" (99).[9] Albert, whom Cecil talks with about Bosch, too, is a white man who leeches on Webb and accordingly attaches himself to Cecil. Perhaps the text does not portray Albert as being as ensconced in dream as the other two, but overall it depicts the relationship among the three men as a "sensual dream" like the painting.

Cecil's Uncle Otis tells him the story of the Visigoths and the Moors in part 3, but while in Spain in part 2, Cecil keeps imagining that he is El Moro, the Moroccan African, to counteract his negative emotion. While it is unclear why viewing the Bosch painting frightens Cecil, his feeling of conflation with his African American ancestors who suffered the oppression of slavery is a possible explanation. Because his ancestors lived it, as Wideman says in the interview, Cecil can sense the nightmare of slavery, imposing its reality as his history and identity, in the disturbingly bizarre painting. El Moro gives him an alternative black identity that entails power and control: "Whatever else they think about [El Moro], they remember in their blood that he once had the upper hand, that they paid him the conqueroo's tribute, that he was a teacher" (64).

Cecil journeys to Africa to reclaim his heritage near the end of part 2, a real journey that once again conflates with a dream. On the way, he has a relationship with an apparently depressed woman who jumps overboard (he does not try to save her); the account of this is particularly dreamlike: "Cecil . . . is suddenly salty-eyed as he dreams of Anisse sea changed, scaly and supple-tailed, of hair growing and her chicken voice gone to pure nightingale" (112). Then, "[t]here is no Africa. Only curtain mist and sea split by prow. Cecil is afraid to approach the rail. A tiny man with a big mouth screams *Man overboard. Man overboard,* inside Cecil's chest. Through the spiraling echoes a pig roots for food. Cecil will not release the voice because Cecil knows, in spite of her freckles and plains, Anisse is not a man but a woman, and in spite of the fact that she is a woman, she doesn't want to dance at the end of any more hooks." In the last paragraph of part 2, "Cecil couldn't decide whether Africa rolled across the horizon or was just some cloud of fog and mist being pushed seaward from the land" (116). The journey to Africa is misty like the dream of the woman, but the image of Africa and the power of the imaginary black conqueror El Moro that oppose oppression may be the most positive aspects of Cecil's dream. Part 3 is a continuation of the dream.

The early section of part 3 is Esther's life story, but parts of her narrative bring to mind Cecil's dreams. Esther's attention to shaping reality with words, a concern of Cecil's, from the beginning associates her story with him: "With the aid of a pocketbook edition of Webster's *New World Dictionary* Esther Braithwaite began her memoirs" (119). "Esther sought the word from Alpha to Omega" (120). Esther seeks her own words, but her "memoirs" at one time repeat words, first spoken in the novel's third paragraph, that are the key to Cecil's identity quest: "Oh Cecil, why did you do it." And in the context of the words, she is also looking for answers about his journey, specifically about why he left her, as he is. Further, although it may not be completely a dream, Esther's story is dreamlike, and merges into a dream about Cecil near the end: "I dreamed he touched me. I dreamed unmaiden dreams of wind in my hair and against my thighs. I was in water and Cecil from nowhere like a hawk plummets through the air, I saw a dark cliff where he leaped from and he was a bullet about to slam into where I was floating and I knew the spray would dazzle, would burst and make ripples and circles and flowers in the water" (129). Pleading for Cecil with God and emphasizing her "words," the very religious Esther says at the end: "Do not renounce him. . . . hear my fervor, my words. He is in Your hands, Your hands" (130). Because of connections to his characterization, such as his preoccupation with words and the journey itself, and its overall dream quality, this could be Cecil's dream of Esther dreaming.

The section after Esther's "memoirs" is Cecil's "journal," which by implication would also distance the narrative from dream and make it a more objective account, but it does not. Always the wordsmith, Cecil takes the pose of the writer classifying his narrative: "There is no novel. I have a vivid imagination, and countless frustrations. Therefore I retreat to illusion, fantasy. Call my imagining my novel. Journal as close as I get. But not even journal, more like . . . like nothing but fantasy, illusion" (154). The "journal" is Cecil's fantasy, imagination, or dream too. The last words are: "So Cecil dreamed" (185).

A stream-of-consciousness form that portrays the main character's modernist life, *Hurry Home* is the most experimental of the early novels. It is a development beyond *A Glance Away* that one might also describe as dream consciousness because it more radically contests the reality of the objective world and leaves what happened in the novel—if anything real or objective did happen—undecided at the end.

The Lynchers is an interesting combination of imagination and external reality. As Wideman describes the book: "The novel started out with these two tendencies—realism and fantasy. *The Lynchers* is in part plot-oriented; I wanted to create drama and get the reader involved with it. On the other hand, the subject of the book is imagination. The novel absorbs some of the philosophical assumptions that caused experiments in form over the last several years, and attempts to merge them with a more traditional plot line" (O'Brien 8). Realities of the past and present strongly drive black imagination, and imagination in turn plays an important role in determining contemporary realities, which are part of the same pattern of oppression that generates imagination. The characters' imaginations of reality are forced on them to some extent by white people's imagination of them, but all the actual atrocities of the past, lynching being central, and actual contemporary oppression play a greater role in black imagination and concomitantly lead to the characters' deaths or to their actions being thwarted.[10] Imagination is as important as actuality, though: "[A] subterranean apocalypse does come to pass because people are changed more by their imagination than they are by actual external events" (O'Brien 9). However, these characters are not free just to imagine like Cecil. Their plan fails, and they suffer the consequences.

After *Hurry Home*'s ambiguous plot, *The Lynchers* really stands out. It deals with the centuries-old issue of black revolution in America from a unique perspective. Four black conspirators—Willie Hall (Littleman), Thomas Wilkerson, Leonard Saunders, and Graham Rice—plan to lynch a white policeman publicly. Littleman expresses the idea: "We must say No, you cannot define us, you cannot set the limits. No, the flunkies you pay to keep us within bounds are not enough. We must show how the cops are symbolic. How they are too few and how these few can be made to disappear. We will lynch one man but in fact we will be denying a total vision of reality" (*The Lynchers* 116). He implies that the lynching of a white man will symbolize black resistance, and will change the black history perpetuated by the oppressive white symbolism of black lynching.[11] White people can respond by attacking black people, or they can ignore the lynching and do nothing. Black people can fight if attacked, or they can live in peace if ignored. Either way, blacks will define themselves as free in the future by taking assertive action that precipitates their destiny. As in *Hurry Home,* imagination is virtually the same as dream, which the characters often do, but generally *The Lynchers* is an experimental work that is relatively accessible because stream of consciousness portraying imagination largely reflects some sense of the characters' tangible contact with the external world.[12] Also, while the novel's theme, tone, and structure are modernist, there are no characters or quotations specifically derived from white modernist works. Everything considered, in line with what Wideman says about involving readers, those without strong literary backgrounds can concentrate more easily on plot and interesting historical and contemporary issues.[13] Overall, *The Lynchers* focuses on the effect of historical oppression, symbolized in lynching, on black imagination as it intersects contemporary actuality. Deviating from the first two novels' overt foregrounding of modernist influences, *The Lynchers* makes black history and contemporary life more vivid and central.

Although his external life is usually depicted, part 1 begins as Orin Wilkerson, Thomas's father, is having a dream in which he is singing sweetly in contrast to the grimy, venomous life with his wife, Bernice, to which he awakens. This connection between song and a more positive dream of life suggests black cultural potential that is not the novel's focus. In a later section where he gives an account of talking to a jazz musician and listening to jazz, Orin envisions an early-morning gathering place called Harold's where he and his fellow garbage men are evil and edgy and still superficially dreaming about pleasures that their hard lives belie. However, Orin's surmise that "maybe jazz dreaming too" (39), accompanied by his speculation about why people like to listen to jazz in dream-inducing dark rooms, casts a different light on the men's dreams and temporarily creates a positive tone. The episode implies that there is a different way of dreaming and imagining associated with black music that may counter the imagination of black oppression. *The Lynchers* picks up on this thematic thread related to black song and jazz most clearly near the end, where Orin and Bernice finally come together more sympathetically after he goes to jail. Bernice can only touch Orin's hand through the bars and "[tell] herself to pray" (258), indicating her reliance on the black religious tradition. The treatment of musical and related religious aspects of black culture that are potentially ameliorating is not one that *The Lynchers* pursues beyond brief episodes, but significantly it does anticipate the depiction of black culture in later works.

The struggle between Orin and Bernice, mainly a result of Orin's (Sweetman's) sexual philandering, is a plot connected to the plan to lynch a white policeman. Orin's and Bernice's lives turn in a direction as tragic as the lives of the conspirators when Orin kills his longtime friend Wilbur Childress, another garbage man, in a stupid fight. One further tragic spin-off of their lives is that Rice hears about the murder and later shoots Thomas, primarily because he distrusts him and the other conspirators, but also because the thought that the murder's publicity will endanger the plan still angers him.[14]

The multiply deadly connection among Orin, Rice, and Thomas shows how the plots intertwine in a cycle of actual white oppression and the black imagination of white oppression, which contributes to it. Orin's bad life to a large extent is a result of poverty and limited opportunity caused by the actual oppression that dominates the conspirators' imaginations. His life leads to his murder of another black man, which is a secondary factor in Rice's murder of Orin's son. These are the real acts of black men, but they are just like the real historical acts of white oppression against black people that dominate the conspirators' imaginations. These acts augment the actual oppression that the conspirators imagine and that they fight in their imaginations. The pattern is hopelessly repetitious; after the traumatic cycle of white oppression and the oppressive imagination of it begins, none of the black characters escape.

The Lynchers documents the history of white oppression of black people at the beginning with the "Matter Prefatory," a twenty-two-page account of atrocities taken from various sources such as a nineteenth-century black petition for justice from Kentucky Negroes and black autobiographies. These are the actual events that enthrall the imaginations of the conspirators, set the plan in motion, and raise expectation.

After the "Matter Prefatory" and another long section at the beginning of part 1 that portrays Orin and Bernice, but deals more with the stories of their sexual exploits told by Sweetman/Orin and the other garbage collectors, the conspirators appear in a vivid plotline as they congregate to plan the lynching. The scene seems very realistic as their tension slowly evolves toward a discussion of the plan. The characterizations of the conspirators are clear. Littleman, who has a powerful upper body but walks with the aid of a cane and leg braces because his lower body is crippled, is the main planner and motivator. Saunders, a street hustler and former athlete, is the assassin who is always close to a deadly violent confrontation with Littleman. Thomas Wilkerson is a schoolteacher and the most formally educated, and although he always seems shaky and apprehensive, Littleman has apparently chosen him for participation in the plan because his difference from the other conspirators complements the group. Rice is the low man whom the others do not respect and whom Littleman uses strategically to keep the guns.

The plan appears as a fairly vivid reality too when the characters talk, but at the same time Littleman's language already starts to push it toward debilitating imagination. The lynching of the white policeman is on one hand graphically visual: "You wouldn't take his clothes off. Nobody would give a damn about seeing his pot belly and flabby ass. Leave him in his obscene blue uniform. Pour a sack of flour over his head while the noose is being fitted. He'd be sweating so much the flour would stick like it does to a wet chicken breast you're dipping to fry" (63). However, apparently because everyone cooperated in a deed defining white community power (62–63), Littleman, "a failed poet" himself (61), says "[a] great artist must have conceived the first lynching . . . from the raw fantasies of his peers." He rhetorically asks, "Do you think niggers could ever get themselves together enough to do a lynching in the grand manner?" (63). The supposed artistic conception has become a historical reality that imaginatively inspires him. Littleman obviously imagines that the lynching is possible, but in the present an artistically conceived lynching by a black person must stay in the realm of imagination and dream.

From this point, the depiction of the characters and their efforts to come to terms with the plan fades in and out of dream and becomes increasingly dreamlike. For Thomas, the plan makes sense because he can clearly see the oppression and sordidness of his life that it would subvert. Littleman's words haunt Thomas, but he still has a hard time seeing them materialize as the plan. He takes refuge in a dream: "When his eyes open the dream of the lynching is still there. He does not know if he has slept ten minutes or ten hours, just that the room is dark and the dream is fresh" (68–69). Thomas "peel[s himself] from the dream" (69), but from a perspective that is part dream, part reality, he thinks about the plan with regard to his unsatisfactory job as a schoolteacher, his romance with his fellow teacher Tanya, and the relationship between his mother and father. He is seemingly there when Orin shows up to meet Tanya and makes a bad scene with Bernice. However, part 1 ends like a dream as Thomas cannot determine whether Tanya actually came to the door and witnessed the altercation or if it was someone else: "She's not coming. Or has been here and will never return" (104). He fantasizes that he will run and get her and they will return to console and reconcile his parents, but then runs down the "shadowy landing" of the stairs through a "slice of light" away from a nightmare that he is not sure really happened. He loses a sense of objective surroundings in the general context of his attempt to grasp the plan, and it cannot be objective for him either.

The world briefly comes back into clear focus at the beginning of part 2. Thomas meets Littleman as he is watching a basketball game that the narrative describes graphically. There is a contrast between the supple bodies of the athletes and Littleman's crippled one that implies that he is dreaming about somehow being like them, but the emphasis is on the action Littleman sees on the court. They have met because Thomas has doubts and needs Littleman to convince him of how the plan will work: "Do you believe anyone would have the strength to start all over if the new day, the emptiness [after the revolution] ever really comes" (114). Littleman answers: "That's the kind of thinking I want to get rid of. I don't need to think about then. Look at what's here. How real it is. Don't you remember what you saw a few minutes ago. Brick and stone and money and marble. All that's still there. You can peek through these ruins and get a glimpse." Overall, the episode depicts a man of conviction trying to convince one who has none that the world around them and the plan are real.

Shortly following this, however, Littleman, the main proponent of the reality of the plan, starts to slide deeply into dream. Before the plan is supposed to begin, Littleman makes the militant speech on the steps of a junior high school that leads to his beating by the police. The speech does not make sense because it should be obvious beforehand that it might preclude Littleman's participation in the plan. The speech does not occur in a dream, but the way it happens, inexplicably and uncontrollably, is reminiscent of one.

The speech takes on additional dream ambiance because it gets subsumed into the dream that increasingly encompasses Littleman. The first description of events begins with a somewhat surreal narrative of the setting as the police close in on Littleman: "Its cyclops eye bloodshot and spinning, the squad car hovered outside the entrance of Woodrow Wilson Junior High School" (119). The initial description continues and finishes along these lines (119–22). The second account starts after the speech and during the beating, and focuses on Littleman as he loses contact with the external world: "I am dreaming or hallucinating. Nightmare lethargy. I want to move my finger but the pain is unbearable" (136). When Littleman awakens, the presence of the conspirators in his hospital room and his beaten body show that the occurrences were not a dream, but everything has an imaginative and dreamlike quality for him.

The possibility that Littleman dreamed a relationship with a woman named Angela colors the accounts of the speech and beating. Littleman's initial memory of his good relationship with Angela comes after the first description of the speech and beating. The relationship sounds as if it actually happened. The second description dealing with the beating after the speech, which did not happen during the relationship with Angela, associates Angela with the speech because she is on Littleman's mind as he leaves home that day. He has probably been imagining or dreaming her: "Angela still a warm blur clouding his thoughts. Image of her sleepy eyes caressing his back as he creaks down the stairs" (133). The relationship starts to sound more imaginary, and later it becomes fully part of Littleman's dream world. He thinks: "Had I invented a life for Angela? . . . If I doubted the [life Angela talks about in the] dream, why not doubt the total memory of Angela, accept the interlude as fiction, a prop, an anchor created by a lonely man? What proof were those hours of waiting [for Angela] beneath City Hall? What proof was Angela's face divided among a hundred women at whom I stared?" (171–72). One could doubt the actuality of the speech and beating too, but Littleman's injuries appear real.[15]

Littleman moves further into dream, then back to a state which is still like an out-of-control dream/fantasy. He has a dream of a black God that "end[s] without a revelation of the God's precise human shape" (188), but with the hope that "I can no longer doubt the spirit has been released and received, a new man born" (189). In Littleman's mind, maybe the God is the young black hospital attendant Anthony, a witness to Littleman's beating at the school whom he now tries to recruit to execute the plan. Littleman's thoughts at the time that he makes the unrealistic effort to enlist Anthony, young, scared, and incapable of conceptualizing the plan, are a distorted, unsettling dream/fantasy: "I sense discontinuity, inappropriateness. A mass of people have been displaced. The stumbling rows of houses cannot contain them. They spill onto the streets and the streets cannot hold them, the people keep slipping away. Rivers are in their eyes. They disappear behind luxuriant trees. Run across wide, grassy fields. Superfluous clothing falls away. Their arms and legs are sculpted by a wind that never aired these streets" (189). At the end of part 2, Littleman hears his own out-of-control voice "shouting [at Anthony as] a nurse and an orderly [rush] into the room" to sedate him (194), ironically laughing and imprisoned now in a physical state where he has even less control.

Saunders in part 2 never clearly focuses his oppression-filled imagination retributively against white people; instead, he most directly hates black people, a manifestation of oppressive self-hatred that is potentially oppressive for other blacks. His always close to deadly violent antagonism to Littleman and especially his virulent feelings about black women, even his own mother, show this. He reveals his hatred for his mother as he witnesses her strip away her clothing in a tortured delusion about her oppressive life: "They had always called him cold. He knew why then. A numbness in his limbs, an icy wind swirling through his chest" (149). His feelings for the prostitute he is stalking and has to kill (so that they can blame and lynch the policeman, her pimp), the prostitute's daughter, the old woman living with them, and apparently all black women are more explicit: "Wipe all the silly bitches off the face of the earth. Walls [of the prostitute's place] were pressing in on him. Had to get out. . . . Business done he was gone forever. That's the way it was with nigger wenches. The stink. The chill. Too familiar to Saunders" (165).[16] Saunders's imagination may not incapacitate him like Littleman's dream, and maybe he could murder the white policeman to initiate the plan. However, one has to wonder if he could carry out this plan against whites if he has such strong negative feelings about black people. Part 3 supports the idea that Saunders's hatred is futile and he cannot utilize it. In the last view of him, he is waiting for the already dead Wilkerson, imagining killing him for not being there when the plan is supposed to start, among other angry thoughts. The plan is in his mind, but the direct object of his rage is someone black once again.

The plan will obviously fail in the end. In a section of part 3 dealing with Wilkerson, his doubts about the plan ultimately lead him to try to stop it by going to Rice's apartment to confiscate the guns they will use. This is when Rice shoots him, helping to stop the plan with the kind of violence against a black person that the plan is supposed to stop. All that is left after the shooting is the portrayal of Saunders's futility, a brief scene showing the abject condition of Orin and Bernice when she visits him in jail, and the bitter death of Littleman,[17] who never emerges from the region of dream/fantasy.

The white modernist influence is strong in this pessimistic novel, but it powerfully portrays African American life. It does not matter that many times the reader cannot tell whether *The Lynchers* is depicting imagination/dream/fantasy or actual external events. This story is very compelling because it so well shows the relationship between the two, and how they can interact in a powerful, potentially deadly, inescapable connection.

3

Hiding Place, Damballah, and Sent for You Yesterday

NEW DIMENSIONS OF POSTMODERN EXPERIMENTATION
IN THE HOMEWOOD TRILOGY

iding Place (1981), *Damballah* (1981), and *Sent for You Yesterday* (1983)—the three works that follow *The Lynchers* (1973)—are called the Homewood Trilogy because they tell stories about the life of Wideman's family and the people in the Homewood community where he grew up. Between 1973 and 1981, Wideman lived with his wife and children in Laramie, Wyoming, and taught at the University of Wyoming. Ironically, he changed the direction of his fiction to emphasize black culture while he was away from the black cultural traditions of Homewood. As he has said in interviews, the stories he heard about his own family and the community when he went back to Homewood on family occasions inspired his change of focus, but having distance from the black communal source gave him the perspective he needed to change.

The focus on blackness marked a departure from a reliance on European tradition, especially modernism, which had been a staple of Wideman's first three novels:

> In my first three books, the way I tried to assert continuity with tradition and my sense of tradition were quite different than my understanding of these matters in *Damballah, Hiding Place, Sent for You Yesterday.* . . . That is, for my first books, the tradition was mainly European, mainly literate. Because I was a black man and had grown up in a black community I sort of divided my books. Blackness provided the local habitation and names; the scenes, people, conversations, were largely drawn from my early experience, because that's what I knew best. But I was trying to hook that world into what I thought was something that would give those situations and people a kind of literary resonance, legitimize that world by infusing echoes

of T. S. Eliot, Henry James, Faulkner, English and Continental masters. . . . But as I grew and learned more about writing, I found, or rediscovered I guess, that what Bessie Smith did when she sang, what Clyde McFater did, what John Coltrane did, what Ralph Ellison did, what Richard Wright did, what the anonymous slave composer and the people who spoke in the slave narratives did, what they were doing was drawing from a realm of experience, a common human inheritance, that T. S. Eliot, Faulkner, Tolstoi, and Austen were also drawing from. As a writer I didn't need to go by way of European tradition to get to what really counted, the common, shared universal core. I could take a direct route and get back to that essential mother lode of pain, love, grief, wonder, the basic human emotions that are the stuff of literature. I could get back to that mother lode through my very own mother's voice. (Rowell 95–96)

A black construction of postmodernism replaces white modernism as the main feature in Wideman's writing, and alters its tone, theme, and form.[1] The work published in 1981 and after focuses on the black cultural tradition, and the rhythms and nuances of the black oral voice become a more dominant structural influence than forms and structures derived from the white modernist tradition, such as stream of consciousness. Alienating modernist states of dream and imagination in the early works are prevalent in the Homewood Trilogy, but are secondary to an emphasis on black cultural stories, told in a black voice, that unite and support.

Similar to what other black and ethnic writers do using divergent approaches, Wideman derives black voice and story from postmodernism's general premise that all art and literature, as well as reading and interpretation, is biased, subjective human construction. In "'All Stories Are True': Prophecy, History, and Story in *The Cattle Killing*," Kathie Birat makes statements relevant to my point about postmodernism in Wideman's writing after the early works. She argues that Wideman uses "strategies which have come to be associated with the phenomena grouped under the terms poststructuralism, postmodernism, and deconstruction" (629).[2] In the context of postmodernism, Wideman "concentrates on reading American history in search of stories which may be turned back upon themselves in a self-reflexive gesture which will liberate them from the frozen discourse of a totalizing vision" (631). "[F]or Wideman the very power of storytelling lies in its capacity to embrace the endless movement of language itself, 'writing,' if not necessarily 'righting,' the wrongs of an 'upside-down' world" (641).

Stories told from a black perspective make white stories "self-reflexive," self-critical, breaking down their dominant, "totalizing," fixed negative perception of blackness; this points toward a broader vision that is truer—though not definitively true—because of its diversity. "All stories are true," which is the title of a later volume of Wideman's short stories, means that every person and group has a self-interested or ideologically inspired version of truth—not *the* truth—that develops from experience, and diverse stories give an overall perception of truth, which is always evolving in the "endless movement of language[/stories]," and which we constantly strive for but never reach definitively. The concept of linguistic movement, one that other postmodern writers share with Wideman, is like both his concept of stream of consciousness, in which thought theoretically flows continuously in the conscious and unconscious mind, including dream, and Great Time,[3] where theoretically everything happens at once and all stories are simultaneous. As Heather Andrade expresses it: "In Wideman's works, narrators, voices, stories, histories, myths, imaginations, readers, are woven together, ebbing, flowing, spilling out onto each other's textual bodies and into the body of the text" ("Race, Representation, and Intersubjectivity" 44). This is Wideman's theory of stories ever unfolding in both a linear and circular fashion.[4] The process bonds those who see the world similarly, and allows others empathetic connection and insight into different realities. Stories are therefore important as stories because of the very act or process of storytelling. Stories can more correctly "'write,' if not necessarily 'right,'" an unbalanced vision of the world. Postmodern stories are as complex as modernist stories, but they lack the implication of definitive truth that underlies the grim modernist vision.

Stories may include facts, but are really more about constructing perspectives of reality. Different individuals and groups can start with the same facts, but they will not tell the same stories precisely because they are different. The so-called facts are only the foundation for the creation of subjective, and thus biased, stories that shape meaning in a larger context. Stories grow into something much greater than facts, and factual sources are in effect obscured, leaving only the stories. Many assume that a historical narrative is factual because it is "history," but according to postmodernism, history is not an unbiased rendering of factual events, but is itself comprised of stories. In both history and fiction, "the meaning and shape are not *in the events*, but *in the systems* which make those past 'events' into present historical 'facts'" (Hutcheon, *A Poetics of Postmodernism* 89). Historians and others write and read history, and along with books that are the sources of their research and everything humanly constructed, they are "systems" structured by ideology, self-interest, and bias.[5] Their subjectivity intrudes heavily on writing and reading to create a story that makes the factual highly secondary to the subjective.[6]

Wideman's postmodernism generally concurs with a range of postmodern theory, but not with critics who say that stories are politically indeterminate. Although these critics would agree that all art forms and responses to art are political because they represent ideology and human interest, they would also state that art is indeterminate in political and social change because the relationships among creator, art form, and reader/observer are too unstable to promote meaning that leads to political action. This aspect of postmodernism does not project beyond its own theory; it does not have an "effective theory of agency that enables a move into political action" (Hutcheon, *The Politics of Postmodernism* 3). It remains ambiguous about "agency" or instrumentality in art and its role in political change. Stories are valuable because they give an experience in language and not because they move people socially and politically. Some critics correctly observe that Wideman's writing "resist[s] postmodern indeterminacy" (Andrade, "Race, Representation, and Intersubjectivity" 45) because of its sociopolitical intention and attempt "to enact social transformation." For Wideman, while stories are not definitive, neither are they politically indeterminate; they are intended to move readers toward a broader, truer, diverse perception of reality that corrects sociopolitical inequity and makes social transformation possible.

In the publications after 1981, Wideman's writing evolved toward this formulation of postmodernism because it has greater social and political potential. Among his main goals in using postmodern experimentation and its politicization of art and all human culture are to show that race is a constructed concept and not natural, and to subvert the allegedly true stories about blackness underlying racism that are also constructed.

Wideman's primary focus is always on a process of writing/storytelling, and by no means does he offer didactic prescriptions for social or political action. Nevertheless, he intends to bring about change by affecting the imaginations of his readers, as the stories in the Homewood Trilogy illustrate. Wideman first appears as a character/writer/narrator telling/writing his own story and listening to stories in the Homewood Trilogy. He does this because postmodern thinking and experimentation allow him to blur the line between fiction and nonfiction as human constructions. This opens up the writing process so that he can reveal the human construction of all stories, and at the same time draw attention to his positive role as a black writer constructing black stories. The stories are often tragic, and in them, black people almost never solve problems permanently and create a happy existence. In spite of much that is bad, however, black people maintain themselves and sometimes triumph in the face of pain and oppression. The stories are always potentially empowering because they project the way that black people think about their endurance and survival in a harsh world, and herein lies the potential that the stories will engage other people empathetically and contest one-dimensional, negative stories about blackness, opening the way for social and political change.

Hiding Place begins the postmodern experimental phase, but is the most accessible of all Wideman's works, probably because he is finding his way in a new direction in his writing. John Lawson, the surrogate character in *Hiding Place*, comes from Laramie, Wyoming, to reorient himself to Homewood and write about it, paralleling John Edgar Wideman's real-life efforts.[7] The character named Clement describes the tentative entrance of John, who feels alienated because he is educated and materially comfortable: "Tall man in a suit ducked in the door [of the Brass Rail Bar] and looked around real careful like maybe he in the wrong place, like maybe he subject to turn around and split somebody yell *Boo* real loud" (98). *Hiding Place* is similar to *Hurry Home* and *The Lynchers* in its emphasis on alienation portrayed through stream-of-consciousness structures representing dream and imagination, but in *Hiding Place* and the other two works in the Homewood Trilogy, alienating dream and imagination merge with stories that restore lives, reconstitute family and community, and build tradition. Modernist influences are still evident in Wideman's work as the new phase of his writing develops, but he also unveils post-modern concerns about black storytelling and his task as a black writer constructing stories about Homewood. Overall, *Hiding Place* unveils family and community stories that portray a complex secular, spiritual, and supernatural folk tradition that has been the source of life from slavery to the present; black people utilize their tradition to fortify against dangers projected from within the self and to unify against racism from outside, emphasizing that they are the tradition's complex, substantive products and creators.

Two of the main characters initially live in both dream and imagination of self, family, and community and physical isolation, but dream and imagination merge into oral stories that restore positive self-identify and reconnect them to family and community. Mother Bess resides alienated on Bruston Hill, the abandoned family home place, because of the death of her husband and the loss of her only son in war. Her relative Tommy, a fugitive falsely charged with murder, absconds in self-imagination separated further by the desperation of flight. The diagram of family genealogy before part 1—also a feature in *Damballah*—shows the connections between Bess and Tommy and others in the family that the narrative development makes more meaningful.

The core of Bess's story that reconnects her is the death of Tommy's niece, whom his sister brought to her shack on Bruston Hill, but through the memory of her grandmother Sybela Owens, who ran away from slavery with her master's son and established Homewood, she is part of a much longer heritage.

The sweet babies [when Sybela was alive and Bess was young]. And some almost as old as me. Takes all kinds to make my people. You pass by a couple years ago you think [Bess's] crazy as a loon rocking up on that porch and grinning like a Chessy cat at herself and rocking and smacking her thigh and talking and ain't a soul up there but her. But that's my people up there and I'm coming and going and sometimes it's enough to make me laugh out loud.

Used to do a lot of that. But I been up here too long now. Two many new [family] faces and I can't see nothing in them. No names, no places. Just faces and I think on them and all I see is Bess, myself behind my eyes and

I mize well be blind as Mother Owens cause I been up here on this hill too long. (32)

Although she was blind as Bess remembers her, Sybela "looked over" positive, productive family relationships when she sat on the porch on Bruston Hill, as Bess does now. The sighted Bess is like her because her negativity to others is figurative blindness, but Bess's blindness fosters sterility instead of productive relationships.

Bess's first stories about family history that include the fugitive Tommy are stream of consciousness. She finds him sleeping in her shed after she refused to hide him from the law inside her shack, and the relationships start to come together in spite of her denial.

> He would be Freeda's daughter Lizabeth's son. Freeda the quiet one raised by my sister Aida and Bill Campbell. . . . Quiet as she was didn't stop her from running away with that gambling man John French. Quiet Freeda marrying a loud man twice as old as she was. . . . Funny how things turn out. [Her sister] Gert had Freeda but Aida more like Freeda's mama. Aida raising Freeda while Gert gallivanting around. Then [Tommy's mother] Lizabeth born dead [to Freeda]. Freeda's [*sic*] first lying there blue as a piece of sky but [her niece] May saved her [by plunging her in snow and shocking her into life]. Little twist this way or that none them be here. They catch Mother Owens keep her down in slavery wouldn't be no Bruston Hill. Now Lizabeth's son out in my shed. . . . (48–49)

After encountering Tommy, Bess's sterile stream-of-consciousness stories become productive oral ones as she recounts bonding family history in an ongoing process. Later, she lets Tommy come inside, and she tells him a story that begins with his sister Shirl and her daughter. Shirl brought the child to her and called her "Mother Bess" because "[t]hey think I'm mean enough and crazy enough and old enough to have some kind of power so they bring the little ones and push em up in my face" (130–31).

> It was your sister, Lisabeth's middle child, the one they call Shirl she one of the last I let in here. Favors her Mama and her Mama's the image of Freeda, my sister's girl. Freeda was the oldest and the prettiest in her quiet

way. But don't you let those quiet ways fool you. She run away with John French quiet enough didn't she? So quiet she fooled everybody till she come back four days later and told Bill Campbell, I'm married. I'm married now. And she was married good. You know John French married her good. Quiet as she was she was married good and you could see the brazen in her eyes you never saw before when she come back after four days talking about she's married to that rogue John French.

She's the one. The one they call Shirl. Don't tell me I don't know youall. I know just who you are. Wrapped up like some Indin Chief in my blanket. Snoring like a hog at my table. (128)

Bess repeats some of the same details, but this time she addresses the story directly to Tommy, affirming his family identity and hers.

The story Bess is telling catalyzes the emotional investment in family she had when she was young that has been waiting to be rekindled since Shirl brought her the baby, who later died. The one they sent to tell Bess "[s]aid they'd bury her on Wednesday and somebody be by in the morning to take me down. Didn't pay no mind to all those words. Heard him talking and heard him getting mad cause I didn't answer [the door] but I wasn't studying him or studying no funeral or no Wednesday or nothing else because [the child's] big black eyes was in this room and I said Jesus and said good God Almighty because that's what I say when there ain't nothing else to even say though I ain't been a Christian for years, Jesus and good God Almighty cause what else you gon say when some old woman ninety-nine hundred years old still living and breathing on the top of this hill and that little baby's gone" (130). The story brings back the feeling, suppressed during Shirl's visit and the baby's funeral, which now affects her relationship with Tommy and the family.

Tommy is alienated in the imagination of self, and Bess draws him out through her interaction and her stories. At the funeral of his niece, Bess saw the signs of Tommy's alienation. Leaving the funeral, he "was alone, moving away from the others as fast as those stiff shoulders and man's suit and grave dust all over his shoes would let him" (54). His exploits when he is building his own image in the streets and his consequent bad treatment of his wife, Sarah, and child constitute the stories that dominate his imagination and alienate him. Tommy also has memories that could be positive family stories, but he recounts them in a frame of romance that shows his discomfort with stories. "Once upon a time. Once upon a time, he thought, if them stories I been hearing all my life are true, once upon a time they said God's green earth was peaceful and quiet. Seems like people bigger then. . . . Aunt Aida talking about people like they giants. The world was bigger, slower and he'd get jumpy, get lost in it." "Once upon a time" then frames him "in a story" with Sarah that ends with him being "[s]maller than nothing and alone" and with the conclusion that "[s]tories are lies" (79). When he runs to Bruston Hill and sleeps in the shed, Bess first symbolically pulls him from his hiding place of imagination: "Someone pulling on his foot. Have him by the foot and dragging him out the cave where he's been hiding. . . . Yes. He is hiding deep in the rivers of his blood. . . . But they have him by the foot dragging him out" (72). After extracting him, she engages him with stories.[8]

Bess's stories will not prevent Tommy from going to jail, but their influence enables him to come out of alienation, talk to her in a positive voice that could tell positive stories, and return to Homewood. The final paragraph of the last "Tommy" section supports this: "This very goddamn dreary quiet ain't got no choice night, old woman. Old Mother Bess. Finish this cup of moonshine [whiskey] and put my foot in the path [for Homewood] and say good-bye. Say thank you Mother Bess even if you don't want to hear all that mess, even if you cuss me with your fine old cold self" (152). They are not separating, however; Bess returns to Homewood, too.

At the beginning of the last section of the book, entitled "Bess," she is in a dream state telling the same family story that she has earlier emerged from dream/imagination to tell Tommy, but this is not a regression for her. The novel's last paragraph emphasizes that she will go back to Homewood to tell people Tommy's story. She will "go down there and tell the truth. Lizabeth's boy didn't kill nobody. He wasn't scared. All he needed was another chance and somebody needs to go down there and tell them. And she was going to do just that. Burn down that last bit of shack on Bruston Hill and tell them what they needed to know" (158). Bess talks more to Tommy than she listens, but as her resolve to tell stories about him implies, both telling and listening are important. Stories from her black perspective are "true" because black listeners understand and because others can relate and understand how black people have struggled and come to places in life where they have acted as they have. These stories oppose negative white stories of blackness, and are the stories Wideman wants to write in his postmodern phase.

Similar to the way Tommy and Bess come together through stories, the novel portrays the men of Homewood perpetuating tradition that unifies the community through different oral forms and rituals, which are modes of storytelling. They engage in mock-adversarial barbershop talk and tell anecdotes and stories about each other and Homewood people. They are already making Tommy's escapade that ended in the death of a white man part of the story of Homewood (142–43).

The tradition that the men are carrying on includes belief in the supernatural; this is in part represented by their stories about Bess being supernatural, just as her family portrays her. According to Big Bob, the barbershop owner who runs the numbers game, she "ain't natural" (139). Saying that "she had power [and] she had magic" (135), one man plays a number based on a dream that he had about Bess. The number hits, and to appease Bess the man sends her a hundred dollars through Clement, the novel's other main character who works in the barbershop. Bess sends Clement back to play a number that hits even bigger, and thus confirms the story of her being supernatural. Bess explains that she was partly lucky, but her explanation seems to put more emphasis on greater power. "[H]ow you [Clement] gon know what I'm talking about. You just a baby. Ain't no way you can get as deep as I'm going and I ain't even wet yet. I'm just playing numberology and trickology" (142). Her ability to summon Clement without directly contacting him is supernatural, too: "Nothing strange about being miles away in Big Bob's and hearing her call him" (33). Beyond what the men believe, the novel implies the importance of belief in the supernatural and the stories that constitute it. In Wideman's postmodern context, these stories are "true" for Bess and Homewood because they believe, just as Bess's other stories and black stories about Christian spirituality are. The stories portray a depth of supernatural and spiritual belief defining cultural substance for everyone who empathizes.

All aspects of the tradition generated through different forms of storytelling, such as song, unify the community to present *Hiding Place*'s postmodern story.[9] For example, in barbershop banter and anecdotes and

Homewood lore generally, the orphaned Clement is the subject of ridicule because he is retarded. However, Clement's negative characterization is paradoxically supportive because it is a way of accepting and giving him a place in community, and having this place mitigates the effect of orphanage. The story that is *Hiding Place* thus conveys how black culture has an underlying humanity larger than its insensitivity. This is another indication of Wideman's postmodern project in which black stories counter negative, superficial ones with perceptions of black cultural substance.

In the short stories in *Damballah,* telling stories and listening to them unify people as in *Hiding Place,* but *Damballah* also includes stories transmitted differently that create a myth of Homewood. In postmodern terms, the mythic stories present "true" black beliefs and worldview. Further, through his appearance as a character, the writer John is blurring the line between fiction and nonfiction, and calling attention to stories as human constructions and to his construction of black stories that balance constructed white ones. The stories are personal family stories and stories of the community that both family and community people know because they tell and listen to them. However, the stories bond everyone together in a larger connection because, in Wideman's words, "the whole rationale of the stories presumes certain kinds of narrative license or imagination, which allows one person to get inside another person's skin" (Samuels 21).

In an analysis of the portrayal of John in *Sent for You Yesterday* that also applies to *Damballah* and *Hiding Place,* Ashraf H. A. Rushdy states that "the boundary between self and Other is problematized to the extent that an uneasy integration between those two entities becomes possible"[10] ("Fraternal Blues" 319). In *Damballah,* John Lawson is the surrogate for Wideman. He is sometimes the first-person character who is the writer and an outsider trying to return to the community and resituate himself by learning to tell stories. However, in the context of Rushdy's analysis, John can theoretically be the third-person narrator with both communal and intimate knowledge of individual characters that he contributes to a Homewood myth.[11] Like the Homewood myth constructed by the community, John's mythical construction includes various kinds of stories (including songs) that transmit commonly sustaining history, beliefs, and traditions of the secular, spiritual, fantastic, and supernatural. It also encompasses the wide-ranging antagonisms, oppositions, tragedies, and triumphs that show endurance. Overall, John's magical ability to share stories and create a tradition is inseparable from ongoing, transgenerational storytelling in Homewood that produces intersubjective, commonly known stories of the past and present. John is theoretically the writer creating a common myth in each story at the same time as family and community. John is inside the characters' "skins," sharing stories with and among them, speaking in their voices, using narrative devices that connect them, producing a body of stories that is a myth. This theory is tenable because of his characterization as the writer in three stories, the connection he makes between the first and last stories that symbolically connects all of the stories, and the similarity of the stories all the narrators tell throughout *Damballah*.

John connects *Damballah's* first and last stories to symbolize the transgenerational sharing of stories that constitute the myth of Homewood; therefore, in his characterization as writer, he implicitly writes "Damballah," the title piece, a story set in slavery about African traditions being passed to African Americans in the process of myth making. It portrays the spiritual connection established between an African named Orion newly arrived from "the Indies" (22) and a boy born into slavery. (The American-born slaves, who hate and fear him because his rebelliousness threatens their safety, call Orion "Ryan.") Through his spiritual link with Orion, whom the white master kills, the boy gets in touch with the voodoo god Damballah, and combines African religion with Christianity, as shown by the reference to the river Jordan from the black spiritual: "Damballah said it be a long way [the] ghost [of Orion] be going and Jordan chilly and wide and a new ghost take his time getting his wings together" (25). At the end, the boy says the word "Damballah," which the other slaves have forbidden him to say, and "listened to Orion tell the stories again" (25). Orion transfers his stories spiritually, which parallels John's creation and that of the family through their Christian spiritual rituals in the last story.

"The Beginning of Homewood," the last story, has a direct connection to the title story through John's reference to the "old heathen Orion" (198) when he recounts Sybela Owens's thoughts about Orion. John dedicates the story to his incarcerated brother Tommy from *Hiding Place*, who is a surrogate for Wideman's incarcerated brother Robby, to whom *Damballah* is dedicated. The characters include great-great-great-grandmother and runaway slave Sybela, who founded Homewood; implicitly Orion and other slaves of that community; Aunt May, who is a great storyteller in the present; and Mother Bess from *Hiding Place,* who has moved back to Homewood and is telling stories; and John.

The story is a linguistic, ritualistic narrative process that symbolizes crossing time and linking many of slavery and the present in the history of struggle. The narrator talks about what he is doing and suggests how storytelling works:

> I wanted to dwell on Sybela's first morning free but the chant of the [Homewood] Gospel Chorus wouldn't let me sit still. *Lord, reach down and touch me.* The chorus wailing and then Reba Love Jackson [from another *Damballah* story] soloing. I heard May singing and heard Mother Bess telling what she remembers and what she had heard about Sybela Owens. I was thinking the way Aunt May talks. I heard her laughter, her amens, and *can I get a witness,* her digressions within digressions, the webs she spins and brushes away with her hands. Her stories exist because of their parts and each part is a story worth telling, worth examining to find the stories it contains. What seems to ramble begins to cohere when the listener understands the process, understands that the voice seeks to recover everything, that the voice proclaims *nothing is lost,* that the listener is not passive but lives like everything else within the story. Somebody shouts *Tell the truth.* You shout too. May is preaching and dances out between the shiny, butt-rubbed, wooden pews doing what she's been doing since the first morning somebody said *Freedom.* Freedom. (198–99)

This is John's mythic story that is like the black community's: His narrative technique and theory make him and all the characters from the past and present simultaneous contributors telling and listening to a common story that is constantly revised and renewed. They are individuals at different times who sometimes complement their narratives with spiritual forms like gospel lyrics, sometimes with spiritual call-and-response rituals and performance. However, like May, they are also at the same time telling and listening, revising and renewing the story "since the first morning somebody said *Freedom*. Freedom." Implicitly, Sybela and Orion, their fellow slaves, May, Mother Bess, the narrator John, Tommy, and the people of Homewood bond in the quest for freedom of Sybela and Tommy and of everyone in the Homewood tradition.

The past is ongoing in the Homewood story. The narrator describes a scene with Tommy in handcuffs and shackles and compares it to a scene from Sybela's slave life (199–200). He tells Tommy at the end that "the struggle doesn't ever end. [Sybela's] story, your story, the connections. But now the story, or pieces of story are inside this letter ["The Beginning of Homewood"] and it's addressed to you and I'll send it and that seems better than the way it was before.[12] For now. Hold on" (205). The stories are an ongoing means of struggle that present comprehensive historical and cultural perspectives from the oppressive past to the oppressive, crime-ridden present. The tradition "recover[s] everything"; "*nothing is lost.*"

"Daddy Garbage" is a third-person narrative, and John has only a minor part, but it is a family story and also a Homewood community story that he is telling according to *Damballah's* paradigm. It starts by placing four generations of Homewood together to emblematize the connection that produces the ongoing construction of mythic stories, one of which is "Daddy Garbage." The story mainly focuses on the earlier lives of Lemuel Strayhorn, an old man now, and his friend John French, the deceased grandfather of John Lawson, who would be a child in the main story. However, at the beginning, when his Aunt Geraldine is walking on the street with the grown-up John, his children, and sister's children and they see Strayhorn, the action unites the generations from Strayhorn and John's grandfather, to his Aunt Geraldine and mother Lizabeth, to him and his siblings, to his children and their cousins.

"Daddy Garbage" depicts the qualities of Homewood through the primary portrayal of John French. He and Strayhorn, drunks and poor men affected by racism, ceremoniously bury a frozen baby that Strayhorn's dog Daddy Garbage discovers. John French's relationship to his own family reveals the same basic goodness. One segment of the story portrays his girl Lizabeth thinking longingly about her father because she knows he will bestow his love when he comes home (36–37). Later, when she is in the hospital having her own child (40–41), her sister has to get Strayhorn to find him because he is somewhere drinking and gambling. Although he is drunk and singing an obscene song when he arrives at the hospital, the love he expresses in his actions is clearly more important than his embarrassing public conduct (41–42).[13] In spite of being a clearly flawed man, he is a fixture in family and Homewood stories and an example of the community's assertion of humanity in the face of racism. "Daddy Garbage" becomes part of the historical Homewood struggle that stories pass through the generations represented at this story's beginning.

A third-person narrative except for short segments at the beginning and end, "Lizabeth: The Caterpillar Story" implies the voice of the narrator/writer John Lawson telling his grandmother's and mother's story about their personal relationship to John French.[14] Several stories comprise the caterpillar story. When Lizabeth was small, John French ate most of a caterpillar after she ate a small part, which was his frantic, comical way of trying to save her from death by killing himself. Later, when she was about six and Freeda was looking out the window and telling her the caterpillar story, a man crept up behind John French to shoot him as he walked home. Freeda saved him by pushing her hand through the window to distract the man, cutting her arm to form a scar that looked ironically like the caterpillar she had been talking about in her story. Another story is Lizabeth sitting up late at night to watch and save John French, who was up with his shotgun watching to kill a man who was dumping ashes on his property. She wanted to save him too since her mother had, and she needed to stop the shooting so that he would not have to run away from Homewood like his friend Albert Wilkes. Later, Freeda and Lizabeth find the gun under the icebox that John French hid for Albert when he killed the white policeman and ran away.

The narrator reveals that it is difficult to find the inception of stories in memory, to organize memory's chronology, and to tell where stories end and begin. Initially, Lizabeth remembers a straightforward scenario: "I remember you [Freeda] telling me the caterpillar story and then I remember that man trying to shoot Daddy and then I remember Albert Wilkes's pistol you pulled out from under the icebox" (48). Near the end, the narrator presents a more complex account: "If a fist hadn't smashed through the window perhaps she would not have remembered the screaming, the broken glass, the shots when she watched her mama drag a pistol from under the icebox" (62). "But Lizabeth did remember and see and she knew that Albert Wilkes had shot a policeman and run away and knew Albert Wilkes had come to the house in the dead of night and given her father his pistol to hide, and knew that Albert Wilkes would never come back, that if he did return to Homewood he would be a dead man." "Lizabeth remembered [the caterpillar story] when the gun was dragged from under the icebox so there was nothing to do but lie awake all night and save her Daddy from himself, save him from the trespassing cart and smoking ashes and the blast of a shotgun and dead men and men running away forever. She'd save him like her mama had saved him." The convolutions notwithstanding, the first-person ending shows the mother and daughter telling a coherent story about their positive remembrance of John French (62–63), which is implicitly the story of the writer John Lawson, who has also literally heard and told it.

While the women's story centers on John French, it extends to other Homewood people, places, and events, and it is implicit that community people will create different versions of the story that include John French, Albert Wilkes, and others as part of an ongoing process. The later novel *Sent for You Yesterday* suggests how the story of Albert Wilkes develops different versions that are ongoing in the present: "You could get a good, loud argument [in the Bucket of Blood] about who was the first to see Albert Wilkes when he came back. Even long after Wilkes was dead and buried, even from people who should have known better, people who couldn't have seen Wilkes first, second or last because they weren't even born that day in 1934 he returned" (56). In *Damballah* and *Sent for You Yesterday*, the narrator is talking about a complex narrative process, but his oral-sounding voice alludes to people, Lizabeth, Freeda, and John Lawson among them, constructing and telling stories of John French, Albert Wilkes, and Homewood that are a myth whose underlying composition is also complex.

John Lawson is simultaneously creating and becoming grounded in the Homewood myth to which everyone in family and community is contributing in "The Chinaman." "Chinaman" is an old black vernacular term for any Asian man, and is an imaginary but powerful reality for his grandmother Freeda. In a state of great agitation, she sees the Chinaman in the room with Homewood community people who are actually there when her husband, John French, dies, and she recalls a nightmare in which the

Chinaman's body disintegrated, foreshadowing her husband's death and also Freeda's (87–88). Her death is the story's central event.

In trying to tell the story, John is showing how he learned his voice. At the same time, he is constructing, in postmodern terms, the Homewood myth, paralleling the community's construction; his implied creation is similar to and even clearer than it is in "Lizabeth: The Caterpillar Story." Shifting, ambiguous points of view reveal this. At the beginning, he is remembering Freeda's story about the birth of his mother, which Bess has already told in *Hiding Place,* and which people in Homewood undoubtedly know. He is speaking partly in his characterization as a writer who is an unsure outsider and partly in a more certain third-person voice like the family and community's: *"Once . . . once . . .* her first baby born premature and breathless" (83). At a different place, his voice seems at least briefly to be first person and sure: "The firstborn, Lizabeth, our mother, saved by May in the snow" (85).

After the beginning section, John almost seamlessly takes over in the first person and indicates how he has used others in family and community to practice his storytelling and situate himself in the tradition. On the way from Wyoming to Pittsburgh, he first tried to tell the story to his wife, Judy: "I began to talk about my grandmother. I wished for May's voice and the voices of my people in a circle amening and laughing and filling in what I didn't know or couldn't remember, but it was just me whispering in the dark hotel room, afraid to wake my sons" (91). He knows the story although he cannot tell it. As she approached death, his grandmother began to mutter the word "Chinaman" to her children, and to them this indicated she was saying a Chinaman was coming to get her when she died. Her son Carl figures this out when he hears her say the word and remembers the "diabolical, menacing" folk jingle about a Chinaman: *"Chinaman. Chinky, chinky Chinaman, sitting on a fence. Trying to make a dollar out of fifteen cents"* (92). Her children believe that Freeda's prediction comes true. There is a Chinaman who is a patient in the hospital with Freeda, and as he is leaving after his release, he comes by her room to check on her because his family and Freeda's have become acquainted. Freeda dies shortly afterward, and the children say that the Chinaman actually came to carry her away just as she indicated. Although John knows the story, his version of it is "stiff [and] incomplete" (93).

Lizabeth finishes the story in the voice of family and communal story-telling. Talking to Judy and John later in her kitchen, she infuses the story with her religious and supernatural beliefs: "Things like that [the mystery of the Chinaman] happen in people's lives. I know they do. Things you just can't explain. Things that stay with you. Not to the day I die will I understand how Mama knew [the Chinaman was coming], but I do know things like that don't just happen. Five times in my life I've been a witness and I don't understand but I'm sure there's a plan, some kind of plan" (94). Lizabeth's voice telling the story complements John's and resonates with May's: "I am sleepy but the story gets to me the way it did the first time I heard it. My mother has told it, finished it like I never can. And the shape of the story is the shape of my mother's voice. In the quiet house her voice sounds more and more like May's" (94).

Homewood people know the story of Freeda's death that Lizabeth, May, and others have told, and will tell it in a similarly resonant voice as an aspect of the Homewood story. On the level of his role as outsider and storytelling apprentice, John has trouble telling the story right because it is hard for him to accept Lizabeth's beliefs: "For her the story of the Chinaman is a glimpse of her God who has a plan and who moves in mysterious ways. For me the mystery of the Chinaman is silence, the silence of death and the past and lives other than mine" (94–95). However, his statement at the end when he and Judy are quiet after the story affirms its importance: "The silence is an amen" (95). In his position as postmodern creator corresponding to the community's creation, he needs to tell the story and has done so.

"The Watermelon Story" affirms storytelling that inculcates values and perspectives that serve the black community in an often painful, frightening, unfathomable world. It starts in the third person at some unspecified time with a boy's account of a wino tipping over a pile of watermelons, falling through the Homewood A&P store window, severing one arm, and surviving to continue drinking wine because someone applied a tourniquet to stop the blood (100–103). He first remembered the story as a dream (100–101) and then that May was telling it (102–3). Addressing her hypothetical audience by asking, "[y]ouall heard about Faith" (104), she then tells a related story that draws on African and African American folk stories that syncretize the religious, supernatural, and fantastic. In the story, watermelons are symbols of a rich, dangerous mystery with which humans must constantly contend. Two old childless people named Isaac and Rebecca pray for a child, and miraculously find a baby boy in a watermelon. They rejoice greatly, only to have the spirit take the boy away (104–6). After this, "[t]he rest was the weeping and wailing of old Isaac and Rebecca" (106) because they had already "[u]sed up [their rejoicing] so when trouble came, when night fell wasn't even a match in the house" (107). Frightened by the story and wanting to "forget the rest," the boy asks if the wino could grow another arm: "May smiled and said God already give him more'n he could use. Arms in his ears, on his toes, arms all over. He just got to figure out how to use what's left." The conclusion is open-ended. The account of the wino can continue as part of the story of a precarious world that is concomitantly full of potential if one approaches it right and finds it.

"The Watermelon Story" is an exemplar of ongoing Homewood community construction of stories that corresponds to the postmodern writer's creation. May compels her audience: She "looked round the room catching nobody's eye but everybody's ear as she finished the rest of her story" (106). Her power is in her technique and in the story's pain, fright, and mystery, and in the substantive concepts she instills beneath the fantastic—faith, perseverance, circumspection, discernment, and equanimity among them. In the context of an ongoing tradition, the boy's initial story and May's are one story that crosses time and generations. First, it flows around an indefinite contemporary time. It is relatively recently that the wino's arm was severed at the store, but "[t]he A&P is gone now" (101). May extends the ambiguous time back "in Africa" or in "old time Georgy" (104–5), "[w]here people talk to animals just like I'm sitting here talking to youall," where she learned storytelling "sitting on Grandpa's knee"; then she moves it forward again and leaves it open-ended with the final reference to the wino.

In the context of stories being shared, the third-person narrator is a Homewood communal voice. He knows the child's, the wino's, and May's stories and all the multilayered stories they could tell, and is, like them, a storyteller. The story is the past and present community's creation that belongs to everyone, as indicated when the boy surmises that it is his property through a dream: "He dreamed it like that many years later and the dream was his, the throne of watermelons belonged to him, green and striped and holding the heat of the sun" (100–101). As in "The Chinaman" and other stories, it is also implicitly the creation and property of John Lawson the postmodern writer. John is part of the community, or trying to engage it by learning to tell stories like the boy, and he is also inside and behind everything that happens. The creative convolutions and connections and back and forward flow are as ongoing and open-ended as the tradition.

In "The Songs of Reba Love Jackson," different voices tell stories that are past and present, individual and collective. In the final analysis, this is another story of Homewood. The narratives include *One for Brother Harris in Cleveland*, which portrays an anonymous first-person narrator answering Reba Love's phone during a gathering when her friend Brother Harris calls asking her to sing because his mother has died. The song is a spiritual sharing of grief among all. A third-person narrator in *For Blind Willie Who Taught Me to Sing* describes the scene when the child Reba Love and her mother, Precious Pearl Jackson, encounter Blind Willie, a blues and gospel singer, drunk and asleep on the street. This story is about the life that has created Precious Pearl's spirituality, the travail of Blind Willie that has affected him spiritually and made him a singer, and the encounter with Blind Willie that impacted the spirit of Reba Love and "taught" her to sing. At one point in *For Old Time Preachin*, a first-person black vernacular paean to the master preachers and singers of the past, the narrator explains the rhythms of the preachers' vernacular that played on Standard English to evoke communal spirit: "And you talk about talkin. Mmmm. They could do that. Yes indeed. *Epistemology* and *Cosmology* and *Ontology* and *Deuteronomy*. They was scholars and men and knew the words" (116). He concludes by placing Reba Love among them. In *For Somebody Else*, the third-person narrator explains aspects of Reba Love's life and worldly experience, especially her first sexual episode, which she could not speak aloud. This reality, and expiation for what she thinks is human frailty, emanates spiritually from her songs instead. *One More Time for Blind Willie* is another third-person perspective on his misfortune that is the source of his song. It is interspersed with secular and religious song references, and ends with Blind Willie's imagination of Reba Love singing and of elevating himself spiritually to sing with her.

Songs are rituals of communal storytelling that evoke an unspecific, commonly accepted story; the community imagines the general story of oppression and hardship through the deep emotion, the spirituality, of the singing. The narrator in *For Somebody Else* reveals how Reba Love's songs relate to the community: "Couldn't speak about some things. She could only sing them. Put her stories in the songs she had heard all her life so the songs became her stories" (120). The last narrative in Reba Love's voice, *This Last Song's for Homewood*, makes a similar point in explaining how her songs are her main expression: "*This is my story. This is my song. Yes. Praising my savior. All the day long.* Sang with a scrub brush in my hand. Sometimes I think I ain't never sung no better than I did all by myself on my knees doing daywork in the white folks' kitchen. But I know something about Homewood. . . . Could tell you plenty about Homewood in those days [when I was young] but youall come to hear singing not talking and that's what I'm going to do now. Sing this last one for Homewood" (128–29). The listeners know only a few specifics of Reba Love's life, but they share the feeling emanating from the spirit of the songs. In turn, the myth of Homewood that resides in the stories told by people in "The Songs of Reba Love Jackson," as well as throughout *Damballah*, depicts the life they share with Reba that she spiritually evokes in her songs. It is not just what those in the present feel; it is the common emotion of all the singers and storytellers in communities of the past. Those who have experienced a similar life and heard the songs know what she means. All of the different voices along with Reba Love's represent the Homewood community that has told its story and heard her songs, including John Lawson, who would have heard her in childhood and on return visits. The third-person narrators and perhaps the speaker in *For Old Time Preachin,* by combining vernacular and high-sounding Standard English to portray the virtuoso black preacher, suggest John's presence most strongly.

The other stories in *Damballah* conform to this pattern in which John the postmodern writer creates the Homewood myth with the community. As stated earlier, in the last story, "The Beginning of Homewood," John dedicates his writing to his brother Tommy, links him to Sybela Owens and her to Orion (198) from the first story, "Damballah," and ends by emphasizing "[h]er story, your story, the connections" (205), thus connecting all the stories and implying his role as writer. The story "Tommy" is similar to the account of Tommy's life in *Hiding Place* and the auto/biographical *Brothers and Keepers* (1984), and an obvious part of the myth of Homewood that John and the community are constructing in "The Beginning of Homewood." "Solitary" is a story of Lizabeth's crisis of religious faith after Tommy's incarceration that compares her life to Freeda's after John French's death, and is very much a family and Homewood story in the tradition.

"Hazel," "Rashad," and "Across the Wide Missouri" do not clearly fit the pattern of the other stories. "Hazel" is about the tragic lives and deaths of Lizabeth's great-aunt Gaybrella and her children Hazel and Faun, whose story has not been previously told as part of the family and Homewood story constructed in *Damballah*. However, the story also significantly focuses on Lizabeth, John French, and the family. "Rashad" depicts another character not presented anywhere else in *Damballah*—Rashad, the dope-addicted, abusive husband of Lizabeth's daughter Shirl, who Lizabeth says is very much like Tommy. But again, the story deals a lot with Lizabeth and the family that is presented throughout the text. Therefore, aspects of these stories still place them in the tradition from slavery and the slaves Orion and Sybela to the present. "Across the Wide Missouri" is the most different. It is about John's painful, uncertain relationship with his father and sons, reminiscent of the auto/biographical *Fatheralong* (1994) and the fictional *Philadelphia Fire* (1990), and does not relate as strongly to the people and events from *Damballah*'s other stories. However, it has a general relationship because it is one of the three stories, along with "The Chinaman" and "The Beginning of Homewood," in which John the writer is a first-person character talking about writing, telling a significant part of the story, and symbolizing and theorizing his postmodern role and the connection of all the stories.

On one level still the outsider listening to communal stories and learning to tell them like John Lawson in *Damballah*, Doot—John's jazz-inspired nickname in *Sent for You Yesterday*—is on another level a writer figure ensconced in Homewood stories, as in the previous text. The difference is that he takes experimental storytelling further than does John in *Damballah*. He highlights the depths of the postmodern writer's creativity to a greater extent than John by imagining stories and recounting ones he has heard, flowing from first to third person in the stories, often submerging himself in past and present characters' stories, dreams, and identities, and also often blending characters into each others' stories, identities, and dreams. Clearly, he is constructing a myth of Homewood, writing the novel in a postmodern sense, at the same time that characters within his story are telling stories and constructing a communal Homewood myth in which they move across generations, knowing each others' realities through conflated identities, stories, and dreams.[15] Further, whereas in *Damballah* John Lawson grounded his myth in his family, as Doot in *Sent for You Yesterday*, John incorporates his family into his myth to make this definitely a Homewood story in this last book of the Homewood Trilogy. Achieving his goal of becoming a communal storyteller, the writer Doot parallels and becomes an inseparable part of communal mythic construction even more clearly than in the two previous works; in a complex postmodern form that combines stories and all emblems of stories, the theoretical author of *Sent for You Yesterday* constructs a Homewood myth that affirms and brings to fruition the storytelling process of *Hiding Place* and *Damballah*.

"In Heaven with Brother" begins the novel with a representation in which converging dreams are a story. Brother Tate talks with someone else, who could be Doot since he is inseparable from all the other characters, about a dream foreshadowing his horror-filled death. The other person also reveals a connected dream about an elephant symbolizing nightmarish threat that Brother incorporates into his dream. The dreams and identities of two people become one, presaging the structure of the rest of Homewood's ominous story that is ironically a supportive and sustaining mythic story of survival too. Their presence "in heaven" also suggests identities crossing temporal and spiritual or supernatural boundaries. Further, in light of the epigraph that states that each person in the present "harbors the spirit" of someone from the past, these could be spiritually connected identities that conflate the past and present. Similarly, Doot will tell his story in the novel by imaginatively assuming many identities that move across the lines between the temporal and the spiritual or supernatural and between the past and present.

At the beginning of part 1, "The Return of Albert Wilkes," the first-person narrator, who shortly after identifies himself as Doot, starts his story. He first portrays an image revealing the trepidation he feels when imagining Brother: "I was always a little afraid of him, afraid I'd see through him, under his skin, because there was no color to stop my eyes, no color which said there's a black man or white man in front of you. I was afraid I'd see through that transparent envelope of skin to the bones and blood and guts of whatever he was" (15). Used often in the novel, the "skin" is a figure for Brother's frightening story, which includes his son's death in a fire and his on the railroad tracks, and the story of Homewood.[16] Doot is already connected to Brother by stories and by his imagination that Brother must have reexperienced the life and death of his son Junebug when he looked at him: "Brother treated me special because he could see Junebug in me. In Brother's eyes I grew up living not only my own life, but the one snatched from Junebug. . . . I would be a reminder of both the life and death of his son. I couldn't help carrying both seeds. And Brother couldn't help remembering . . . what he'd lost" (17). However, Doot must pursue this troubling connection through stories and imagination by telling his own story that goes into more depth.

Doot begins at an earlier time that will give a broader creative perspective on Homewood, and emphasizes his imagination as he starts to construct a mythic story. He places his Uncle Carl and Brother in an imaginary place that is also partly Homewood before Doot was born and assumes the identity of Carl: "I am not born yet. My Uncle Carl and Brother Tate hurry along the railroad tracks. . . . Carl is daydreaming of running away. He feels the sun on the back of his neck . . . but his mind is on the ocean, an ocean he has never seen except in pictures and daydreams. If he closes his eyes he can see an ocean, red and wild as his blood, an ocean surging past the shimmering curtain of heat rising from the steel rails, an ocean rushing to the end of the world. He would run away that far if he could. To the place where the waters roar over the edge and the sky is no thicker than a sheet of paper" (17–18). The rest of this first story of Brother and Carl is about them looking for John French after Freeda learns that Wilkes has returned (17–29).[17] Although he primarily tells this part of the story from Carl's perspective, Doot continues to highlight his role as creator, alluding to his imagination and use of words and making Homewood clearly mythic by comparing it to Noah's ark and an isolated island of life: "That's the way it must have been on Cassina Way. Rows of wooden shanties built to hold the flood of black migrants up from the South. Teeming is the word I think of. A narrow, cobbled ally *teeming* with life. Like a wooden-walled ship in the middle of the city, like the ark on which Noah packed two of everything and prayed for land. I think of my grandmother and grandfather and the children they were raising in that house on Cassina and I see islands, arks, life teeming but enclosed or surrounded or exiled to arbitrary boundaries. And the city around them which defined and de-limited, which threatened but also buoyed and ferried them to whatever unknown destination, this city which trapped and saved them, for better or worse, never quite breached Cassina's walls" (20).

Doot maintains his role in which he imagines stories and constructs them from other stories, and continues his focus on the complex process in which stories and emblems of stories merge. Portraying Freeda, he says: "That's what I see, invisible in the alley, trying to remember. When I lived on Cassina Way I couldn't have been more than four or five, so my image of the inside of the house comes less from what I saw than from what I've been told since. Yet the cobblestones are real under my feet, slippery and cold from last night's rain, cold and damp until the sun gets high enough to light the shadowed stillness behind me. There must have been a cur-tain at the front window but the glass is bare now as I peer through" (30). Looking in at Freeda through the imaginary window of his story, which he develops from other stories, Doot briefly merges into the identities of Freeda and Lizabeth, identities that are inseparable from their stories about John French eating a caterpillar and a man shooting at him, which are important parts of the Homewood story: "This is the window my grandmother smashed with her fist. She watched a man sneaking down Cassina, a man with a gun, a skinny, pigeon-toed somebody whose eyes were fixed on her husband's back, a sneak with a pistol in his hand get-ting closer and closer to where she sat with Lizabeth on her lap. Lizabeth was smiling. She loved to hear her mother tell the caterpillar story. When the man in the alley raised the gun her mother's fist punched through the glass, her mother screamed, and Lizabeth screamed and John French gone like a turkey through the corn." Throughout *Sent for You Yesterday*, stories will continue to blend into Doot's stories and the stories of others, and stories will be inseparable from identities and dreams and other emblems of people's stories such as their arks, islands, songs, spirits, and skins. That is, stories and emblems or symbols of stories will constantly fuse and flow together in a complex process.

In part 1, the central story in Doot's stories is Albert Wilkes coming back to Homewood after he shoots the policeman, and Wilkes's songs are his story that is a main symbol holding the overall story of Homewood together.[18] Later, Doot calls less attention to himself as he merges further into Freeda's story and identity and also into the connected stories and identities of John French, Wilkes, and many others who are also the story of Wilkes's songs and Homewood. In John French's story, "All Homewood coming apart" since Wilkes went away (67): "It was after he got it just like he wanted it and the music started coming out that you could find yourself, find your face grinning back at you like in a mirror" (68). Wilkes has a comparable story of his own music as a story within a story. He hears the woman who raised him, old Mrs. Tate, telling the story of her life that includes him and that he takes over and makes it his story when he plays: "You push up your gray sleeves. Then you are stepping right dead in the middle of her story and you play along awhile, measure for measure awhile until the song's yours. Then it's just you out there again by yourself again and you begin playing the seven years away" (60). Playing his music is like giving people self-realization by telling their story, and in telling their story, he also tells the story of his seven years away from Homewood and of his whole life. At the end of "The Return of Albert Wilkes," remembering the way "Albert puts together the chords, the phrases, the bits and pieces into a whole song" (86), John French feels relaxed and promises Freeda he will stay home instead of going to help the fugitive, whom the police will murder. All of this is in the story and in the music too, which is the story of Homewood, and ultimately a myth that transcends tragedy.

"The Courting of Lucy Tate," part 2, more clearly reveals that Doot is the postmodern writer and the parallel construction of the Homewood myth by him and the community. Part of Doot's story is set in the present when he is thirty years old in the Velvet Slipper Bar listening to Carl and Brother's adopted sister, Lucy Tate, tell stories (117). This is the depiction of the writer who is an outsider and novice learning to tell stories the way that the community does, and implies that he is secondary to the community in the construction of the Homewood myth. When Doot is in this role, Carl understands better than he the great complexity of reality encompassed in a story. Referring to "the way the world turns," another emblem of a story, Carl says that everything is "[c]ircles and circles and circles inside circles. . . . Just a circle going round and round so you getting closer while you getting further away and further while you getting closer" (118).[19] At other instances, Doot makes his presence explicit as the writer imagining the story, and blends into his own narrative that emphasizes Carl's metaphor in which stories are never-ending circles of black mythic construction. In the final analysis, neither Doot nor the community is separable from the stories and their emblems and from each other.

In "The Courting of Lucy Tate," three of the primary characters of the next generation of Homewood, Carl, Brother, and Lucy, all carry the identity or spirit of Albert Wilkes, and he and his story live through them. The spirit of Wilkes is most obvious in Brother, who one night at the Elks Club mysteriously played the piano exactly like Wilkes (89–93). Doot speaks briefly in the first person about what "my Uncle Carl said" (90), but mainly recounts the story of Brother's feat as a third-person narrator retelling a story that Carl tells. Carl says that he was "surprised" and "scared" by the mystery of what Brother did, and that "Lucy knew better" (91) than her explanation: "Must of been Albert Wilkes taught you. And you hiding it all these years. Hiding it all this time then getting up on the bandstand and showing out tonight. Ain't you something, lil brother." There is an explanation for Brother's ability to play other than that Wilkes must have taught him when he was six or seven; in the context of people connecting through their stories and figures of stories—songs in this instance—Brother plays because he essentially becomes Wilkes by carrying his song. Carl weaves in an allusion to black folk stories to move to the end of this part of the story. "Everybody setting Brother up [after he played] and setting up his table [where Carl and Lucy sat] so why not? Didn't spend one more dime that night and drank till dawn. Shucks. I've heard there was a time when niggers knew how to fly and knew how to tell the truth. And if people could manage all that and forget all that then I'd be a fool not to listen when the listening good and drink when the drinking's good. Nothing but a party anyway. Whole thing ain't nothing but a party so why should I be a fool and sit there and fret?" (92–93).

Maybe he is skeptical about the "truth" about black people flying and is not sure that Brother played, even though he was there; however, he believes there is a mysterious reality deeper than concrete truth conveyed in black stories like the tale about supernatural flying in the tradition, Brother's supernatural musical performance, and the story about the performance. Listening to the music and enjoying the celebration afterward shows Carl's acceptance of the reality of Brother's musical story. Further, Carl implies that he knows instinctively that a person's life can be passed supernaturally from generation to generation in a process of connected stories like the folk story and Albert Wilkes's and Brother's musical stories. In fact, Carl's own story about the music passing to Brother is a supernatural passing of stories in the tradition to Doot in the Velvet Slipper, and Doot is demonstrating the passing by telling this story within a story, which is like the "circles and circles inside circles" of Carl's figure of speech. Doot will begin to tell his own story when he gets up to dance at the very end of the novel, and will in a sense be standing on his own feet independently and moving beyond the connection of stories. However, he will also be finding another way of telling a story that is similar to the performance of Brother and Albert Wilkes, showing that he supernaturally shares their spirit from their stories, and going deeper within the "circles."

In his story that continues Carl's, Doot's creative powers, the content of the story, and its atmosphere are similarly supernatural. When he emerges fully in the first person, he again invokes time magically: "I was born about six months before that evening in 1941" when Brother played (93). Then his story recedes even further: "But it's spring now. Spring one more time in Homewood. I'm not born. Not even thought of, let alone born, as somebody would remind me if I needed to be reminded" (94). As Doot assumes the third person and goes back in Carl's story, he tells of the passing of Wilkes's identity to the next generation when Lucy tells Carl the story of Wilkes's murder in the Tate house while he was playing the piano (101–2). In the story, Wilkes's blood and bone fragment that Lucy shows Carl to symbolize Wilkes have the magical power to capture his spirit, as the story itself does (103–7). Doot later reemerges in the first person to witness Carl's construction of the Homewood story as the mysterious and supernatural continue to unfold and as the story goes deeper into tragedy. Carl explains why Brother killed himself: "They kill everything" (120). "Found Brother dead on the tracks. Wasn't no blood so he was dead before the train hit him. It was something else or somebody else killed him, killed him just like they killing everything worth a good god-damn in Homewood."

As "The Courting of Lucy Tate" develops, stories continue to evolve within stories and figures of stories. Doot says that "Carl's voice gets busy telling the story his way" (123), and Lucy is "telling it to herself[,] [h]er way" (124), and then Doot in the third person takes over and tells Lucy's version of the story. Brother, who never talked much anyway except in the scat-singing musical sounds such as the one that he named Doot with, stopped talking altogether (and stopped playing the piano too) after the death of his son Junebug (121–22), the child of a woman named Samantha. Samantha wanted to save Homewood from the death that Carl talks about by having all the children she could. She had so many children that she called her house an Ark: "When this old Ark docks be whole lotta strong niggers clamber out on the Promised Land" (132). She had never had a relationship with a light-skinned man before Brother, and Junebug turned out to be white-looking like Brother and different from his brothers and sisters. They persecuted him and, in a dream that Samantha had about it (140–43), set him on fire and burned him up because of his difference. Samantha ended up in Mayview insane asylum where Lucy visited her and watched her fall apart over the years, and all of this pain had a catastrophic effect on Brother. The ark, headed to the promised land with all of her children, and the dream of the child Junebug are emblems of Samantha's story, just as Junebug's skin, like Brother's, is an emblem of his.

The text clearly makes the point about dreams and skins of existence that are like stories within stories. Junebug was born with Brother's skin, and also "was born with the secret" (137), an additional layer of skin, a "caul, [a] gauzy web clinging to [his] see-through skin." Reminiscent of the way that Brother spiritually becomes Albert Wilkes when he plays his music, Junebug is Brother's spiritual double because he is born in skin much like Brother's. Junebug has two layers of skin, Brother's skin—a story in itself—and a caul that gives him more access to the "secret" stories of others and of Homewood. Looking through Junebug's transparent skin could be scary, as looking through Brother's was for Doot (15), because it meant looking at the tragic aspects of Homewood's story that he and Brother represent. (His siblings kill him because the pain of his story is unbearable.) Samantha is Junebug in the dream of what happened to him: "[I]n the dream I'm him. I'm little Junebug" (141). Further, Lucy "had to be Samantha to understand," and "[i]f [she is] Samantha [she is] waiting for Lucy" to visit her at Mayview (127). It is impossible to separate stories and realities: Lucy lives within Samantha's and Junebug's stories/ dreams/skins, Samantha within Junebug's and Lucy's, and consequently Junebug within each of theirs. Lucy has to "shake like a dog to get [the] skin off, those pieces of Mayview and Samantha still sticking to her. If you tell Junebug's story you have to be Samantha and you have to make that long trip" (145).

Carl has already incorporated into his version of the story Brother's death on the railroad tracks[20] and other tragic elements that are the myth's malevolent forces that Homewood will ironically survive by dealing with and accepting them in the myth. After Carl talks near the end of part 2 about his, Brother's, and Lucy's drug addiction precipitated by white racism, in the last sentences of this section he invites Doot to take Brother's place and participate in this kind of mythic construction that builds survival from tragedy: "Old cream-of-wheat Brother. I know I'm supposed to be telling you his story. But how Ima tell his without telling mine. And Lucy's. Cause yeah. We was the three musketeers, all right. . . . Brother's gone and it's just me and Lucy now and it's time to get off this stool cause I'm hungry. You ready, Doot? You come over to the Tates' [house] and it be three of us again just like the old days (154–55).

In part 3, "Brother," Doot does not reveal himself in person until the end, but throughout he *is* Brother, inside his identity/skin/ dream/spirit telling his story, the story that Carl has said is his and Lucy's and that is Homewood's. Doot gets much deeper in the first section of part 3, "1941," by in effect dreaming Brother's train dream, and the conflation of stories inside dreams and of stories that are spirits connecting time takes an even more complex form. In the dream, Brother is Albert Wilkes, and Wilkes's song that Brother is playing is at first comforting, as his music was for John French earlier (86). Finally, though, it is the pain of Wilkes's life that is dominant:

[Albert Wilkes's] song like a window Brother could see [through] way down the tracks. To now when he is dreaming. To the time when he will speak to a son. To the time he wouldn't speak to anyone anymore. To the lives he would live and the lives he would be inside. Albert Wilkes's song like a hand over the troubled waters, and then the water was still and he could see everything. Everything gone and everything coming not mixed up together anymore but still and calm. Albert Wilkes's life was hanging on him like a skin to be shed, a skin he couldn't shake off, so it was squeezing, choking all his other lives. It would kill him forever if he didn't shrug it off, so he ran from the living room and up Tioga to Homewood and Frankstown and said to a white policeman he'd never seen before that Albert Wilkes was back. (163)

Brother cannot shake off the song/dream/skin that is Wilkes's tragic story, his story, Junebug's, and Doot's, and Homewood's tragic history. When he tries to escape by informing the police on Wilkes, "they stomped in and blew away his skin . . . and the lights went out and the boxcar rattling and the blood and the bodies" (163). Inescapable tragedy perpetuates itself back and forth in time leading to Wilkes's murder, which is ironic because it is the main aspect of the tragedy that forces Brother to try to escape, and further stories of tragedy evolve. There is a coffin in the boxcar holding Wilkes's body, but the coffin turns into a cradle with Junebug in it: "A tiny babyboy in a cradle rocking and a black hand tipping the cradle back and forth and it's a boy, a boy child white as snow." The cradle contains the living body of the newly born Junebug, but also ironically portends his death and, in supernatural convolutions of tragedy moving back in time, the deaths of Wilkes and Brother. Still part of the train dream, an image of Junebug's death near the end of the next section, "1946," is so profoundly painful that it stops Brother from talking for the rest of his life (172): "*Youall see that ambulance come through here. One them little childs got burnt up over to Samantha's. Say the poor little thing ain't nothing but a cinder, time the ambulance got there*" (169–70).

As the history of Homewood unfolds that is signified by the section headings of part 3 designating years, the significance of Doot's conflation with Brother is that Brother's tragic story enables Doot to carry on a positive Homewood legacy, which is how survival grows out of tragedy in the myth. The section "1946" concludes with a reference to Brother's silence; however, "1962" ends with him at the railroad tracks hearing the voices of John French and others and talking to Junebug (182). He is going to play the dodge-the-train game that he played with Carl as a child (23): "Listen here, boy. Listen to me. Watch me. Cause ain't nothing to be fraid of. Ima win this one for you. Ima be the best for you. I ain't gon back down." "Watch me play" (182). Playing is surviving tragedy, and his literal death notwithstanding, the spirits of Brother and Junebug live because Doot *is* Brother playing (dancing) at the end of the novel, which is symbolic of Homewood's very serious survival response to the force that is attempting to destroy it. The "1970" section switches from Brother's tragedy to Lucy's story, and progresses to the affirmative ending.

At the end of the novel, Doot is the third-person narrator narrating the past, then the present, and finally the first-person narrator narrating the present. He describes the past of Lucy's story: "Lucy remembers how hard it had been to clean up after they killed Albert Wilkes and how much harder it had been when she was alone in Brother's room cleaning up again" (193). Lucy situates Carl in the Homewood tradition in the present, invokes the past, and moves the story in a positive direction: "I love you more than any man, but the old Homewood people taught me you don't have to give up. I mean John French, your daddy. And Mrs. French and Albert Wilkes and Strayhorn and the rest of them. The old folks. The ones dead now. And Brother. He's one of them now. Always was one" (198). Later, "Doot [is] quiet in the chair" (200), and asks for "the story [Lucy] promised" when she points out his silence (202). She continues the positive Homewood story with an account of the time when he was young and she got him up to dance: "Then we are back in the Tate's living room and Lucy finishes the story and says, The song you danced to was 'Sent for you yesterday, and here you come today'" (207). Doot takes over in the first person in the novel's final sentences and concludes Lucy's story. He imagines Brother and Albert Wilkes coming into the room, and Carl and Lucy urge him to dance. As he does, "Everybody joining in now. All the voices. I'm reaching for them and letting them go. . . . I'm on my own feet. Learning to stand, to walk, learning to dance" (208). Doot's story is now clearly Lucy's, Carl's, Wilkes's, Brother's, Junebug's, Homewood's, and his transcendence and survival of tragedy is theirs.

Sent for You Yesterday culminates the Homewood Trilogy with an extremely provocative portrayal of black storytelling in which the roles of the writer and the community are parallel and virtually inseparable. Using storytelling methods and secular, spiritual, and supernatural sources from the black tradition, the community has skillfully constructed and passed along its story. In postmodern terms, that story is a myth that makes sense of life from black people's perspective of their struggle and survival throughout the generations. The educated, accomplished writer returns to his community to become part of it by constructing this same story. The writer utilizes postmodern techniques and approaches, but the community is just as imaginative and creative as the writer. He merges his techniques and approaches with the community's, and learns from the community as it constructs the story, which is the only way he can construct its story and integrate the community.

4

Reuben and *Philadelphia Fire*

PROGRESSIVE EXPERIMENTATION AFTER
THE HOMEWOOD TRILOGY

erhaps Wideman's most esoteric novel, *Reuben* (1987) is a link between the Homewood Trilogy and *Philadelphia Fire* (1990). It reflects a different, new phase of the creative life apparent in Wideman's writing after Doot becomes part of the community in *Sent for You Yesterday.* From the perspective of the white power structure at least, the character Reuben is an ersatz lawyer without a degree, but he is really an odd amalgamation of philosopher/necromancer who constructs postmodern "fictions" that help black people. The terms "fictions" and "stories" are interchangeable in *Reuben,* and *Reuben's* fictions are not false in much the same way that the Homewood Trilogy's nonrealistic, sometimes supernatural, fantastic, and magical stories are not. However, fictions call attention to reality's creation even more than these stories do, and have even less connection to apparent or assumed realism. The main focuses in *Reuben* are the imaginative and intellectual fictions inscribed on paper by white Western culture, and the novel's own imaginative, intellectual, and magically ritualistic fictions inscribed on its pages. As portrayed in the novel, fictions can be spoken or can be composed and enacted only in mind and imagination, but the text highlights the idea that fictions are linguistic constructions that only symbolize and do not concretize or actualize reality—the reality of blackness, for example. Fiction makers are presented in the novel as serving their own self-interest, not portraying inherent truth, when they symbolize reality. In *Reuben,* white culture is a fiction maker that has positively symbolized itself, and thus accrued the power to generate the persuasive, self-interested fictions negatively valorizing blackness that Reuben must oppose. A major problem is that negative, powerful fictions of blackness constructed by whiteness can always challenge and negate Reuben.

The text identifies Reuben's task of constantly devising postmodern fictions:[1] "[Reuben and Kwansa] needed to start again. Go over familiar territory until it wasn't familiar anymore, till it was a starting place unlike anyplace either of them had been before. Unless they started fresh they'd be caught up in one fiction or another, and that fiction would carry them wherever it was going. And its destination would have nothing to do with where they needed to go. . . . [T]hey should sit and listen, learn the first words of the story they need to tell" (17). A third-person narrator presents Reuben's fictions, and through them he often connects with the dreams and identities of others, somewhat as Doot does from multiple complex intersubjective narrative perspectives in creating stories in the communal setting of *Sent for You Yesterday*. However, focusing much more on the abstract, abstruse, and arcane intellect than on communal tradition, Reuben takes the next step by conceptualizing, imagining, ritualizing, and articulating fictions that are even harder to understand than Doot's stories. Reuben's fictions are an attempt to constitute a new myth, one broader than the myth of Homewood in *Sent for You Yesterday*, that is indefinite in time and the starting point for liberating him as a black creator and also freeing blackness from negative symbolization. Although he is not a writer, Reuben is just as creative as one and performs similar tasks in his guise as a lawyer. In the self-interest of blackness, Reuben creatively manipulates reality by devising experimental constructions that disrupt or *de*-familiarize the usual linguistic patterns of negative, self-interested white fictions of blackness; in turn, Reuben tries to help Kwansa and others create "*[de]*-familiar" black fictions or stories that are the potential beginning of positive new liberating black portrayals.

In "Thoth," the fourth of twelve fictions that comprise the novel's chapters, Reuben constructs his reality partly as an imagined, magically ritualistic beginning in which he is separated from his brother and symbolically reconnected at an ambiguous time:

All that heady double-talk about time makes his gold watch heavy this morning. If it's morning. Guiltily he consults the ivoried face of his timepiece. Ten-thirty. Has he been asleep at his desk, in his clothes? And if sleeping, how long? Rip Van Winkle years or just a few, sweet nods? An old man's oatmeal head drooping into the pleats of his turtly neck, his skin bunched under his chin like the bib his mother ties round his neck. Here, baby. Take this, baby. Her face is broad and round as an Eskimo's. He can't be remembering that woman born in another century who lay down and spilled him out upon the damp earth. Like a doe in the forest. Not only him. Two of them all spotty like fawns. A dark one and a light one. Twins on a bed of soft earth and leaves and grass. He cannot be remembering because it happened too long ago. Was he ever that young once? The cries, the shivering, light slitting open his eyes. It began when a crossbar pried loose sky from earth and he was just there, where he'd always been, under the rock of darkness waiting. Light. A terrible weight lifted and then levered down again on his shoulders. He thought his heart had been broken in two when his brother was stolen from his side. Always he had heard only one heart, strong, firm, its beat a fire within him, warming, pumping light. Then the sound was halved. Two hearts beating, the slightest syncopation, his brother or himself off by a quarter beat as he discovered he was two, not one.

At the bottom of his watch a brass charm was attached by the thinnest gold wire. Reuben fingered the bullet-shaped object. The wire passed through a hole bored in the bullet's nose, then through a loop on the watch. To see the charm Reuben had to pull his watch from his vest pocket and to check his watch he had to drag out the charm. Since the watch was linked to a chain and the chain pinned inside his vest and his vest fastened around his midsection, the container of his heart, lungs, liver, et cetera, Reuben sometimes thought of the charm wearing him. Conceived of himself as an elaborate headdress flowing from the pointed helmet crowning his brother's skull. Because the charm was an image of his brother. (64–65)

Later, oneness with the brother fictionally segues to an invocation of Thoth, the ancient Egyptian god of learning, wisdom, and magic, the scribe of the gods who merges into a figure of the writer with magical, creative powers to help Kwansa:

So each night Reuben frees the chain and watch and charm from the pockets of his vest, converts watch chain to neck chain, stretches the gold noose round his neck, fastens its circular clasp, then lays back on his bed to sleep. Circles within circles within circles linked over his bony chest, which rises and falls almost in time with his brother's.[2]

Awake or asleep his boon companion. His cut buddy. Reuben dangled him closer to the desk's surface. Walked [the brother also named] Reuben to Kwansa Parker's sorry papers.

Oh Thoth, patron of scribes. Full moon springing from the head of Seth, god of darkness. Thoth the "reckoner of days" in his moonship. Time and light and writing overseen by Thoth, and in his spare hours, as protector of Osiris, he aided the dead. Perhaps he'd help with this flood of papers drowning Reuben's desk. Reuben couldn't recall how or why the baboon became Thoth's totem animal. Yet a baboon, brow furrowed in deep thought, middle finger searching his asshole, was a perfect emblem of the writer. Thoth and sloth. A baboon marooned in the moon. (67)

Reuben invokes Thoth, the writer-figure who creates through imagination, intellect, and magical ritual, because this is what he wants to do.

However, the "emblem of the writer" is an uneasy reminder that white fictions have created a clear, powerful definition of his reality; as the text goes on to show, Reuben feels that negative white "Philadelphia" fictions are a genre that clearly defines him and others, in spite of his complex fiction making and the general subtlety and complexity of language. At the end of "Thoth," this white definition is "the foolishness sleeping in the white soup of the bone's marrow" (71): "You are what you are. Mountebank. Charlatan. Fool. Witch doctor. They say it again. He hears again. Nods to the empty trailer [where he lives]. Scans every well-traveled square inch. You are what you are. Their voices taunting him. All of Philadelphia laughing him out of existence again."[3] The novel asserts a context in which the sound of the "Philadelphia voices" talking and ritualistically taunting *is* the reality in which Reuben lives; this is the reality of powerful white fictions constraining Reuben and all black men. Collectively and individually imprisoned in the language and consequent psychology of fictions that negatively define them, black men in turn reconstruct the same fictions that negatively portray them, which is what happens later when Reuben and his friend Wally characterize themselves and their reality negatively.

From another perspective, however, black men have the potential to negate, or certainly manipulate, imprisoning white fictions. Reuben initiates the process by starting over. The narrator alludes to this early in the novel when Reuben first thinks about defamiliarizing powerful white fictions. He realizes that "[u]nless they started fresh they'd be caught up in one fiction or another, and that fiction would carry them wherever it was going" (17). He then refers to the photography of Eadweard Muybridge, the English photographer who invented the zoopraxiscope, and whose techniques are Reuben's model for stopping motion by making it a series of still shots: "He must study each link of the chain. Like Muybridge with his stop-time frames of animal locution, he must break down the process into discrete, manageable units. Then he could prevent it, stop it from happening by creating a counterillusion." Muybridge had been successful in showing the motion of horses as a series of photographs with all four feet above the ground. However, this is only "[f]reezing things into unnatural frames. Forestalling an inevitable conclusion by the logic of another conclusion, just as inevitable if the dice are given a slightly different spin."[4] He cannot decide whether the pictures are motion or stillness and whether the illusion is meaningful. However, he leaves open the possibility that Muybridge's series of photographs is a model for slowing down white fictions.

The words of the text, particularly the images created by his counterfictions, can be like photographs that break the illusion of white fictions by briefly disrupting them; in this context, Reuben successfully forms at least the beginning of positive black fictions within constraining white ones. In "Flora," his description of love in the midst of horror is an example. He tells Wally that "[a]ll black men have a Philadelphia. Even if you escape it, you leave something behind. Part of you. A brother trapped there forever. . . . My Philadelphia's strange because for all the horror, more of it's about love. Have you had yours?" (93). The "brother" is the symbol Reuben created earlier that stands for his ability to love another person and potentially to love Wally, but Reuben is primarily talking about finding love in the strangely horrible fiction of his tragic relationship with Flora. When he chooses to emphasize love in this story, he disrupts its negative pattern and makes a positive fiction possible. Wally ignores what Reuben says about love in "Flora." In "The Recruiter" (98–124), "abstract hate" detaches Wally from his emotions and makes him an "abstract" person who lives by constantly meditating the fiction of murdering white people (116–19). Wally went to school in Philadelphia, but "abstract hate" represents his "Philadelphia" fiction that contrasts Reuben's love and reveals the negative influence on black men conveyed in white fictions.

Wally still has the potential to move beyond "abstract hate," however, because Reuben influences him, and he lives off the fictions of his "brother" Reuben. Wally realizes the following in "The Recruiter": "You could tell Reuben anything because he's liable to say anything back. Like fairy tales. . . . You think you got the old nigger's attention, then he come back at you grinning with some off-the-wall mess. In Egypt, when Egypt was Egypt and Pharaoh the Sun King, they had priests could empty your whole brain through your nose hole and never leave a mark on you. One curved needle all they used. . . . Stick it in a baboon or a falcon or a leopard. Then they could talk to the parts of God in these animals and yes indeed, the animals could answer" (108). His conclusion about the seemingly nonsensical fiction is that "[m]aybe the point wasn't answers. Maybe the point was having somebody to ask. And maybe that's why he'd missed Reuben before he'd met Reuben" (109). Wally feels the timeless human connection of participating in Reuben's fictions, although they are abstract too.

Wally is also part of Reuben's fictions on a deeper, unconscious level. In his detached fiction, "Wally treats his life like a memory so he won't have to worry about what's happening to him. . . . He could tell any lie he needed to get by. It's all in your mind. A dream made up as you go along" (102). The dream, the fiction of his life, includes Reuben, though: "Reason he asked Reuben how long he stayed in Philly was because there are times, now, looking back, when Wally has memories of those school years that don't make sense without Reuben around. If not Reuben, somebody like Reuben talking to Wally. . . . Wally had never spoken to Reuben till he returned from the university so he couldn't have carried Reuben's conversations to Philadelphia. Couldn't have missed him because he didn't know him yet" (113). Wally did carry Reuben with him to Philadelphia: Wally's entire fiction is not a "lie" because it is inseparable from Reuben and his "Philadelphia." At one point, Reuben's "dream taking shape inside another dream" (104) segues to Wally's feelings of love that are a reminder of Reuben's words that Philadelphia is "about love." In this instance, Wally's memory of his childhood is like a blanket that is the odor of his grandmother, "her love inseparable from the smell of her body soaked into each of the blanket's fibers" (106). Wally lives in "abstract hate," and that is why the feeling of love is unsavory,[5] but love unconsciously develops from the association with Reuben.

In the final analysis, Wally, Reuben, and others, like Wally's friend Bimbo, are connected "brothers" or "twins" in terms of their existence in the overall context of imprisoning white fictions *and* oppositional black fictions. The text clearly implies that Reuben knows this; it also clearly reveals that Wally senses it. Wally and Bimbo "hung out together without getting in each other's way. As close to alone each could be and still be with somebody. . . . Bimbo good for Wally because Bimbo was easy. Bimbo let Wally lead him" (169). "Not Bimbo running beside him today. Not anyone else Wally could see. Yet he'd heard footsteps solid as his own. Someone dogging him, matching him stride for stride. . . . In Reuben's riffs there was a brother, a twin the old man sometimes mentioned. Wally had never sorted out the truth. Whether Reuben was one of an actual set of twins or whether Reuben had talked himself into believing a phantom existed somewhere, Reuben's double from Planet X or wherever spooks like that came from" (170). "Reuben always talking about doubles, twins, other lives he might or might not have lived. Wally wondered about his own doubles . . . . Wally made up a million other Wallys. Kept in touch with some of them." "Reuben said your twin didn't have to live in a body exactly like yours." Given his awareness, Reuben can potentially free himself by defamiliarizing white fictions, but Wally's latent consciousness of his connection to "twins" or "brothers" in the context of Reuben's black fictions gives him potential too.

The potential to tell a liberating story still exists, but the text makes it possible that imprisoning white fictions prevail. The fiction after "Bimbo" is "Mr. Tucker," which is about another "brother" or "twin" for Reuben/ Wally. Mr. Tucker has been arrested for theft at the same time that Reuben has been arrested for impersonating a lawyer, and is a prisoner in a white newspaper fiction like Reuben. The fictions are separate, but Reuben first treats them as essentially one fiction that imprisons both of them. He tries to free himself and Mr. Tucker: "A Reuben chained by words, Reuben locked up forever. So he played for time. Let the words above the house-stealing story [about Mr. Tucker] float free until they told another tale" (191). Later, Reuben has great difficulty because the powerful newspaper fiction about him is "[h]is life story in three hundred words or less staring back at him. The unvarnished truth" (195). After this, Wally begins a negative fiction that indicts Reuben as a "pile of shit" (195–96). Then as words from the newspaper fiction about Reuben appear at intervals in the text (197–98), Wally continues to assault Reuben with the negative fiction, and Reuben tries to construct a positive fiction in which he and Wally can "[m]ake things better" (196–201). The third-person narrator then presents a "device in old movies for dissolving from one scene to the next" (201), and describes Reuben using this "*[d]issolve to*" device to escape from Wally and perhaps all negative fictions (202): "Reuben makes it a ranch. . . . Blue Wyoming sky. . . . climbing a ladder of stars and bars to heaven and back. Yippee. I. Oh . . ." However, at the end of "Mr. Tucker," it seems that Reuben has not escaped. He dreams the fiction of a disastrous accident that seems to prefigure continued imprisonment in negative fictions (204–5): "And would his brother ever be free?" (205). Would Reuben, Wally, and Mr. Tucker ever be free? The answer is hard to find in the complex, fragmented narrative.

The narrative moves away from Reuben and his "brothers" following this, and anonymous, indeterminate, disembodied male voices tell the story of Kwansa and her girlfriend rescuing Kwansa's son from abduction by his father, Waddell. Early in "Toodles," the narrators say the following: "From a great distance, longer than the time it's taken all the voices that have ever told stories to tell their stories, in the welcome silence after so much lying, so much wasted breath, [Kwansa's and Toodle's] voices reach us. Where we sit. Imagining ourselves imagining them" (207–8). At the conclusion, Toodles cuts Waddell's throat, and they take Kwansa's son: "I wasn't more than a few feet away. Saw everything, man. [Waddell] tried to squeeze his neck back together. Hold hisself in. . . . [Toodles] stepped across him like he ain't nothing but a sack of potatoes and kneels down to where she can help Kwansa Parker up off the floor" (213). Reuben returns in the final section, "And," to pick up Kwansa's son Cudjoe: "Imagine a short, gimpy, immaculately dressed, bearded, brown man in the piss-colored hall of a public building" (214). The novel ends: "Hello. You're Cudjoe, aren't you? . . . Your mother sent me. She said she loves you and will see you soon and everything's going to be all right. My name's Reuben. I'm here to take you home" (215).

Wideman has commented on the ending of the novel and his intentions to create a myth. He says in an interview: "Take Toodles, for instance —actually I saw Toodles as a kind of goddess, and I saw the book as a kind of mythological tug-of war for Kwanza's [sic] soul, between a male principle and a female principle, and a female principle wins out. There's the literal battle where the dragon [Waddell] is slain, somebody is restored. In that scene, *Reuben* is kind of allegorical—there's the myth of Osiris, the Egyptian myth that underlies and gives you the kind of plot-line, or story-line. But I wanted to be optimistic; I wanted that last scene to recall Michelangelo's ceiling, especially God touching Adam. That was Reuben and the little boy" (Olander 172).

If one views the ending in light of Wideman's words about mythic symbolization and the text's imagination of Reuben speaking as a savior bringing love, then Reuben may be liberated. However, Wideman also implies that Reuben becomes free only in fictions that emphasize the victory of the "female principle," which also means the throat-cutting defeat of the male. In the novel, the last time Reuben was with his "brothers" in "Mr. Tucker" he was struggling to escape white fictions of blackness and Wally's repetitious negative fictions. In this context, one could read Reuben's lame, well-dressed appearance in a "piss-colored hall" at the beginning of "And" ambiguously and ambivalently, and wonder at the end what happens to Reuben and the "brothers."

At the same time, *Reuben* takes the next experimental step after *Sent for You Yesterday*. It goes beyond family and Homewood community stories and focuses more on the individual artist's attempt to create fictions that open up a larger black myth. I return to Kathie Birat's statement about Wideman's postmodernism quoted at the beginning of chapter 3: "[F]or Wideman the very power of storytelling lies in its capacity to embrace the endless movement of language itself, 'writing,' if not necessarily 'righting,' the wrongs of an 'upside-down' world" (641). In terms of the characters' primary existence in fictions that are words, "And" suggests open-endedness and perhaps Reuben's freedom to continue his never-ending fictional opposition, in spite of the apparent continued imprisonment of the "brothers" in language, part of which is their own repetition of negative black fictions spoken by white voices. Reuben's connection to the apparent agency of Kwansa and black women aids his political pursuit of "'writing,' if not necessarily 'righting,'" oppositional fictions in "the endless movement of language itself." *Reuben* is a fiction that begins a new mythic construction of blackness that can liberate in the context of Wideman's writing. To achieve its goal, the novel breaks down or defamiliarizes customary linguistic patterns even more than most of Wideman's other works, and this makes it an unusually difficult work to read and interpret in his generally challenging oeuvre.

Philadelphia Fire opens with an evocation of myth as the main character, Cudjoe,[6] a writer, tells the story of a tour boat pilot he knew named Zivanias[7] who had a deadly accident in a storm trying to sail from the Greek island Mykonos to "Delos, the island sacred to Apollo where once no one was allowed to die or be born" (4). However, when he returns to Philadelphia from the Greek island steeped in myth, Cudjoe has lost his mythic thread and lost his story, except, as revealed later, the story's negative parts like the desertion of his sons, which is apparently related to Zivanias's story of desertion (3). He feels incapable of creating the story of a mother, children, and lost boy, victims of the police bombing of MOVE members in Philadelphia on May 13, 1985, who are the foundation of his black myth. His grandmother's crystal ball, which he used to hold and imagine was a mythic matrix, is "long gone. He can't recall the first time he missed it. Nothing rests in the empty cup of his hands. Not the illusion of a chilly winter day, not snowfall or a dark-haired woman's face, her skin brown and warm as bread just out the oven. *Ladybug, Ladybug. Fly away home. Your house is on fire. Your children burning.* He is turning pages. Perhaps asleep with a book spread-eagled on his lap, the book he wishes he was writing, the story he crisscrossed an ocean to find. Story of a fire and a lost boy that brought him home" (7). The story of the boy would be central in his myth because of his story of deserting his sons. Because he lacks creative inspiration, the book that will be a new black story initiating a positive myth is only a wistful reality in a dreamlike region of consciousness, but Cudjoe will attempt to write it in spite of his doubts and grave misgivings. As part of the process, he will even go as far as trying to rewrite Shakespeare's *The Tempest* to change the negative image of blackness that the play forged in white Western cultural tradition.

Cudjoe's characterization is similar to Reuben's. Reuben's words describe Cudjoe: "All black men have a Philadelphia. Even if you escape it, you leave something behind. Part of you. A brother trapped there forever" (*Reuben* 93). Later, Wally remembers Reuben "talking about doubles, twins, other lives he might or might not have lived" (170). Returning to his Philadelphia, Cudjoe has "brothers," "twins," "doubles" trapped in their "Philadelphia fictions" as Reuben does. Conflated with him, the writer/ character John Wideman is Cudjoe's main "brother," "twin," "double" in *Philadelphia Fire*.[8] Their abstract, experimental intellectual ruminations do not separate them from a semblance of reality as much as Reuben and his "brothers" seem separated, but at the same time they do not connect with others through the process of storytelling like Doot in *Sent for You Yesterday*. Importantly, like Reuben they feel the destructive power of white fictions. Reminiscent of Reuben thinking about constructing defamiliarized fictions, but expressing more self-doubt about his ability to create than Reuben, John asserts the need to imagine fictions that will begin a new, empowering myth opposing negative white fictions and a negative white myth of blackness: "Pretend for a moment that none of this happened. . . . Pretend we can imagine events into existence or out of existence. Pretend we have the power to live our lives as we choose. Imagine our fictions imagining us" (97–98).

There are broad similarities and differences in the texts of *Philadelphia Fire* and *Reuben*. Generally, *Philadelphia Fire* is related to *Reuben* by specific textual reference[9] and common theme, and is the next stage after *Reuben's* attempt to construct a positive black myth. Compared to *Reuben*, *Philadelphia Fire* focuses more on fictions written and (re)written on the page and composed in imagination and less on narratives of magical ritual that are oddly based in intellect, like the ones Reuben creates in "Thoth" (64– 65, 57). Like Reuben, the writers in *Philadelphia Fire* have great difficulty trying to create positive black fictions because of the power of negative white ones. They cannot rewrite the story of the boy tragically lost in the fire, which is also inseparable from the story of their lost son(s), which is further inseparable from a dominant tradition of Western stories like *The Tempest* whose negative characterizations of blackness impede the writers from telling a positive black story. However, much as the ending of *Reuben* does, the stories of part 3 in *Philadelphia Fire* present open-ended potential by disrupting or defamiliarizing the usual negative linguistic patterns of Western stories characterizing black men and black life. Part 3 also concludes with Cudjoe's imagination of possibilities including liberation, perhaps implying the power to initiate a new, empowering myth of blackness along with his "brother" John,[10] which is like the conclusion of *Reuben*.

In part 1, Cudjoe totally lacks the ability to imagine a story leading to a positive myth for reasons he does not understand. Early in part 1, he fails to get a victim of the fire named Margaret Jones to tell him the story about the lost boy so that he can rewrite it. Then, like Reuben attempting to find a new starting point for a fiction, he tries again. He "must always write about many places at once. No choice. The splitting apart is inevitable. First step is always out of time, away from responsibility, toward the word or sound or image that is everywhere at once, that connects and destroys" (23). "Many places at once. Tromping along the sidewalk. In the air. Underground. Astride a spark coughed up by the fire. Waterborne. Climbing stone steps. To reach the woman in the turban [a victim of the fire], the boy, he must travel through those other places. Always moving. He must, at the risk of turning to stone, look back at his own lost children, their mother standing on a train platform, wreathed in steam, in smoke. An old-fashioned locomotive wheezes and lurches into motion. His wife waves a handkerchief wet with tears. . . . [His sons] hide and sniffle, clutch handfuls of her silky clothes. It hurts him to look, hurts him to look away" (23–24). However, he has only seen the train station "in movies. A new career for his wife and sons. Wherever they are, he keeps them coming back to star in this scene. Waving. Clinging. But it's the wrong movie. . . . Caroline had never owned a silk handkerchief, let alone a long silky skirt" (24). Cudjoe ends up seeing a painful vision of his own negative story as a black man when he tries to initiate a black myth from a place in time that is both multiple and ubiquitous, but although he did separate from his wife, this is not the memory of what happened. His negativity comes from some reality that is not actual events. His feeling that he must move "away from responsibility" suggests he could know that he must escape a false, debilitating image of himself that stops him from telling his story. Without the help of his "brother" John at this point, though, he cannot prevent its abrupt, "[stone] turning" intrusion, explain it, or prevent it from taking over his new mythic "place."

Negative musings about himself and other black men and visions of his lechery toward Caroline and other women take over Cudjoe's consciousness. At the basketball court, he talks to the younger brother of a friend named Darnell who is now incarcerated, and doubts the story of the younger brother, a college dropout, when he says he will go back to school. He sees no potential in the brothers: "Did anything get better instead of worse? Why couldn't he believe Darnell's brother? Why did he hear ice cracking as O. T. spoke of his plans? Why did he see Darnell's rusty hard hand wrapped around his brother's dragging him down?" (38). He continues to be negatively preoccupied with Caroline and his children, and becomes transfixed with self-accusation about his lustful gazes at Caroline and other women. At one point, he asks, "why did [Caroline] always close her robe or shut her knees if she noticed his eyes . . . peering between her naked legs?" (56). He also broods about disparate memories of looking under the dress of a woman in the park (25–26) and looking at a woman walking naked in an apartment close to his (54–55). In a long episode, he remembers staring at his best friend's eighteen-year-old daughter taking a shower, going back to bed, turning his back on Caroline, and masturbating (62–67).

The rest of part 1 is a series of similar fragmented visions, musings, and uneasy interactions that contribute further to Cudjoe losing sight of the positive black myth that he started. Sparked by the cynicism of a friend named Timbo at lunch near the end of part 1, Cudjoe imagines a "[a] wave of shame and humiliation. Where are his children? Caroline? What would any of the people living and dead whose opinions he values think of this lunchtime debacle?" (92). Right after this, Cudjoe's account to Timbo of his nightmare of a black boy hanged in the park ends part 1 (93–94). Like most of the first part, this scene intrudes as an uncontrollable, disjointed fragment of consciousness that separates Cudjoe from the positive story of the black boy; the concluding story of a dead boy is the antithesis of the one he tried to initiate. The graffiti of Kaliban's Kiddie Korps that he and Timbo see in the city (88–92) could give Cudjoe at least the notion that iconic works of the past negatively impact his writing of a modern-day story,[11] but in part 1 he never undertakes the analysis he is capable of as a writer and intellectual to affect his story positively.

Cudjoe does change positively to examine the tradition and its iconic representation of the negativity of blackness in part 2 with the help of

John, another self, a "brother or "double" essentially, who refocuses him. Entering at the beginning of part 2, John lays out his problems, which are also Cudjoe's, alludes to their roots in white tradition, and later identifies himself with Cudjoe. Using fictionalized details from Wideman's life, he explains how he learned about the fire while he was in Laramie, Wyoming (97–104). In *Philadelphia Fire*'s typical fashion, John intersperses this with a fragmented account of his inability to write his lost son's story, which evolves into his tortured recollection of the son (104–20). Different voices speak. Sometimes John speaks in the first-person voice; sometimes third-person voices speak that are both anonymous and identifiable as John's; and sometimes quotations from other texts "speak." The latter is the way that *The Tempest* is introduced (105, 115). Following the introduction, Caliban enters with a stage direction and speaks a part protesting his adversity in the play (120–22), and an anonymous voice speaks in a short fragment about Caliban being confined in a story in which he always loses his island to Prospero (122). Then, in another fragment, John identifies himself in Cudjoe: "Why this Cudjoe, then? This airy other floating into the shape of my story. Why am I him when I tell certain parts? Why am I hiding from myself? Is he mirror or black hole?" Despite hiding behind multiple unidentifiable voices, John is uneasy with Cudjoe's. Nevertheless, he must know that, instead of a "black hole," Cudjoe is a "mirror" "double" and also an "airy other" who can help write the story by being, in Cudjoe's words, "many places at once."[12] Briefly worrying about his sons when first identified in part 2 (117), Cudjoe reenters, in *place* in Philadelphia, already rewriting *The Tempest* (125). John's contrivance diverts Cudjoe from the directionless fragmentation that subsumed him in part 1 and sets him in a positive direction. They are now "brothers" initiating a new black myth with a fragmented story of son(s). Also, in moving away from Cudjoe's preoccupations with his negative traits, the fragments potentially begin to disrupt or defamiliarize an apparently seamless, believable white myth of blackness started by stories like *The Tempest*.

However, because *The Tempest* is the center of a very persuasive white myth of blackness, Cudjoe and John continue to struggle to rewrite and stage it, and to construct a black countermyth, as they analyze the play's mythic effect. John explains how the play is the center of a myth that is "many places at once": "This is the central event. I assure you. I repeat.

Whatever my assurance is worth. Being the fabulator. This is the central event, this production of *The Tempest* staged by Cudjoe in the late late 1960s,[13] outdoors, in a park in West Philly. Though it comes here, wandering like a Flying Dutchman in and out of the narrative, many places at once, *The Tempest* sits dead center, the storm in the eye of the storm, figure within a figure, play within play, it is the bounty and hub of all else written about the fire, though it comes here, where it is, nearer the end than the beginning" (132). Sounding diffident, John, "the fabulator," analyzes the hidden, insidiously powerful effect of traditional white writing like *The Tempest* that is a "figure" or "play" woven within others facilitating oppression at the center of the seemingly timeless white myth of blackness. His reference to Cudjoe is a reminder of what he said about him as an "airy other" who assists John from multiple places.

Earlier, Cudjoe talked in the same terms about how *The Tempest* created a Calibanic symbol that assigned blackness universal inferiority enabling oppression and exploitation. Imaginatively addressing the ten- and eleven-year-old black children whom he would instruct and cast in the play, Cudjoe says that Caliban's bestiality is the symbolic foundation of an oppressive white myth of blackness that has been passed down through time:

Today's lesson is this immortal play about colonialism, imperialism, recidivism, the royal fucking over of weak by strong, colored by white, many by few, or, if you will, the birth of the nation's blues seen through the fish-eye lens of a fee fi foe englishmon. . . . [L]ong before various events, each of which is a story in and of itself worth learning, studying . . . long before a Third World when there was only One and it was cakewalking, expanding by leaps and bounds, big fish swallowing little fishes and little ducklings, in Bermuda, near the fabulous, infamous, mystical Triangle, your Godfather Caliban was hatched. And it was a playwright, a Kilroy Willie who fabulated the plot. Who saw the whole long-suffering thing in embryo, rotten in the egg, inscribed like talking book on the tabularasa walls of the future. Sentient. Prescient. Yes, Willy was now. Peeped the hole card. Scoped the whole ugly mess about to happen at that day and time which brings us to here, to today. To this very moment in our contemporary world. To the inadequacy of your background, your culture. Its inability, like the inability of a dead sea, to cast up on the beach appropriate role models, creatures whose lives you might imitate. (127–28)

Cudjoe's words imply that in the white myth of blackness *The Tempest's* bestial images work along with similar ones in the Western cultural imagination that come from different times and from various oral and written sources.

In similar language, Cudjoe more directly talks about his job as a writer in exposing *The Tempest's* symbolism of truth about blackness and reversing the effect. He says further that "one of my jobs as model and teacher is to unteach you, help you separate the good from the bad from the ugly. Specifically, in this case, to remove de tail. Derail de tail. Disembarass, disabuse, disburden—demonstrate conclusively that Mr. Caliban's behind is clean and unencumbered, good as anybody else's. That the tail was a tale. Nothing more or less than an ill-intentioned big fat lie" (131). He is talking about debunking the intentionally constructed lie that Caliban is a beast with a tail, which justifies his oppression in the play, and which through the power of his black symbolism justifies black oppression in the white myth of blackness. The power of this broad-reaching construction of blackness makes John and Cudjoe diffident and causes them to think negatively. It is the crux of their self-accusation about the loss of their son(s), which as much as anything comes from the negative imagination of their own character *and* angst about the efficacy of their writing.[14] This construction of blackness is the underlying reason that, in the legal system, John's son is a criminal instead of a child with grave problems. In the novel's broadest terms, it stands behind the brutal burning of black people in the Philadelphia fire, the subject of Cudjoe's book in part 1 and a cryptic subject of part 3 that focuses on a mysterious Book of Life. Cudjoe's play on words and the general style and form of his language in the analysis of *The Tempest* in part 2 imply the rewriting that will undercut its symbolic, all-too-real message and change its oppressive effect.

However, in spite of understanding how it works as a central symbol and rewriting parts of it, Cudjoe cannot stage *The Tempest*, and at the end of part 2 the question is what this means. After Cudjoe rewrites a section of the play (138–43), he makes excuses for why he never staged it: "Things happened. Time ran out. I quit the teaching job [with the black children performing the play]. Went to grad school. Whole business just petered out" (149). As Madhu Dubey points out, his project is "in fact a rehash of fairly common interpretations of *The Tempest*" (590) among postcolonial critics who subvert it. Black writers have rewritten *The Tempest*, too. Stacey L. Berry notes that "Wideman's incorporation of an all-black production of *The Tempest* shares similarities with Haitian writer Aimé Césaire's 1969 rewriting of Shakespeare entitled *A Tempest*, which Césaire adapted for a black theatre" (170). Cudjoe and John are intellectuals and writers in the fictional world of *Philadelphia Fire* that always incorporates real-life people and events such as writers and intellectuals who have rewritten and subverted *The Tempest*. Particularly in the context of the novel's amalgamation of the real-life and fictional, it is somewhat peculiar that Cudjoe does not seem to know of anyone who has rewritten *The Tempest*, and cannot stage his subversive rewriting as others have done. However, maybe the important point is not the actual staging. Leslie W. Lewis writes that "as a production that never happened it remains full of possibility in Cudjoe's mind, remains suspended in an always already present that does not allow it to slip into memory" (151). She further states that the play stays in an "ever-present aspect of the performance [that] allows Cudjoe to continue to imagine the children's Elizabethan English as a living language that has shaped and reshaped itself, ultimately into the poetic rap he hears as children's voices in the park."

I would adapt what I understand Lewis to mean and say that the novel focuses on an imaginative *(re)*writing, an ongoing, open-ended imaginative process, because the imagination is where the symbolism of *The Tempest* has done its work in the first place. However, *The Tempest* has power over the imagination because it has the illusion of truth of an iconic white Western text inscribed on the page. It is hard to write a black text that displaces the power of white writing on the page; however, hypothetically at least, the (re)writing importantly should be a process of "shap[ing] and reshap[ing]" linguistic symbolism in imagination that has the comparable effect and illusion of truth of Western iconic writing. Further, as Lewis perhaps suggests by referring to the children's voices Cudjoe hears in the park, the imaginative (re)writing is a collective effort and not solely the individual writer's. Cudjoe's role at the end of part 3 where he contributes to a collective imaginative (re)writing of a text by nontraditional writers indicates this.

The depiction of John and his son at the end of part 2 is consistent with the idea of (re)writing stories imaginatively in an ongoing, collective effort. First, in the penultimate paragraph of part 2, John tells his son that he will continue to write: "I will write you soon again" (150). Then, in the section's last paragraph, he implies the importance of imagining stories in a continuing process of "shaping": "We do have a chance to unfold our days one by one and piece together a story that shapes us. It's the only life anyone ever has. Hold on" (151). The son's imagination of stories makes him a "writer" along with John the individual writer, and opens the way for the imaginative creation of other "writers" in part 3.[15] Also, John's exhortation of the son to create his life sounds like the second paragraph of part 2 where he says they must "[i]magine our fictions imagining us" (98). John is anxious and uneasy at the beginning and end of part 2, but in each instance he has the implicit support of his "brother" Cudjoe. In this context, part 3 ends with a portrayal of Cudjoe/John, but most of it depicts other equally troubled "brothers" who will similarly be involved in an imaginative (re)writing process nevertheless. Further, their stories are imaginative fragments of collective writers that have the potential to unite, and thus thematically the stories counter and connect the novel's fragmented written structure.

The primary character in part 3 collectively and imaginatively involved in a (re)writing process is J. B.; extending the work of John in part 2, he does what Cudjoe could not at the beginning of part 1 by engaging the story of the Philadelphia fire from multiple places where he can, at least potentially, initiate a story that is the beginning of a new black myth. "[J. B.] is always everywhere at once. Never a rush, a reason to leave here and go there. He inhabits many places, no place" (184). "His name is James. James Brown. They teased him forever when the singer stole his thunder" (156). The popular entertainer is a general reference for the name, but the singer's life provides no clue as to who J. B. is. J. B.'s ubiquity is mythic, and his anonymity makes him congruent in a collective group of imaginative writers that includes Cudjoe/John and other anonymous writers. The main emphasis in J. B.'s story is Philadelphia burning. "Philadelphia's on fire" (157), but the city is more than just contemporary Philadelphia. It is one among all the cities that he has seen burn in his mythic existence: "He remembers all the smoke from burning cities he's ever sucked up the four-lane blues highway of his nose. The stink and putrefaction. The flies. He'll miss this city. He always misses them. It hurts to just walk away. Leaving everything behind. Nothing" (156). His story of the Philadelphia fire is the timeless, mythic story of the godlike creator who still sees a very real present: "This job, like God's, of making a city had wearied J. B. Light every morning to tame. Playing father son and holocaust to the kids running wild in streets and vacant lots." The reality of the kids is an aspect of the story of the fire J. B. is (re)writing to change the white mythic text of blackness that controls the present.

It seems clear that acts like J. B.'s attempted imaginative (re)writing have turned the controlling white mythic text into a defamiliarized palimpsest that still inscribes evil but maintains a continuous developmental process too. After the description of a mysterious Book of Life (167–68), the narrative suggests that part 3 is a palimpsest when an unnamed narrator/writer, who wrote in the Book of Life along with others, compares layers of semen on a sheet to "starting that palimpsest you build layer by layer" (169). Part of the palimpsest's defamiliarization is thematic. J. B.'s imaginative children break the stereotype of bad, destructive black children. In one apparent episode of his story, uncontrollable "little white boys" set J. B. on fire (188), also ironically taking retribution on white people and all of society by contesting the idea of essential white goodness. As will be shown later, however, J. B.'s imaginative, palimpsestlike layering of the story's versions also implies structural defamiliarization that keeps the process of storytelling open and shares it with other writers. Part 3 is a fragmented, defamiliarized structure like parts 1 and 2, but it is also a somewhat different one that has a palimpsest's layered possibilities.

The Book of Life first appears as a palimpsest of good and evil. The narrator/writer, probably a man named Richard Corey, sees a "kite. Wavering, flickering, silly, ominous, blowing in the wind" (167):

Here is the story it writes: I am an informer.[16] I tell tales on my friends. Who become my enemies. Because I am a snitch. I squealed on my former soul mates, my comrades huddled in the arms of the Tree of Life. Squealed to the pigs. Revealed all our good hiding places, secret springs of potable water, the edible roots and berries. Translated our secrets, stored in the sacred Book of Life, into the grunting, rooting, snarly pig tongue. Stood by aiding, abetting as Porky Pig snouts bulldozed and leveled and angry pointy Porky Pig hooves stomped.

I betrayed our good mother Earth. Betrayed her anointed dreadlocked King. Switched allegiance, planted incriminating evidence, stranded my good brown brothers out on a limb, high and dry.

I feel terrible. Together, black and white and yellow and red and brown together, all the rainbow children of Life, all born to Life's bounty, Life's sacred trusts and duties, together we learned the message of the Book. To read it and pass on the teachings and keep the Tree alive. So when I turned, when I shifted loyalties, the most hurtful twist was the knife in my own guts, the disemboweling hari-kari wrench of my own self exposed inside out and stinking to high heaven.

Forgive me, brothers. I didn't know what I was doing. Still don't. Never will. Forgive me.

When the fires blaze highest at noon, smoke rolls in from the west, till it's damned by that upthrust of green hills. Smoke thickens to a wall, then slowly disintegrates during those long summer afternoons. A dusky kingdom suddenly risen then gone to rags and tatters which night swallows. I watch it intently. Read the smoke again and again for what it says about me, my fate. The only truly interesting, engaging story anyone can tell me, after all. My fate. (167–68)

Bribed by the power structure, the informer treacherously switches allegiances. Through his descriptions of the power structure's subornation that ensnared him, he (re)writes a story in the Book that changes the supposed, always implied good of whiteness to evil, and (re)writes a counterstory that changes the essential evil of the betrayed "dreadlocked King" and "rainbow children of Life" to good. Obviously, however, the process of (re)writing must go beyond portrayals that are still totalized oppositions, and the informer's writing in the Book is not enough.

The book is a palimpsest in which J. B. continues imaginatively (re)writing his story in different versions when he gets it from Richard Corey after his suicide. J. B.'s unclear vision of the form of the book, which is not capitalized now, symbolizes its multiple, nontotalized versions: "The book's a kind of journal or diary. Handwriting squinchy small. [He] holds it close, then at arm's length, then pulls it toward him till it wavers into focus" (187). *"The Tree of Life will nourish you. You need only learn how to serve its will. Its will is your best self speaking the truth to you. The seed of truth is planted in all of us. You only need to listen. Let it grow. . . ."* J. B.'s imagination of wild children associated with Philadelphia burning at the beginning of part 3 is the same as the book's portrayal of vengeful children:[17] *"It's time, my friends, to reap what's been sown. The Children's Hour now. The Kiddy Korner. What have they been up to all this time we've left them alone? Over in the shadows with Buffalo Bob. Mister Rogers. The Shadow knows. But do we? Are we ready to hear the children speak? Ready or not we shall be caught. We are pithed. Feel nothing. Children have learned to hate us as much as we hate them. I saw four boys yesterday steal an old man's cane and beat him with it. He was a child, lying in his blood on the sidewalk. They were old, old men tottering away"* (187–88). When he imagines little white boys setting him on fire, he does not know if it is real, but goes on imagining the palimpsest-like layering of his story: "[M]aybe [the fire] was somebody else's dream in a book, maybe a book he, J. B., was writing. All were possibilities, possible worlds he was sure he was remembering" (188).[18]

Stopping the process of creating the palimpsest's possibilities is the main problem to avoid at this point in the novel. Anticipating Cudjoe at the rally for the fire's victims at the end, J. B. "surveys the multitude. Begins to preach" (189): "This is my story. This is my song." "The book he's singing from snaps shut. Is smoke in his hands. Ashes. He beats down flames on the crackling pages." The book snapping closed on J. B.'s account of the fire and J. B. having to beat down flames could possibly mean that he will burn up: "When he reaches the fountain he trips over its raised lip, flailing into its dry center. . . ."

However, J. B.'s thoughts and the oral voices that appear occasionally symbolize imaginative (re)writing throughout part 3, and the possibilities will continue to develop in an imaginative palimpsest that J. B. and others build. J. B. hears a rap song: *"You're a separate nation/Under their domination/Takes you for a ride/Peel away your pride/When your skin's gone, children/Are you black inside"* (159). Just before the rap, J. B. "thinks of young black boys shotgunning other black boys, black girl babies raising black girl babies and the streets thick with love and honor and duty and angry songs running along broken curbs, love and honor and duty and nobody understands because nobody listens, can't hear in the bloody current that courses and slops dark splashes on the cracked cement, how desperate things have become. How straight the choices, noble the deeds" (158). The rap J. B. hears tells a story of oppression that leads to the positive possibility of being "*black inside.*" In line with this, J. B. imagines a negative story that, if we listen, includes "love and honor and duty" and the "desperate" along with the "straight" and "noble." The rap voice seems to be distinct from J. B.'s. However, his thoughts are substantively similar and directly precede the rap, and it could be a product of the collective culture that is inseparable from his imagination. This is consistent with the idea of collective imaginative (re)writing in part 3. Later, J. B.'s blues song implies pain, but also perseverance and endurance: "J. B. sings the blues: *Poor boy long way from home. Poor boy long way from home*" (178). Overall, black imaginative (re)writing portrays white domination and destructive black violence and sexual activity that are parts of the totalized negativity of blackness in the white myth; however, it also tells a story with a range of positive possibilities that will continue to unfold.

Now (re)writing imaginatively like J. B. instead of writing his own book or the script of his play as in parts 1 and 2, Cudjoe imagines the ongoing possibility of societal change at the end of part 3.[19] Like J. B., he is now "many places at once"—in contemporary Philadelphia on the day of a sparsely attended memorial service for black fire victims, but also imaginatively in 1805 at an Independence Day rally in Philadelphia. At this point at the end, he is one among different storytellers who can contribute to a palimpsest that has endless layers. Envisioning the 1805 rally, "[f]or a second he populates [the scene] with ghosts. All of Philadelphia crammed into Independence Square" (190). White people chase the black ones out of the square on that day in 1805. Later, in the present, drums "bound them [the victims], braided them, infused them with the possibility of moving, breathing, being heard" (198). In the last paragraph, "Cudjoe hears footsteps behind him. A mob howling his name. Screaming for blood. Words come to him, cool him, stop him in his tracks. He'd known them all his life. *Never again. Never again.* He turns to face whatever it is rumbling over the stones of Independence Square" (199). Cudjoe imagines succeeding figures of liberation and oppression, and ends facing an ambiguous, ominous sound. Tracie Church Guzzio concludes that "now Cudjoe is ready to confront history no matter how painful. 'Never again' will he run away from who he is or from his past" (187). I would say that the oppression is by no means over, but neither is the possibility of liberation.

The ending of part 3 implies that Cudjoe, John, J. B., and all the writers can begin a new liberating myth of blackness in the layers of their complex story; they can defamiliarize white stories like *The Tempest* to make new ones possible that initiate a different black myth. They do not have to write their stories in books only; they can spread them throughout the culture as nonformal texts of imagination as well. Hypothetically the stories will achieve what black formal, written texts have failed to do by (re)writing the myth of blackness on the level of cultural consciousness where it has become most deeply inscribed. As always, Wideman's writing is difficult for a reason, and in this case the structure represents a complex process and theme of liberation.[20] This is the goal in line with the postmodern agenda of the creator and writers in *Reuben* and *Philadelphia Fire*.

5

The Cattle Killing, Two Cities, and *Fanon*

EXTENDING EXPERIMENTAL WRITING, MAKING IT CLEAR,
AND EXTENDING IT FURTHER

ike the "brothers" in *Reuben* and like Cudjoe, John, and the other
writers in *Philadelphia Fire,* the writers in *The Cattle Killing* (1996)
(re)write stories formally on the page and also through the imagination. *The Cattle Killing* is many stories told by many writers (re)writ-
ing and subverting pervasive white Western cultural stories about
black character and the black historical past and present. The white stories constitute a negative white myth of blackness that Western culture
purports is definitive. Like *Reuben* and *Philadelphia Fire, The Cattle Killing* defamiliarizes the white myth. It displaces the familiar themes and
structures of the white stories that negatively define blackness with black
stories that are structurally and thematically difficult, hard to interpret,
open-ended, and generally nondefinitive.[1] Because they are nondefinitive,
the stories in *The Cattle Killing* avoid the mistake of portraying blackness
as essentially good. At the same time, their open-endedness can start an
ongoing interpretative process that makes a new myth possible in which
blackness can never be essentially bad. Further, the stories begin a process that can save black people from oppression caused by the belief that
blackness is bad.

The Cattle Killing happens, in the words used to describe the story in
Philadelphia Fire, in "many places at once." The idea that open-ended,
ongoing stories develop simultaneously in multiple places informs the
concept that Wideman calls Great Time. As Heather Andrade argues, the
concept is more prominent in, but not unique to, Wideman's later works.
As early as the works of the Homewood Trilogy, published in 1981 and
1983, there is an "interfacing of 'mosaic memory' with the concept of
'Great Time'" ("Mosaic Memory" 343) in which "storytelling functions
as a bridge between the past, present and future, and between myth, his-

tory and memory" (344). *The Cattle Killing* takes the experimental use of Great Time further than *Philadelphia Fire* and the works that precede it and highlights it more. In the words of a writer/character, Great Time in *The Cattle Killing* means that the novel is *"all the books it might have been, could or should have been, buried in its pages"* (9). Further, Great Time is palimpsestlike layers of narrative like part 3 of *Philadelphia Fire*, but it is also simultaneous movement of time back and forward in which "[a]ll time's always present" (*Hoop Roots* 104). Generally, events and people have inseparable realities, and all stories are a concurrent, ever-changing linguistic form that holds liberating possibilities. Therefore, Great Time is a technique Wideman uses to fulfill his postmodern agenda of "'writing,' if not necessarily 'righting,' the wrongs of an 'upside-down' world"[2] (Birat 641).

The narrator/writer at the beginning of *The Cattle Killing* becomes a composite of people who tell first- and third-person stories, interact with listeners, and listen to their own stories and other people's stories. By both listening to stories and telling them, the narrator/writer either merges into or relates to many different stories and oppressive histories, those of women as well as men. One is the eighteenth- and nineteenth-century story/history of Bishop Richard Allen, founder of the African Methodist Episcopal Church, who played a prominent role in the 1793 Philadelphia yellow-fever epidemic in which white racism plagued black people. Among other important stories/histories is one about the nineteenth-century South African woman named Saartjie Baartman, called the Hottentot Venus, whose exposed body exploitive white men exhibited in England and France for over five years beginning in 1810. Another is about white people taking the Xhosas' land in the historical event known as the South African Xhosa cattle killing of 1856–57. There are other people and major and minor events that merge with these structurally and thematically to represent an entire story/history of white oppression of black people in Great Time. Theoretically, *all* the history of Africans and the black Diaspora happens simultaneously, and the narrator/writer and others are black men and women who are inseparable stories/histories in *all* of it. Talking about the complexity of *The Cattle Killing*, Fritz Gysin says that the novel has a "dynamic structure in which stories weave in and out of memories, dreams, and epileptic fits, reappear embedded in other stories, and reach back to first-order 'reality,' to create a web of stunning complexity and seemingly limitless metamorphosis" ("Do Not Fall Asleep in Your Enemy's Dream" 623). *The Cattle Killing* is Wideman's most ambitious novel thus far in his postmodern phase. It builds on *Reuben's* and *Philadelphia Fire's* concept of writing formally on the page and also writing in the imagination; and, utilizing experimental techniques based on the concept of Great Time where everything happens at once, it combines history, fiction, and *all* kinds of stories of black oppression to (re)write them simultaneously in an ongoing interpretative, saving process.

In regard to writing in imagination or sometimes by or through imagination, Wideman writes: "You are naked and chained to others who look like you, under the merciless control of brutal strangers who look and act nothing like you and . . . do not speak your language. . . . You realize you're learning a new language even as you swallow the bitterness, the humiliation of learning the uselessness of your own. Much of this learning and unlearning occurs in silence inside your skull, in the sanctuary where you're simultaneously struggling to retain traces of who you are, what you were before this terrible, scouring ordeal began. . . . When you break your silence, are you surrendering, acknowledging the strangers' power to own you, rule you? Are you forfeiting your chance to tell your story in your own words some day? . . . Silence in this context is a measure of resistance and tension. A drastic expression of difference that maintains the distinction between using a language and allowing it to use you" ("In Praise of Silence" 548).Wideman is alluding to aspects of his writing and of storytelling by black people that constitute a black language of "silence" that subverts the oppression inherent in English. His implication of the story of slavery and all the stories of oppression since then is particularly relevant to the narrative of *The Cattle Killing* and to this discussion. In the context of this analysis of the novel, writing and storytelling in "silence" means in imagination or by or through imagination: It indicates the effort in *The Cattle Killing* to use a liberating black language created within black being and experience in a process of telling all the stories of oppression from slavery to the present. This language supplements the language that the black novelist has learned in oppressive white culture.

The idea that a book is all stories is hard to explain, and such a book is hard to write; early in the novel, the narrator calls himself "Eye" to begin to explain the concept of the narrative and how he will write it. He listens as he conceives himself as "Eye" writing black stories/histories in Great Time:

> *Eye. Why are you called Eye. Eye short for something else someone named you. Who named you Isaiah. What could they have been thinking of. Not this story. Not this place. Not this book all the stories bound together might equal if one of the narratologists at the conference decides you're attempting something like Sherwood Anderson for Ohio or Faulkner for Mississippi or something even more exotic-sounding and harder to pronounce than Yoknapatawpha. Not quite stories. True and not true (check out the facts, dates, murders). Not exactly a novel. Hybrid like this old new ground under your feet as they pound up Wylie.*
>
> *You are Eye because you grew up in this city. And fifty years later you've returned once more as you always do and your mother and father sister brothers aunts uncles cousins nieces nephews still live here and remember you and remember what they named you and call you by that name. So why not. In a half a century you've invented nothing better or more prophetic than Eye.* (8)
>
> *Eye is a convenience, a sort of in-person once-upon-a-time convenience when I write his name.* (11)

The narrator's words have broad implications for the theme and structure of the novel. "Eye" is partly John Edgar Wideman and the character John, and partly a different construction, which ultimately includes all black stories/histories; its text is both fictional and nonfictional, written both on the page and in the imagination. The imagination includes the supernatural world of dreams and other worldly visions from sources such as epileptic fits, to which Gysin refers. The italicization of the first fourteen pages and other devices and references to narrative in the novel symbolize the creativity of "Eye" that encompasses all.

Because "Eye" is all lives lived simultaneously, all stories/histories taking place at once, it must blend the writer's story and that of young black boys in the contemporary community, the story of the Xhosa cattle killing, which was an act of self-destruction like those of the boys who are shooting each other, and later the story of an anonymous eighteenth-century African in Philadelphia:

Shoot. Chute. Black boys shoot each other. Murder themselves. Shoot. Chute. Panicked cattle funneled down the killing chute, nose pressed in the drippy ass of the one ahead. (7)

A brave, elegant African people who had resisted European invaders until an evil prophecy convinced them to kill their cattle, butcher the animals that fleshed the Xhosa's intricate dreaming of themselves. (13)

What he shared with the eighteenth-century African boy whose story he wanted to tell, the thing he would try to write, the thing that must replace names only the boy could give to what it felt like to be moving through clangorous streets, dead for two hundred years, what he could construct, would be testimony witnessing what surrounds them both this very moment, an encompassing silence forgetting them both, silence untouched by their passing, by the countless passings of so many others like them, a world distant and abiding and memoryless. (13)

"Eye" must, in the final analysis, capture the totality of black oppressive experience, much of which is now lost. Throughout the opening italicized section, the writer, "Eye," imagines his portrayal of the ongoing presence of everything past, setting up the rest of the narrative.

"Eye" tries to be endless in the narrative: As a repository of all stories, including the writer's, it has to imagine into being forgotten, silent people and stories/histories, and merge their realities with other people and histories that are supposedly nonfictional. For example, multiple fictional and supposedly nonfictional lives, histories, and biographies come together through clear connections and general associations. The character Liam is an artist, and thus like the narrator who is the writer at the beginning and like other writer figures later in the book. Aspects of Liam's story situate his life near Philadelphia and sometimes in the city in the eighteenth century. Since he is an African, this relates him to the *"eighteenth-century African boy"* in Philadelphia described near the beginning (13). The African boy does not have a specific identity, but his existence in the eighteenth century also connects him to a young preacher, a major character who walks the same Philadelphia streets that the African boy walks and that Liam walked in the eighteenth century. Events in the life of the young preacher, such as his leadership of a black church congregation that secedes from a white one, parallel those of Bishop Allen in the novel and in history. Also, in *The Cattle Killing*, the first white master sold the preacher, his abused mother, and his brother to a benevolent master. The wife of this master influenced him to convert the preacher and his brother to Christianity, and taught them to read the Bible (64). The general details of this fictional biography clearly are similar to historical accounts of Bishop Allen being sold to a second master and converting to Methodism. Further, Liam's life is like the religious lives of the preacher and Bishop Allen. He and ten others were "gulled from [their] African families, taken up by the English to be trained as holy men" (103).

The first fourteen italicized pages are largely the theory of the book's narrative; the book whose construction "Eye" explains in those pages is comprised of the following two parts and epilogue. In part 1, the preacher in the eighteenth century creates the world through imagination as he awakens: "He waits, holding his breath while the house that is the world remembers its shape, erects itself again, all the stone and brick and wood piling up without a sound. He goes to sleep alone in an empty place and next morning the cities of his past, the cities of his future, are spread around him. People step over him, around him, through him, always on their way somewhere else. They wear strange shoes, unimaginable shoes, so he understands immediately he is not dreaming, he is awake in a familiar town filled with nameless faces. People wearing shoes cobbled by devils" (18). Later, fits that turn "the world [into] one sight, one luminous presence inventing his eyes" are part of his imaginative creation, too (69).[3] He sees "[p]eople everywhere. People in outlandish costumes. Shoes from my dreams. A bazaar of people milling about. More African people than I'd ever seen in one place at one time. A throng far too numerous to be contained in the small space of the brush arbor [where he is preaching]. Different faces, groups differently appareled in each direction I scan. Replaced by newcomers if I glance away and then back at the same spot. Swarms of people drifting, shuttling, filling the clearing" (75). Implicitly, the preacher and the writer are one embodiment along with all the text's artists, who are imagining everything and being imagined by others in their ongoing creativity.

Through the narrative process, the interwoven stories/histories that the text is (re)writing oppose the effects of oppression by always inculcating virtue and positive struggle. A primary story is about an unnamed woman afflicted by oppression to whom the preacher tells stories about attending people in the countryside surrounding Philadelphia during the 1793 yellow-fever plague; he is trying to save her with the message about his saving acts. At the same time, listening to and sharing her stories of travail will potentially teach lessons that will save him.

Everything is a constant process from every perspective: The woman is synonymous with other women and men in his stories, and implicitly the preacher merges into men and women in hers. There is a precarious line between moving in many directions and moving forward to avoid deeply digressing and losing narrative focus completely: "I must choose to go on with my story or digress. Endlessly digress, because if I follow where [the woman's] feet lead, I will enter her skin and then there is no end, only the maze of her in which I lose myself forever" (38). The maze of the woman represents an interminable number of people, and the versions of the stories are potentially as interminable as the people. "When I omit parts of the story, do I relinquish my hold on you. When the tale jumps to a different place, where do you go" (39). "How many times have I begun this story. Reaching out again and again. Are you offering me your foot to touch. Or are you sleeping. Your bare foot straying from the covers, in another story perhaps, far from here, a stranger's dream I can't enter even if I dared to stroke your foot, take it in both my hands and lift it to my lips" (39–40). The woman in one dreamlike story walks into the lake with a sick child, and he does not see her return. However, "[s]he returned. I know she did. If I'd waited, I might have found you sooner" (48). He is telling many stories simultaneously in Great Time: One woman in the present is also the woman who walked into the lake in the past and many people. His references to entering the woman's skin and the woman in the story from someone else's dream suggest the never-ending multiplicity of stories/histories, and how inseparable he is from both female and male realities.

As is true in the preacher's fits, the imagination that consists of supernatural/dream realities combining the dead and living, the past and present, is an important aspect of stories told in Great Time. At one point, the preacher feels that his "[e]nterprise [is] speaking into the dark as if it would raise [the woman] from the dead" (78), "whispering in your cold ear—words, words, words, as if silence isn't enough." Part of the woman occupies the supernatural "world of special seeing" (76) that the preacher envisions, and her request for a happy story to "cure her" (78) projects him into another story where the people die (148–49) and live again in the process of (re)writing in part 2 (179–82). The people in the story he tells the woman are Liam and his white wife, who are living outside Philadelphia in the eighteenth century. The wife's victimization by racism because she loves a black man connects her to black women and the collectivity of black oppression; this implies that whiteness is an artificial classification that so-called white society can abrogate. White men have control in society, and are the only ones the novel portrays as oppressors and not victims.

The story the preacher tells the sick woman about Liam and his wife is one that restores on multiple levels, as is typical in the novel. To heal her, the preacher starts telling the woman about Liam and his wife finding him nearly frozen at the door of their house in the remote country outside Philadelphia; shortly, this story interweaves into Liam and his wife's stories that resurrect the preacher and also their own love (79–94). The preacher's voice articulates the transformation of Liam's wife in this process: "[Y]ou began to change" (95). "Perhaps I turned away an instant. Perhaps in that brief, brief absence, another woman, no, girl, took your place." At the end of this section marked by a space separating parts of the text (96), the preacher's narrative seems to suggest that Liam's wife tells him stories through an intersubjective process of imagination that is an integral part of what restores him: "You told me I wasn't going to die. Said it without words and I believed you. You didn't say you'd saved my life, but I knew you were the one" (96).

The writer's portrayal at the beginning as an author of novels and his later embodiment in the preacher and others imply that stories are being written on the page, orally *in* imagination, and *by* imagination, the preacher's supernaturally envisioned stories that bring the world into existence for example (18, 75). The preacher's words further suggest the power in the endless pattern of all stories, including those told orally and imaginatively "without words." It is unclear how stories are written intersubjectively between imaginations as the preacher seems to indicate. However, here and throughout this novel as well as in Wideman's recent novels, the greatest potential seems to reside in stories about the reality of blackness that can be written *in* imagination by other oral and formally written stories, and also in creative stories written *by* imagination such as the preacher's.

The preacher's story about Liam and his wife continues within the freedom stories Liam told his wife when they were in England in their youth. Liam's stories were a "gift of his words painting worlds for [her]" (102). The church, which stole him from Africa, sold Liam to "[a] Mr. Stubbs" (104), who made him "manservant and companion" to his son George Stubbs. In Liam's stories to his wife, he "voyaged round the globe, fought in great naval battles, escaped the chains and torture of a dungeon, lived among savages in faraway lands" (102). The stories of adventure and escape led to her falling in love with him and escaping adventurously across the ocean to freedom in the remote area where they are, privately living as husband and wife, publicly disguised as Mrs. Stubbs and the faithful servant of her dead husband.

However, a perhaps unexpected potential turn in the process of the stories occurs. The power of white oppression in black freedom stories overburdens and infects black imagination; freedom stories paradoxically evolve into stories of oppressive white power that are the common story of black men and women. The story of Saartjie Baartman, the "Hottentot Venus," is a strong influence on Liam and black imagination. According to various accounts, Baartman allowed Europeans to display her naked body to marvel at her physical features, particularly her genitalia, for her own financial reward, and when she died white people cut her up and put her body parts on display. Baartman was a victimized individual, but certain aspects of her story resemble other stories of European oppression of black groups in which the oppressed inadvertently facilitate their oppression. For example, she apparently unwittingly cooperated in the oppression that led to the butchering of her body similar to the way the Xhosa furthered their oppression by butchering their cattle in the Xhosa cattle-killing story. Although many people do not know the Baartman and Xhosa stories specifically, their general content has infectiously inseminated black imagination through oral and written sources, and implicitly this is what happens in the novel.[4]

Liam does not specifically mention Baartman, but his language shows that her story is the basis of one he tells the preacher about his life in the elder Stubbs's slaughterhouse and as the assistant of his son George Stubbs, an artist who used human dissection to try to discover the essence of life. He reacts to the pregnant body of a "Hottentot" "Venus" (136, 135) the young Stubbs examines to purchase for dissection in an English charnel house: "My legs trembled. I pressed my hands into the wall. . . . The African woman on the table was my sister, mother, daughter. I slept inside her dark stomach. . . . She'd been stolen from me and now I was about to lose her again. Knives would slice her open, hack her to bits. They'd find me cowering in the black cave of her womb again, dead and alive, alive and dead. I wished for the fiery breath of a dragon, for tongues of flame to leap from my mouth and consume that terrible cellar where the auctioneer had already begun his obscene chant" (137). Liam is speaking, but the narrator is also the preacher telling stories within Liam's stories and other narrators telling stories within stories. Saartjie Baartman, her fictional re-creation, and all the oppressed women to whom the narrator(s) tell stories are one and have the same story that they do, the same infectious, devastating story of blackness.

More than anywhere else in the novel, the oral/auditory/visual and imaginary/dream/supernatural are indistinguishably integrated, as are the realities of the narrator, Liam, Liam's wife, and others, and the stories encompass more in another massive oppressive convolution. The narrator "knew I must be in the Africa of Liam's stories. I was the boy he'd been before he was snatched away forever" (143). He sees the dream about the Xhosa girl Nongqawuse (144–48), the young woman in the historical accounts of the Xhosa cattle killing of 1856–57.[5] In the dream, the girl tells how the voice of a strange spirit told her to prophesy to the Xhosa to kill their cattle, the symbol of their tradition and way of life. What spoke to the girl "was a spirit of despair grown strong inside our breasts, as the whites had grown strong in our land, during years of fighting and plague and hate" (147). White victory in war gives power to the white spirit's words, and the Xhosas eventually believe the false prophecy and kill their cattle.

Accepting white reality in a story is central to the Xhosa downfall. As the narrator later understands, the inescapable danger of language is that it is invested with white power, and narratives in all forms are potentially white stories that oppress black people. Thus, Liam's oral stories transport the narrator to Nongqawuse, to the Africa of the Xhosas (148), and to the white spirit's dream that caused the Xhosas' destruction, which the narrator dreams along with Nongqawuse (144). The oppressive power of language works in oral stories, written stories, and stories told at the deep level of consciousness that is dream. So Nongqawuse warns, "Do not fall asleep in your enemy's dream" (147). Caught up in the stories, the narrator has fallen asleep, and because of this the white oppression embedded in would-be black freedom stories becomes his story. He "awakens" from the Africa of white story/dream where the Xhosas slaughtered their cattle as the spirit advised, thereby destroying the central part of their existence. The story he "sees" when he wakes up is white: White people from the surrounding rural area burn Liam and his forbidden white wife in their cabin (148–49). All white stories are the same, and that story of black butchery will be his story if the narrator is not careful and "falls asleep."

A feeling of oppression engendered by stories overwhelms the narrator when he sees Liam die. The stories expand and contract endlessly: "Circles within circles. Expanding and contracting at once—boundless, tight as a noose. God's throat, belly, penis, cunt, asshole, the same black ditch. The people an unbroken chain of sausages fed in one end and pulled out the other. A circle without and within, the monstrous python swallowing itself, birthing its tail" (149).

Remember the writer's device "Eye." When Liam burns in the white story, "Eye" is words infused with white power inseminated at the deepest level of nightmarish perception; however, this nightmarish figure at the end of part 1 does not negate hope because "Eye" is also the novel's process of (re)writing. The figure's circles are endlessly outward as well as inward, destroying but constantly reproducing and maintaining the potential for ongoing, liberating storytelling. In part 2, "Eye" continues (re)writing Liam's story (179–82) and, in the process, all black stories.

Part of the (re)writing in part 2 is its ongoing, open-ended treatment of the black religious story told through the preacher and Bishop Allen. Part 2 begins with a focus on the weight of black oppression suggested in the last paragraph of part 1. The narrator is sitting on the bed beside the sick woman (153) telling the collective story that is his story, the preacher's story, Bishop Allen's story, and the story of "the dead" speaking to him. He imagines Bishop Allen sitting abjectly on his bed (153), locked

The narrator focuses on the basic source of oppression in his stories when he addresses the oppressiveness inherent in words. He struggles to speak near the end:

> As you hear, I've begun to stutter. Even when I'm not speaking. Stuttering. Losing my facility in this language that's cost me far too much to learn. Cost too much of this life and countless other lives. A stutter. Between what I want to say and the saying of it, a shadow passes. A ditch opens and the words crumple and drop into it. Fly away, fly away home, my words a face in the mirror I do not want to recognize. (205)

> Time now to give it up. This speaking in a strange tongue, this stranger's voice I struggle to assume in order to keep you alive. The stories are not working. I talk, maybe you listen, but you're not better, not stronger. (205)

Earlier in the novel, the preacher's memory of the words of a white preacher indicates how white people use the negative images of blackness inherent in their language to oppress black people: "Vagabond preachers [like the young black preacher] . . . cast an undiscriminating net, drawing unsavory types to the bosom of the church, including Negroes free and slave, women, the shiftless and untutored, whose undisciplined enthusiasm mocked true faith" (60). Castigating women too, the white preacher is basically telling a story in which negative characterizations of black people inhere in many of the words and the entire narrative. Words are foreign to the narrator because they are from the language that white people have successfully infused with black oppression and that they use as the white preacher does.

The narrator hears his spoken and unspoken words escaping his control in a process of telling black stories that is liberating, instead of supporting the pattern of oppression in white stories. However, the sick woman, who has been telling, listening, and imagining too, saves him by continuing to imbue the stories with love: "No matter, no matter, it's fine, baby. You're fine. Letting him know she understands and it's all right. Either way. Everything. Any way. As long as you tried your best, baby. Fine. Fine. Fine" (205–6).

In this context where there is still hope, the narrator in the last paragraph of part 2 again describes the potential of storytelling. He does not stutter: "Tell me, finally, what is a man. What is a woman. Aren't we lovers first, spirits sharing an uncharted space, a space our stories tell, a space chanted, written upon again and again, yet one story never quite erased by the next, each story saving the space, saving itself, saving us. If someone is listening" (208). He introduces contingency that opens up endless possibilities.

Then in the epilogue, the stories continue to proliferate and imply multiple forms of narrative as fiction and history merge. First, the epilogue portrays Dan, the son of the author of *The Cattle Killing*, discussing his reading of the novel with his father (209–12). When Dan reads the words Liam's wife uses to greet the narrator—*"Tea, sir. Hot tea. Here you are, sir"* (209)—Great Time collapses the past and present, the real and imaginary. The "real-life" Dan in the present listens to the story of Liam's wife in the eighteenth century, and thus all the women's stories, just as the eighteenth-century narrator did. A writer finishing his own book about the African slave trade, Dan has been to the British Museum's African archives in London and found a letter from the brother of a "nameless narrator" (211) in *The Cattle Killing*, the unnamed preacher who was the property of two masters along with his mother and brother. The brother voyaged to Africa after their mother died and later worked with the Xhosas during the cattle killing. He is thus another "real-life" character who reinforces the "reality" of all the "fiction." *The Cattle Killing* ends with a quotation from a letter of the narrator's brother: *"This note, the others I intend to write, may never reach you, yet I am sure a time will come when we shall be together again. . . . Hold on, Your Brother* (212).

Storytelling does indeed reach continuously backward and forward and everywhere at once, amalgamating everything, binding people, and keeping open the potential that it can save and liberate. Jennifer D. Douglas says that in *The Cattle Killing* the "process of articulation, transforming images into words, effects some healing even if it cannot cure systemic evil. Perhaps over time, the accumulation of stories is what prompts change by denying the possibility of forgetting" (217).The process is agonizing but positive at the end.

* * *

Two Cities (1998) may be Wideman's least known and acclaimed novel, and it is the easiest to read among all of his books. Wideman has said that the life of the central character, Mr. Mallory, "opens up great time, the past that's always present. And not only has he traversed spiritually that immense distance and stayed connected, but he has the means to communicate that journey and some of the places he's been to other people" (Berben-Masi, "From *Brothers and Keepers* to *Two Cities*" 572–73). Mr. Mallory is a photographer, a creative artist whose pictures are similar to the creative "fictions" of Reuben. However, instead of building complexity as he does through the depiction of Reuben's "fictions," Wideman uses Mr. Mallory's pictures as central symbols in a structure that breaks down the complexity of Great Time and the narrative generally. *Two Cities* is the one work in Wideman's career where he, in a sense, slows his writing down and reduces its density. The work's more conventional formal and thematic structure is the key to its accessibility.

Like *The Cattle Killing*, *Two Cities* is a love story that is also a political critique of black oppression in white culture. The primary characters are a woman named Kassima, her lover Robert Jones, and her tenant Mr. Mallory. What connects the characters' lives, the two cities of the title (Pittsburgh and Philadelphia), and approximately fifty years of African American history are the memories and photographs of old Mr. Mallory. Among many other things, Mr. Mallory remembers World War II, in which white soldiers murdered his friend Gus and tried to murder him because of their tryst with two white women; the murder of his friend and MOVE leader John Africa in the 1985 Philadelphia fire (the subject of the novel *Philadelphia Fire*); and his desertion of his own family. When he is old, he moves from Philadelphia to Pittsburgh, where he finds self-destructive black youth-gang violence. Kassima takes him in as her tenant after losing her incarcerated husband to AIDS and her two sons to gang warfare, and he dies in her house after she has started and then tried to end a relationship with Robert Jones. Mr. Mallory's death brings her and Robert Jones back together. Near the end, Kassima uses Mr. Mallory's photographs of what he has seen living in Philadelphia and Pittsburgh to stop a horrible black gang ritual at the funeral home.[7] As is typical in Wideman's work, the process of the love story that is also about the historical oppression of black people continues in Great Time in "Zugunruhe: A Postscript."

In light of Wideman's comments about Mr. Mallory "opening up" Great Time, *Two Cities* most importantly makes it clear how stories are told in Great Time. The primary narrative perspectives are those of Mr. Mallory, Robert Jones, and Kassima, but ambiguously placed narrators are also listening to the story and contributing to it in Great Time. Toward the end of "Playing Ball," where the story is primarily Robert's third-person narrative, multiple voices of "Baxter," "Monroe," and others intrude from unspecified places: "Whoa. Man's telling a serious story here and youall acting like clowns. Hush. Let the man talk" (77). "Hey, I'm just trying to be helpful. You know. No disrespect, brother man, but these boo-boo loved-and-lost stories a dime a dozen. You want somebody to listen you got to jazz them up." The idea is the same as in other works; the story is always multiple stories being told at many different places from many perspectives. However, the difference is that the language and the overall structure are clear and straightforward, and the idea of Great Time is easier to grasp than in a more complex novel like *The Cattle Killing*. Although reading *Two Cities* may not make reading *The Cattle Killing* easier, it may help to clarify one of the major concepts underlying the latter work.

Throughout *Two Cities*, Great Time and other major ideas about story-telling are described more clearly than in Wideman's other works. Near the beginning, the narrator explains how Mr. Mallory's reality encompasses past and present people, including the dead John Africa: "Maybe he doesn't have to lose his friend after all. Maybe these pauses a chance for John Africa to slide beside him again, real as the memory. A choice, an offer. Just take one teensy giant step over to John Africa's side. You're dizzy because you're in two places at once or too many places and maybe it's your own fault you're stuck here where you are and he isn't" (12). Again, the basic concept is that all time is simultaneous, but the direct statement and the novel's transparent structure make it easier to understand. The same is true later when the text portrays how stories merge people across the lines of gender and life and death. Kassima looks in the mirror and sees "her features and Mr. Mallory's blended, white-haired like him, skin dry and wrinkled like his, faded to ashy gray like him dead in her bed" (203). Similarly, talking about Romare Bearden's art, Mr. Mallory explains the multiple layers of reality in his own photographs and, by implication, in Wideman's writing: "His paintings are many paintings in one, overlapping, hiding and revealing each other. Many scenes occur at once, a crowd hides in a single body. Time and space are thicker. I'm seeking the truth of his painting when I stack slices of light onto each square of film. Different views, each stamped with its own pattern of light and dark but also transparent, letting through some of the light and dark of layers beneath and above" (117). Also, Mr. Mallory remembers a story set in Philadelphia involving someone going to jail that John Africa told him, and merges people in that story with ones in a story about Pittsburgh. He imagines John Africa's response: "Two cities, old man. You've got everything all mixed up, friend. Two slams in two different cities. Hundreds of miles apart. Years apart. How those guys spozed to meet" (173). They are supposed to meet, though; through irony, Mr. Mallory makes the point about storytelling encompassing many realities and about the two cities of the title as a representation of this idea.

The novel ends similarly to other Wideman novels by emphasizing the ongoing process of storytelling. Kassima throws Mr. Mallory's photographs on the ground to stop the gang members from desecrating the body of a rival gang member: "Then some of them started coming up, looking at us beside the coffin, looking at the pictures all over the ground, picking up pictures, looking at them, looking at each other, handing them around, talking, walking off with pictures in their hands. Who knows what they were seeing. What they said. Who knows what they thought. And that was the beginning of the end of the worst part of that day" (239). The text largely portrays the gang members telling their own intragang stories that separate them from other black people, but at the end there is the clear suggestion that they have a story that is an important part of the larger ongoing black story. One bad part of a bad day is perhaps ending, but the stories told in the pictures continue for endless days with the possibility that the gang members can contribute to a liberating narrative instead of a destructive one.

Two Cities' straightforwardness notwithstanding, its characters and themes sometimes have complex, subtle, or ambiguous connections to other Wideman books, a typical feature of his writing. And theme and structure in *Two Cities* can sometimes be complex as in his other works. For example, the ending and overall portrayal of the gang members suggest that they speak mostly to each other in their own language, often with hand, head, and body signs. Maybe J. B. in *Philadelphia Fire* (158, 159) best implies that young black people in the streets can write a text in imagination that has liberating possibilities as well as negative ones. Talking in signs could indicate that they are writing a liberating language in imagination. Perhaps their language can be the basis of a text written in imagination that is potentially liberating as it is in *Philadelphia Fire* and *The Cattle Killing*. Further, in "Dancing at Edgar's," the narrator says that Robert could have lived in the house where the much younger Kassima now lives (26–28, 31–35). This is a house in Pittsburgh on Cassina Way where the writer/character John Wideman lives in previous novels and auto/biographies. Implicitly, fiction and auto/biography intersect, and male and female characters merge and embody each other across time and between "real-life" and fiction. This is most clear in "Mr. Mallory" when Robert recounts the story of his grandmother saving his grandfather by screaming to distract a man shooting at him on Cassina Way, which is the story of John's grandmother and grandfather in *Damballah*'s "Lizabeth: The Caterpillar Story" and elsewhere.

Also, "Zugunruhe: A Postscript," which imaginatively describes Mr. Mallory's move from Philadelphia to Pittsburgh and explains the reason for it, is more cryptic than most of the novel, and it highlights some of its underlying complexity. "Zugunruhe" is a term from ethology referring to the migratory patterns of animals. By going from Philadelphia to Pittsburgh in the postscript, Mr. Mallory represents the migration and continuation of the story in Great Time, which merges Mr. Mallory's past and present and combines Gus's past life and present life in death: "Pittsburgh a city where he knew somebody dead. And that's another good reason. Gives him a history there. He wouldn't be a stranger, not a newcomer or johnny-come-lately. Hey, Gus. You come lately. How you doing, soul" (241). The very last appended words give the date and place when John Edgar Wideman completes the narrative, "*Sunday, August 10, 1997—Naples, Maine*" (242). This brings him into the book as a character, reminiscent of the character John entering the narrative through his embodiment in Robert Jones earlier. The narrative remains open in the broader terms of many fictional and "real" stories as well as all of Great Time's stories.

* * *

While *Two Cities* is the easiest Wideman book to read and one that potentially elucidates other works, *Fanon* (2008) is probably the most difficult, even more experimental and ambitious than *The Cattle Killing*.

From beginning to end, *Fanon* is distinctly different from other works by Wideman. John the writer/character creates the book's unique fictional course. Early in the text, he writes: "I realize time's running out. I won't be writing many more books, if any" (5), expressing an apparent desperation to write this book that has not been there in his discussions about writing other books. This work will turn out to be important for the liberation of many people John knows and for black people generally. However, he badly wants to write a successful story about Fanon and his constant struggle for liberation because writing it is also his way of connecting with Fanon and liberating himself at the end of his career.[8] In earlier works, the writer spends a lot of time participating in a process of writing, telling, and listening to potentially liberating black stories. In comparison, the writer here is more acutely aware of metafictional problems with sterile, self-referential words. As he engages in a painful attempt to write, he reaches the point where he explores ways to tell Fanon's story. He mainly explores through intertextual relationships, primarily with David Macey's biography *Frantz Fanon* (2000) and Fanon's books and writings, particularly *The Wretched of the Earth* (1961). He bases large parts of his story directly or indirectly on Macey's book, and draws on Fanon's writing to create his life. The heavy, close reliance on other texts is a new approach in Wideman's works that grows out of the writer/character's desperate attempt to write this very hard story.

At the beginning, John focuses on the difficulty of writing Fanon's story because words defy the writer. However, as the novel develops, the focal point of his problem evolves and shifts: Fanon is central in this story of many lives, and it is so difficult to write because the reality of his life grounded in meaningful actions that expressed human commitment totally defies words. One could say that Fanon's whole life grew from questions that were inseparable from committing and doing: "Will this choice free souls from their chains? Or better, will this step move humanity toward greater liberation? His answers led him to war with the Nazis, to struggle with himself, to labor against mental illness, and to a bloody and painful revolt against French colonialism in Algeria" (Ehlen 11). John believes this is true of Fanon too, and a primary thing the book about Fanon must do is somehow to capture the actuality of his committing/ doing. Near the end of *Fanon*, the character Dr. Frantz Fanon implies some characteristics of the book that *is* committing/doing when he describes the text that he is imagining and dictating and his wife is transcribing. It is a text that is partly the words of his patients and that is "hopelessly compromised by any form of writing" (191): It is a "sort of bricolage of free-floating fragments whose authorship is unsettlingly ambiguous."

This is at least a partial description of John's fictional text *Fanon*, which is the model for the novel *Fanon* that Wideman is attempting to write. Devising a multifaceted text that is a bricolage is always important for Wideman,[9] especially in *Philadelphia Fire* and *The Cattle Killing*, but part of *Fanon*'s overall difference is that it takes even further the already difficult effort to write this kind of text. *Fanon* is about writing that is not just more than the words on the page, like recent novels; it is about breaking the bonds of the page-centered formal text. By part 3, the writer is trying to create a highly imagined, improvised, many-voiced, multifragmented text that represents the seeing, speaking, feeling, acting, and nontraditional discoursing of *living* people; also, by the end, he is trying to write the *living* book that virtually leaves the page by animating many people acting and reacting purposefully along with him.

One of the most intriguing aspects of *Fanon* is an ambiguous tone that ranges from playfully anguished to highly serious and pessimistic; this applies to and coincides with John's project of writing Fanon's life and relating to him from the outset. At the beginning, the sixty-five-year-old John is sitting in a house in Brittany writing a letter to Fanon "trying to save a life" (3). "Whose life and why are other things I'm trying to figure out." The letter turns into the book about Fanon. John realizes that Fanon understood better than he when he was young how writing isolated him from others as much as race did (5), and wants to write Fanon's life "to be free . . . to write a life for myself, fact and fiction, to open possibilities of connecting with your life, other lives" (6–7). The task of freeing himself from isolation by connecting to Fanon's vividly lived life through writing is difficult and presents the risk of failure. Fanon risked failure through revolutionary action and human participation, in addition to his writing. John will never accomplish what Fanon did, but maybe if he takes the risk of failing and tries to engage Fanon and others through skillful writing, he will achieve some of the feeling of liberating human experience he wants. Quickly however, John's insecurity about writing becomes clear when he creates his "double," a "man named Thomas, who lives only in his stalled novel" (7), to bear the weight of his own apparent pending failure.[10] He asks Fanon to "[t]hink of me, of Thomas, as your age-mates . . . playing a deadly serious game of chasing your spirit" (9). This begins the last paragraph under the first heading of part 1, "A Letter to Frantz Fanon"; the second heading, "The Bell Rings," starts with the seemingly farcical scene of Thomas hearing the doorbell and "imagining how a head, bloody and real, might arrive at his door."

The severed bloody head in part 1 symbolizes *head*ings representing sections that are seemingly disparate or severed from each other, and it increasingly stands for the seriousness of John's severance from Fanon and human contact by his immersion in words.[11] Placing part of the responsibility for writing on Thomas, he shows the futility of using self-referential words: "The narrative forges ahead. And doesn't. Giving Thomas a headache either way. A bad head. Stop, Thomas. Nothing funny here. One more atrocious head pun and it's off with yours" (13). Thomas would isolate himself in words describing an imaginary head and not open the package with the real bloody one that the delivery man would bring to the door: "No. You would rather write about an imaginary head, right. . . . Writing it until you get it right. Until its words, a story, not Thomas coming apart, not something words can't grasp. Maybe you only need to tell the story once. If you can write it perfectly once, the horror will be the words, the words appearing, the horror disappearing" (16). A writer can never describe a bloody head in words and make it a real one. However, John will still be trying to break through the limitations of the writer isolating himself in words as Thomas is; he will be trying to find better ways of portraying the external world and engaging Fanon and others than the textual maneuvers that he attributes to Thomas.

The writer's consumption in language dominates part 1 through John's projection onto Thomas, the "double" who is afraid to come out of alienation in a world of words, but movement toward a different text that alludes to Fanon's life of committing/doing also begins in part 1 through the relationship between writer and surrogate. Fanon first appears in the seemingly directionless story of the head through a quotation found on a note in the package: *"We must immediately take the war to the enemy, leave him no rest, harass him. Cut off his breath"* (17).[12] John questions the decision to use a quotation that contributes to Fanon's reputation for supporting violence. However, he later says that "[i]f the Fanon quote fits, if it pumps up the action . . . so what if Fanon guilty by association" (18), and concludes "A Note" with "[l]et's say the Fanon quote, *take the war to the enemy,* etc., [will] . . . heighten suspense. Thicken the soup. Teach somebody a lesson. Who. Who knows. Who sez" (19). Cloaked in an ironic and mocking tone, Fanon's words begin to form a pattern alluding to human action, commitment, and feeling that becomes the positive text that develops throughout the novel.

The following sections—"Point of View," "Thomas Teaches Writing in My Old School," "Thomas Leaves," and "The Head Devours Thomas"— continue subtly to develop toward a story that can at least approach the expression of human life. "Point of View" compares a Romare Bearden collage to John's mother's stories that "flatten and fatten perspective. She crams everything, everyone, everywhere into the present, into words that flow, intimate and immediate as the images of a Bearden painting" (21). Writing words so that they animate as his mother's do in storytelling is one technique in writing the unwritable human immediacy and intimacy of the story of the long-dead Fanon and others that John must create. John further says that for his mother "[m]eaning equals point of view" (22). He means that point of view in her stories covers life and its action expansively, and he will later rely significantly on the mother's voice to establish his point of view that presents people living, feeling, and interacting. John asks at the end of "Thomas Teaches Writing in My Old School": "Why couldn't he write this novel. Or even better, why not live it. Love it or leave it, Thomas" (26). Although the tone is ambiguous and ironic again, the emphasis here is on action, most importantly living and loving, which are part of the human substance that John's mother encompasses in her point of view. The title "Thomas Leaves" indicates Thomas actually moving, which sounds trivial, but this is an aspect of the accruing pattern of action. This section portrays John moving too; he is walking and describing New York City as concretely as possible to gain a broad perspective of the outside world (28–32), thus contributing to the point of view that he needs in the effort to portray human life. Before abruptly and briefly introducing the voice of his incarcerated brother (32), which also contributes to point of view, John intimates how in describing the city he is also moving toward the successful engagement of Fanon's human life: "I can manage, more or less, to guide myself through vast stretches of utter darkness by drawing imaginary maps, like this one I'm sketching for you, Fanon, connecting the dots . . . connecting the emptiness between dots" (33). "The Head Devours Thomas" ends with "[w]ords delivering messages over and over again, scripts for plans doomed to fail" (36). However, the words here also indicate developing action that goes beyond Thomas's earlier effete practice of language. John is breaking free of the limitations that he projected onto Thomas, and the potential exists that he will not fail.

A real sense of this potential begins to come through in the writer's sudden imagination of "Africa," which uses Macey's biography of Fanon to open up perspectives on his life actions. Macey's is one of the "many voices [Thomas will borrow] to disguise his voice" (36) in writing about Fanon and imagining the broad, diverse range of his life experience. John says that it is a "simple plan": "As simple as accepting a face in the mirror as real. Simple if you don't ask who is gazing into the glass or who's inside staring back, simple if you don't insist that it's impossible for a face in a mirror to be real unless the one who gazes fabricates a history for it, a story no face in the mirror can take shape without." John seems to be emphasizing the *act* of accepting the face as real and the *act* of writing following acceptance instead of the intellectual analysis that turns back on the image in a paralyzing process. The will to act does seem to work because immediately following this, "Africa" depicts Fanon riding across Mali to find routes to Algeria so that other Africans can aid the Algerian revolution.[13]

This story of Fanon in "Africa" is full of the writer's doubt and cynicism, but in the end turns from the negative to the positive direction that the narrative should go. An example of the negative is the writer self-consciously breaking in on his imagination of Fanon's reconnaissance work, playing on words, and undercutting the narrative: "Good golly, Miss Mali, you sure love to ball. Blasts from the past in my earphones, not Fanon's. Before his short life ended, will end just a few months from this moment we're imagining together, did Fanon hear our Manhattans, our Mr. Penniman, our glossy-topped star Little Richard sing 'Tutti Frutti' or 'Send Me Some Lovin' or 'Good Golly,' etc., or are these tunes anachronisms inserted into Fanon's stream of consciousness in a Range Rover in late September, early October of 1961" (39). John moves past this interruption by reminding Thomas not to analyze too deeply: "Good golly. No fun, Thomas, to think too much about Fanon's story or what you think you're going to make of it. No rules for scoring a life" (40). Then, he tries briefly to go beyond the limitation of writing on the page by using Fanon's journal as a different kind of writing "score" that at least projects the immediacy of reality. Fanon's journal "scores his vision of Chawkwi" (42), a man with him on the African mission: *"Eyes like this do not lie. They say quite openly that they have seen terrible things: repression, torture.... Very difficult to deceive, to get around or to infiltrate."* The important point is that the "vision" of both men "scores" life, albeit horrible, by opening encompassing, realistic vistas that are much more than writing can produce. John is later able to present a richly imaginative "vision" of Fanon in the African night (43–47) that ends with the admission that it is imaginative speculation: "Whether Fanon slept that night or dreamed his dream of Algerian independence or didn't sleeps with him in one of his contested graves" (47). However, at the end of "Africa," the quotation from the conclusion of *The Wretched of the Earth* is a call to action (311) that focuses on the immediacy of life. It is similar to the other Fanon "vision": *"Come then, comrades ... it would be as well to decide at once to change our ways.... The new day which is already at hand must find us firm, prudent, and resolute"* (48).

"Pittsburgh—a Prison" is a shift to John's mother and brother, whose lives and stories represent the immediacy of living in ways that John can imaginatively relate to Fanon and also draw upon in his own living and writing that portrays Fanon. As stated, life as lived and written by Fanon, and as John wants to live and write it, cannot be adequately captured on the page. Nevertheless, John must break the habit of writing in isolation so that he can engage people in an effort to create a text that reflects human feeling and action that go beyond words. He must resituate his imagination in human life and take the risk of using words to allude to the diversity of positive living expression that exceeds formal writing. Along with accessing formal resources as intertexts that help him to refer to life, an important way that John writes this text is by imaginatively accessing the living resources of his mother and brother with whom he is a life participant. In a portrayal of his visit to the prison with his mother near the end of this section, John asserts the imaginative link between her and Fanon that will significantly inform the attempt to express life in the rest of the novel: "Guess what. Your mother over there claims she met Fanon during one of her stays in the hospital" (63). He says his mother insisted Fanon "wasn't dead when she talked to him" (64) and told him about the meeting, which is "going in the book." This book is still writing, but John has a growing ability to imagine a text in which actions and interactions point the story outward to actual living beyond the usual limits of writing. The fact that John's mother did not meet Fanon is not important; what is important is that they exemplify the actions and interactions of living in the outwardly directed story John is trying to create.

Robert suggests how using words in stories can engage actual life as John tries to do by "writing those buggy books" like the one about Fanon:

> Being locked up, you know, I got nothing but time, plenty of time to read. Pick up your weird shit and whoa, sometimes it makes perfect sense to me. Probably because you're my brother. Plenty times I don't agree with them knucklehead ideas I been hearing from you my whole life, but I like to hear your bullshit anyway. Funny, you know, the craziest shit's what I like best. When you get off on words and get to rapping and signifying and shit. Getting off on shit like we do in the yard. Just to hear our ownselves talking sometimes, just to say goddamn words we ain't gon hear less we say em. Guys hanging in the yard talking crazy stories. Know what I mean.
>
> Mom's the storyteller in the family. Wish I had half her gift. I said you're the best storyteller in the family, Mom, and I see you over there pretending to sleep so you can eavesdrop and get more stories to tell on us. (64)

Robert implies how John in the language of his books relates to living reality when he says John's words remind him of prisoners "talking crazy stories" that reflect their lives. John says that the mother is always trying to get new stories to tell, and by calling her the best storyteller, he affirms that her stories engage life too. At the very end, John tries to describe his mother: "[F]amiliar as I am with her face I can't sharpen the image of it, of her, can't bring her more clearly into focus than to think the words *soft-*

ness, freckles, pale and I know better than to worry her image past the peace offered by these few words said to myself into the space between us, the peace for this moment in these brutal, war-torn surroundings" (64–65). The effort to see his mother's face and the emphasis on the words that focus on her physical features further suggest the actual engagement of life.

His mother bestowing a sense of peace in the midst of war initially seems to separate her from Fanon, who was a revolutionary warrior, but in this context in which John brings them together, they are similar in their participation in life and even in storytelling that elicits its reality. John disagrees with the implications of his mother's story of the death of Esther Morris from Homewood (61–63), but it still leads to his feeling that she represents a calm place in the stealthy war against black people that he, unlike her, believes killed Esther. In spite of the fact that his mother would deny the idea of a political conspiracy, her story about Esther shows empathy and implies a long life in which she has immersed herself in interaction with people and learned to take in and respond to whatever happens, which in this instance simply means not eating things that will kill her like Esther killed herself. Her empathy is generally reminiscent of Fanon's call to comrades that John has imagined and will later imagine again (48, 71). John earlier talked about point of view in his mother's stories, the way that she includes everything in them. The very short Esther Morris story approximates this in the broadness of the mother's perspective that covers everything with a sense of peace. Unlike the mother, Fanon is very political, but later through Fanon's description of his "bricolage" (191), John characterizes him as a storyteller with a point of view that is similarly encompassing.

John's text continues to shift imaginatively and to represent his development through it. In "New York," he belies the engagement with life he is trying to attain in the Fanon book (66–67); he reveals how he is still one who watches the news on television separated from people to order his life superficially in clear terms of right and wrong, good and bad. "Counting" continues along these lines when he and Thomas walk the Williamsburg Bridge from Manhattan to Brooklyn alone. However, at the end of "Counting," after connecting Fanon to the births and deaths of Malcolm X and Patrice Lumumba, John wonders if Fanon is on the bridge with him and Thomas feeling empathy for the lives of Malcolm and Lumumba the way they felt for and interacted with others: "Was Fanon grieving, recalling the murder of his birthmate, Malcolm, the murder of his deathmate, Lumumba" (71). John can see Fanon's words that he quotes from the conclusion of *The Wretched of the Earth* (312, 313)—"Fanon's words visible on invisible pages" (*Fanon* 71)—that lead to the vision of Fanon connecting with John and Thomas, calling them from death to life: "Fanon on the bridge that morning admonishing us, Fanon addressing us as comrades, saying, Don't jump." Seeing the words and the vision in which Fanon talks and pleads with John and Thomas alludes to life and human action that connects people.

The role of Fanon here relates to a positive development in "New York–Paris–Pittsburgh," the last section of part 1.[14] Still using Thomas as his surrogate because commitment to life is frightening, John reveals his love, whom he associates with the Fanon story: "And speaking of my new woman, the real one I won't name for fear of jinxing our love, I decided the morning after Fanon saved my life that Thomas needed love and I needed a love hook to jazz up the story of going to France to peddle the Fanon script" (86). The possibility that John can express love, as his mother does in her nonpolitical way and as Fanon does in his very committed political life, will be important by the end. The script is an imaginary one that will be the subject of part 2; the depiction of love for the woman, who is imaginary too, but represents real-life commitment that John wants to experience, will begin part 3 (139–45) and propel John toward the ending.

John concludes part 1 with the implication of Fanon's immersion in life through action, interaction, and writing. His imagination switches from Thomas on the train to France to a conversation in which he is frustrated by his brother's question about why he wants to write about Fanon (94–95). Before the final sentence, he abruptly and very briefly refers to an everyday example of strong life action from the Homewood community where his mother also lives her highly engaged life: "I recalled old black-as-a-bowling-ball, roly-poly Reverend Frank Felder strutting the pulpit of Homewood AME Zion, preaching himself into a sweat" (95).[15] The last sentence answers the question about why John writes about Fanon: "Fanon because no way out of this goddamn mess, I said to my brother, and Fanon found it." This apparently self-contradictory statement is true because, whereas he died like everybody else, Fanon's life of total action and commitment was a very meaningful one that in a sense still allows him to "live." His life is like Frank Felder's and John's mother's life, and in spite of his question, maybe his brother's life too since prison reality has also made him engage it seriously. However, it is important to John as a writer that he significantly portray their actuality. The beginning of part 2 connects to this central concern about writing life.

John prefaces part 2 by speaking somewhat unsurely and ironically, but also showing that he has a developing understanding about his project of writing Fanon's life: "Discovering more about Fanon as I continue this project of writing a life, it becomes clear that Fanon is not about stepping back, standing apart, analyzing, and instructing others but about identifying with others, plunging into the vexing, mysterious otherness of them, taking risks of heart and mind, falling head over heels in love whether or not there's a chance in the world love will be requited or redeemed. At least I think that's what my mother understands about Frantz Fanon, what she shares with him, something like that anyway expressed in her own words, in the actions of her life" (99). He understands what Fanon's life means, the connection between Fanon and his mother, and the need to link them imaginatively in writing. He implies that "writing a life" means he is trying to make formal writing express the actual life of people, and also to make it express his own action and feeling of love for the woman that he also referred to earlier (86). Writing to express the lives of others and his own life of love, in a sense to make them "live," may be what he is talking about at the beginning when he says he is "trying to save a life" (3). That life may be his own most urgently, but also certainly Fanon's life of revolutionary and political greatness as well as his mother's life of everyday greatness need saving in his writing. He risks failure because by writing he can only hope to allude meaningfully to human being and experience, and cannot portray their fullness.

Following this, part 2 is about extending the boundaries of writing in line with John's goal of "writing a life," which is "like me trying to get words to speak in my fiction" (105). To accomplish this in a process that he knows will be imperfect at best in the end, he imagines that the French filmmaker Jean-Luc Godard is in Homewood, and he uses him and his cinematic techniques as symbols in his exploration of the boundaries of writing.[16] Obviously, the documentary images of film represent people and life more directly than words, that is, "speak" life and make it "live" better than words do, or at least that would appear to be true. However, it does not take long for John to reach the point where he concludes that film is a language too:

> Can Homewood's language be reduced one-on-one to another language —film for instance. What's the point of language if another language renders it transparently, disappears it. Why pretend anything can be established by words except other words, either in the same language or different, and if different and they establish the same thing, how and why are they different, except arbitrarily, *they* being the two languages reduced, elided, identified, passing away, redundant, the words of both languages pointing to the same referents, a verifiable reality that finally strips away each language's pretensions to difference, any language a slow boat to China, groaning under the weight of its slowness, inconsequence, its inadequacy because what everybody really wants is China. (108)

In spite of its apparent realism, film is images/words that are inseparable from and dependent upon words/images: Images are never clearly distinct from words that name or classify them; images do not clearly precede words in any instance. Film leaves the world knotted in language and its reality inaccessible just as words do.

Then, in film there is also the problem of hegemonic meaning embedded in images/words just as there is in any other language:

> Nothing stands still, does it, [Mr. Godard]. Including meaning. The light beam interrupting the darkness of the theatre, the darkness of the screen only appears to break a stillness. The world never stops, never slows down for us to catch up. During the split second when darkness becomes light, the audience pretends to slip into a movie's flow, riding the light that propels the camera's gaze, then our restless gaze, across a moving field of images. We focus on the first frame and the next and next, as if we're being born again, born innocent of meaning, but the first frame's full, not empty of meaning. Too much meaning erupts. The meaning for instance of you, your person, your history, your culture, Mr. G., your language and ideas at

a given moment all packed up into the first frame, a frame drowned, satu-
rated with meaning. . . . (112)

Part of the problem, along with the incapacity of language to "speak" life
adequately, is that some images/words have accrued positive meaning
and some negative meaning. In this instance, French filmmaker Jean-
Luc Godard/French history/French culture/French language are positive,
and Homewood/poor/black community are negative. The world is always
continuing, being accessed by images/words that impose meaning; thus,
meaning is an ongoing process. However, the relationship between some
images/words and their positive or negative meaning seemingly remains
constant.

Nevertheless, John continues his imaginary conversation with Godard
as he tries somehow to make Homewood/poor/black community "speak"
and "live" its life beyond the hegemony of images/words. He refers to
film techniques to indicate transitions in his story, but more substantively relies on Fanon's writing to "speak" and then on his imagination
of his mother "seeing" and "feeling" Homewood life to make it "live."
First, "voiceover" and screen "crawl" bring into view passages that include
transcripts from a case study taken from *The Wretched of the Earth* (*Fanon*
114–15; *Wretched* 270–72).[17] The case study is about the murder of a European playmate by thirteen- and fourteen-year-old Algerian boys who had
no apparent motive, reporting that murdered boy was "a good friend of
ours" (*Wretched* 270). *Fanon* rewrites *The Wretched of the Earth* in different
words and somewhat different form, but repeats what it "speaks" in both
its direct quotations of the interview of the Algerian boys and the summary that precedes it, which states that "the event giving rise to the illness
is in the first place the atmosphere of total war which reigns in Algeria"
(*Wretched* 270). Although there would seem to be no connection between
the Algerian war of independence and black gang war in America, by re-
peating Fanon's text, John is trying to allow his text *Fanon* to "speak" the
same underlying causes. The Algerian boys are not mentally ill, but are
reacting to the fact that "the Europeans want to kill all the Arabs" (271).
In *Fanon*, the black gang violence in Homewood that the text then "dissolves to" is a product of a similar "atmosphere of total war which reigns
in [Homewood]" that is a continuing legacy of racial oppression. This

is the larger society's "illness" which is literally and substantively killing black people too. *Fanon's* portrayal of black gang violence in Homewood/ poor/black community must break society's hegemony to "speak" black human being. Still, repetition of transcripts is writing that can only go so far in conveying the reality of black people's lives.

The main device in part 2 is John's mother's "seeing" and "feeling" that *are* what he would say about Homewood's humanity if words could say it. He "dissolves to" a filmlike vision/story of Homewood by his mother in which she is a character (115–34). His imagination of Homewood, how-ever, starts with his own description of a boy on the streets he associates with his nephew Omar, his incarcerated brother's son who was murdered in gang violence (115). It is beneficent imagination that seeks to restore its visualized life as the imagined mother would try to restore it: "Where do you go if someone thinks of you as dead. To be in someone's thoughts or stories keeps the dead alive, the Igbo say" (116). He soon starts to imagine his mother in his efforts to imagine life and save it at the same time.

> Why doesn't [the boy] begin walking the . . . what, twenty, thirty steps from the corner to Mason's or better yet why not go in the opposite direction, any other direction, go the twenty or thirty steps across Homewood Avenue, go, go, go young man, go that way please, please run, run away please she begs grandson or great-niece or great-grandnephew whom the streets make strangers for that instant when they first appear and the shape at a distance could be anyone coming or going down there in the street till the next in-stant a heartbeat, heart burp, or sigh away when the miracle she's watching for is something else again, not a lost one returning, not one saved, but the same old regular thing again happening. (119)

In spite of the mother's vision, the next scene is the boy lying dead in the vacant lot by Mason's (120).

Still, if John can capture the expansiveness of his mother's human be-ing, which is also representative of Homewood's humanity, he can "speak" a story from her perspective that defies the meaning of Homewood/ black/community. He initiates the attempt with a close-up film shot of his mother speaking a monologue. The text "dissolves to" *"a tight focus on her face the entire time she delivers her monologue. Her features should more or less fill the screen, unnaturally large at first, monstrously oversized features, a wasteland of skin so the viewer doesn't feel comfortable, confronted on an exaggerated scale by the mix of familiarity and strangeness any human face expresses"* (120). It ultimately comes to portraying the community in the context of the mother's compassion and love that are inseparable from accepting, understanding, and supporting people in difficult circumstances. In the imaginative depiction of the mother witnessing the boy's murder, she sees his family. She wonders "could a person hold open in their mind the dead boy's place in those weeds for his people to find and drop down on it like I saw them drop. Could it have been me thinking of him lying there, right exactly there, me leading them, guiding them to him so they see him though nothing's there" (128). However, the potentially positive portrayal of empathy ends. John "dissolves to" his dialogue with Godard, and then says, "I don't need you to remind me that getting my mother's stories on film next to impossible." The same is true about getting the stories in words in the text of *Fanon.* He continues, though.

He then attempts to express the human being of his mother that encompasses the humanity of Homewood and breaks the negative stereotype of blackness by focusing on her relationship with him. He portrays their mother-son love in a figuration that begins with his conception and birth (131–34). This, however, leads to John undercutting his own narrative by analyzing and conceding the illusion and contrivance of his words, ending with a negative narrative of the present: "These are not precisely [my mother's] words, of course. Not mine precisely either. A mix, we'll say. As everything turns out to be. I'm making up words. Exchanging words with her to teach myself whatever might remain to be said. At times anything's better than silence. Better than silently abiding her illness and loneliness, the slow, sure progress of losing touch. Better than the silence of sitting alone, crippled in a goddamn wheelchair above those bare streets watching for miracles" (134–35). The "miracles" may be still there in the mother's vision, but John has, for the time being at least, lost his vision. He ends this section in an apparent fit of sarcasm and futility, alluding nonsensically to Godard being the father and his mother birthing Fanon (135).

Overall, the writer's task seems hopeless in part 2. At the beginning, John talks about trying to capture the reality of Fanon's life by portraying his mother's, which was similar in its human involvement. He symbolizes the actuality of this involvement through references to film techniques and speaking and acting in Godard's films. The mother will continue to be important throughout *Fanon*. However, as John goes on to show, film is an image/word language that inadequately accesses the substance of reality and that has certain hegemonic, biased meanings like word/image languages. He cannot maintain the positive, living vision of his mother and of Homewood based on symbolic reference to film. He cannot do it through traditional literary genres either. The last paragraph of part 2 is a letter to Fanon telling him how literary genres such as fiction, nonfiction, and memoir are what he has been trying to "write [his] way out of" (136) not only in writing *Fanon,* but for his whole career. He confesses that he is "dazed . . . by the . . . implacable either/or categories." In the last sentence in part 2, John hears the doorbell and expects a package (136), which is the first implied reference in a long time to Thomas and his debilitating metafictional preoccupation. However, unlike the mother, Thomas will not be an important person in part 3, which will again try to achieve the actuality of life that John has been attempting to write. As John says at the end of part 1 (95) and implies now, Fanon's *living*—speaking, interacting, acting, feeling, committing, and writing—was the "way out" of the limitations not only of literary genres, but existence confined by writing itself, which is the topic of *Fanon*. This is important in spite of the fact that it is impossible for writing to portray life and important in the context of John's *living*. The ending of part 2 sounds negative, but its negativity is not conclusive.

The beginning of part 3 focuses on John as a *living* lover, and starts to define the project as it applies to his ability not only to write the *living* of Fanon, his mother, and others but his own too. He first refers to the beginning of *Fanon* where he describes himself in the evening sitting in the garden of a house in Brittany (3, 139). What he did not say then and says now is that he is trying to make words portray his feeling of love and all the action and interaction that accompanies it. He plunges into this task by writing several pages of free-flowing description (139–45) that emphasizes the word "reluctantly." He is trying to capture what he feels about "let[ting] the day go" (140) "because it's been full of proofs of love and simple good living and promises more of the same still to come" (144). However, he also has stated that "*this thinking all fine and dandy but it's not the book, where the fuck's the book*" (143). In spite of his awareness of the impossibility of writing this book of *living*, he closes this section by focusing on the words "reluctantly" and "*love*" (145) as he imagines Fanon going to war "in another region of this country, this France, where I sit tonight in a time of peace you could say, or say I'm lucky to be peaceful this moment in it. Lucky as you, Fanon, or anyone watching snow fall even though war's never-ending."

John persists by trying to depict the actuality of his own *living* love in a world that continues to be war-ridden. Maybe writing cannot portray human life, but John does imply that naming things with words has power, just as he does at the end of part 1 when he says that he will not name the woman he loves "for fear of jinxing our love" (86). Here he talks about being "happy doing whatever it is you're doing together and you don't even need to give it a name, don't want to give it a name that might jinx it" (141). This notwithstanding, words that he is using—"reluctantly" and "love" are the main ones—are at least an approach to a human perspective that is hopefully more than words usually give and as much as words can do. This use of words is also leading to John's imagination of Fanon going to war, which is ironically inseparable from loving because it represented his commitment to others.

Both John's and Fanon's human commitments along with John's mother's commitment will constitute *Fanon*, the composite book of *living* by the end. John has mentioned the incongruous combination of war and love at the ends of part 1 (94–95) and part 2 (135–36). In the context of love and war, Fanon fought worthily and loved, and John now wants to love and wants war to end, although he knows it will not. Unlike Fanon whose essence was committing and doing that included writing, John only has writing to portray what *living* is, whether that may be his loving, his mother's, or Fanon's loving, warring, feeling, writing, and interacting in many human ways.

The following imagination of Fanon first leaving Martinique to fight for France in World War II, which happens before the earlier imagination of him in "Africa" (36–48), draws heavily on Macey's biography of Fanon;[18] although the self-consciousness of John about the limitations of writing are still very much there, he moves toward the overall development of the narrative in part 3. A short distance into part 3, John first mentions Macey in a context that is sarcastic after he has already started using accounts from his biography of Fanon's first departure in his own story: "I learned the details of his getaway in a book Fanon never had the opportunity to read so the information's thirdhand at best, an outsourced search for truth, documented by the plausibility of facts, facts unconfirmed by Fanon, untouched by his hand dead forty years before the book published. Welcome information in any case (thank you Mr. David Macey, assiduous historian), welcome as some of the facts might have been to Fanon on those fitful nights conflicted, stalled on Dominica [after leaving Martinique]" (153). John earlier addresses the subject of writing in a similar tone: "Are there semblances of plot, of direction, purpose, and necessity, in Fanon's story. Someone or something in charge—weird sisters, a deity, Progress, History. . . . Why not you in charge, Doctor Fanon. A physician who first cures himself, then cures us, the world, of its ills. Why not you. Seize the bit in your teeth, horse and rider, and ride" (151). In spite of these sarcastic interruptions, Fanon is in a sense "in charge" because the imagination of his story in the predominant body of part 3 is developing and continues to do so in an overall positive way that it did not in parts 1 and 2.

John proceeds as he tries to imagine the aspects of Fanon's human commitment that are tantamount to loving and the key to John's life and others. He imagines that Fanon's life is "many fates in one." (157): "Paris burning in an African campfire. Fanon's journey from Martinique to the metropole to America crackles there too, smoke rising into the darkness, the false start to Dominica burning like all the stories true and false, threads that a curious, determined boy must follow, teaching himself to risk anything, everything, even squeezing out of one skin into another, his life, his fate always unknown, always in his hands" (157–58). Fanon was like anyone else who is subject to fateful forces beyond human control. However, his greatness was his natural proclivity to think of others—in a broad sense, France in World War II, Algeria in the war of independence, his patients who had been tortured in the war of independence—and thus take risks for them. This is also the loving that exemplifies the *living* that the text tries to portray.

John moves toward the completion of the book of Fanon's life that tries to do more than the typical book by portraying *living* human being. He reminds himself that he cannot capture Fanon's experience through the conventional scenarios that writers use to encompass the lives of other revolutionaries. Fanon's "life evades those myths of martyrdom so handy for settling accounts. For closing the book. Fanon's accounts of his life prevent him from being written off in other people's accounts. We have his words; we can count on them. Fanon uninventible, or you might say resists invention. He's no more or less a fiction than any person writing about him. Fanon's been here and gone. Free. Played the game till it was too dark to see the ball. You can't touch that" (163–64).

Perhaps the most important point in this quotation is that Fanon has left his words, and because of them "resists invention" does not mean that John cannot reinvent him through radical imagination. Right after the quotation, Robert raises serious questions about whether John should write this kind of challenging book that breaks conventions because no one will read it (164). In later sections (175–78, 182), however, he implies why such a book should be written. He implies that conventional narrative forms and scenarios make human problems a consumable commodity, but do not attempt to achieve greater substance by portraying human reality more deeply. Fanon was always concerned with human problems, as the conventional stories supposedly are, but the genuine commitment to human *living* that was part of the solution and went beyond the desire to sell a commodity is not anywhere in the purview of these stories.

In part, John imagines an unconventional book of the *living* Fanon that relies on the primary intertextual connection with Macey's book and also on Fanon's words from his books. He later says the following about the words in a Fanon book: "Another's life shaped into words—Fanon's book . . . how much of it can anyone else really use. Its truths belong to the witness. Darkness abides. The witness's words are evidence of a known world closing down, its light, however bright or small, piercing or shallow, swallowed by the unknown" (181).

John clearly implies that his imagination is just as necessary when it comes to creating Fanon based on his words in his own book because these words fail to be a transparent window to who he was as a *living* human being. John takes an unconventional approach to Fanon's committed *living* by imagining it in people's words about Fanon in written texts or imagining it firsthand in people. This vision of Fanon reflected through the lens of other lives provides none of the illusion of life that one would associate with conventional narratives, whether fictional, historical, autobiographical, or biographical. Instead, it gives sporadic glimpses of people—John's brother and mother, Fanon's family, and others—perceiving the world and interacting in it in ways that suggest the *living* Fanon. Focusing on other people or on their words implies the importance of imagination in creating Fanon's *living* commitment to people. Imagination is the key, whether John is using Fanon's book or books about him, or creating him through his vision of people perceiving and interacting in the world. He will not try to be definitive, and will leave the story ongoing and in progress.

Using Macey's account in his book (65–66), John imagines one of the sporadic glimpses at Fanon's *living;* it is the perception of his uncle Edouard Fanon based on his direct observation of Fanon. The short section in the novel (178–80) is about Fanon and his brother living with and being instructed by Edouard, a teacher and strict disciplinarian, in Le François. Edouard did not punish his nephew when he failed to return from recess until very late in the day, which, normally, he absolutely did not tolerate. Edouard "learned later that he had sneaked away at recess to spy upon the autopsy of a drowned man being performed in the basement of Le François's municipal building. . . . he'd . . . witnessed . . . the horror accumulating until he became ill watching the slicing and draining, watching the scalpel digging deeper and deeper, the prying and sawing, dead flesh peeled, split, butchered till it was nothing but gore, nothing more, nothing, not man or woman, not horse or cat, nothing. The nothing I saw in his empty eyes when . . . he materialized in my classroom" (180). Macey concludes his account: "As a medical student in Lyon, Fanon would never be good at dissection" (66). In comparison to Macey's, John's imagined story reaches no clear finish or conclusion, but perhaps suggests what one could see in Fanon when looking at him in this *living* moment. Apparently, the empathy expressed in his eyes is as all-consuming and inexpressible as the butchery he sees and realizes exists beyond this specific instance. This is a view of Fanon's *living,* human commitment that is so vast as to be impossible to write, a commitment this novel tries to approach, suggest, or make briefly visible through the "nothing" in Fanon's "empty" eyes representing its devouring power. John imagines that Edouard also lives through his own empathy for Fanon in this powerful momentary glimpse of life.

John moves ahead as he imagines Fanon. After the final section portraying Robert, John addresses his mother as his "island" in a vast, uncharitable sea (183). This leads to a section in which he confesses that he writes because he is lonely (183–84), which now also coincides with greater resolve and strength, however. Thomas, the surrogate who symbolizes his insecurity about writing, then appears explicitly for the first time since part 1. Thomas throws the severed head into the New York East River in "Thomas Disposes of the Head," the last section with a *heading* since part 1 and the last in the book. As a device to get rid of the head, Thomas refers to a young boy throwing away a severed head at the end of his story "Damballah" (published by Wideman in 1981): "The ending had worked once. . . . Why not recycle a good thing" (184). Thomas the older writer does not naively believe that endings work in his writing as he believed earlier, but he still throws away the head. He has matured in the process of writing *Fanon* to the point that he can stay focused on his task, no longer needing the head as a symbol because he feels inadequate as a writer. John is using Thomas to talk about himself, and disposing of Thomas and the head because he no longer needs them.

As John approaches the end, it becomes clear that along with imagining the *living* Fanon, he is also imagining a book written by Fanon as *living* writing that is more than a staid formal structure on the page, and this will be a part of completing *Fanon* and trying to make it *living* writing too. Having progressed to this point, John now tries to produce instances of this *living* writing that are Fanon's and that are his as he completes his project. Immediately after Thomas throws away the head, John portrays Fanon's *living* writing using *The Wretched of the Earth* as the primary model. Talking about Fanon writing, Macey says: "Fanon never learned to use a typewriter and dictated his text to [his wife] Josie as he strode up and down the room like an actor declaiming his lines. Traces of the oral origins of the text are visible in the sudden breaks and changes of direction, as Fanon suddenly recalls or thinks of something. If there is an element of free association here, it is Fanon and not his informants who is free associating" (Macey 134). John imagines Fanon in "Lyon pacing up and down the cage of his mind, like a lion in Lyon pacing up and back, he listens to her pounding nails into his book, pounding nails into his cross, his coffin. Fanon's voice rises and falls, louder, softer as he tells his wife his book, his thoughts flying almost" (187). The description of Fanon moving, listening, thinking, interacting with his wife, and modulating his voice suggests a *living* discourse that is more than written words; this discourse is "his cross, his coffin," Fanon's common plight within and inseparable from the lives of others. (The imagined Fanon book is a fictional version of *The Wretched of the Earth*. Macey writes about Fanon dictating *The Wretched of the Earth* (454), but John's reference to Fanon "pacing" and dictating clearly echoes Macey's remarks above, which are about *Black Skin, White Masks* (Macey 134). John's text *Fanon* (187–91) merges the two passages from Macey about both Fanon books in a portrayal of him dictating the fictional *The Wretched of the Earth*, which is clearly indicated by quotations from Fanon's actual book.)

The character Fanon later explains possible written features of the fictional *The Wretched of the Earth*, the *living* text that represents him and others:

> Stop a moment, Fanon says. "Nerve specialist" is the patient's way of saying *psychiatrist*. Be certain the text distinguishes the patient's voice from mine. When I quote him I'm reading from notes transcribed during interviews. . . . In this book I want readers to hear precisely the language with which a patient describes his or her situation. Perhaps you could insert an extra space to separate blocks of text when one voice gives way to another. Perhaps the patient's voice typed single-spaced to contrast with the normally double-spaced format of the narrative. Underscoring or brackets or quotation marks perhaps around short phrases of the patient's I include in my summaries of their cases. . . . I don't want to fall into the trap of treating my patients as the *beke* [the white Creole ruling class in Martinique] treat me. Never letting me speak for myself. . . . The proper representation of these cases is immensely complicated. Perhaps hopelessly compromised by any form of writing. I suppose in some sense I'm always speaking for my patients. Though, in fairness to myself, I often feel the patients speak for me. Not only do I quote them at considerable length. I also find myself splicing into my accounts their exact words or words not exactly theirs not [sic] mine either, words I try to imagine the patient might employ in a par-

ticular situation. An odd, secondhand, alienated structure's being formed as we proceed in these book sessions. A process that controls me as much as I control it. A sort of bricolage of free-floating fragments whose authorship is unsettlingly ambiguous. Two men or perhaps several attempting to go about their business, each with a leg in the same pair of baggy trousers. (191)

Fanon describes the book more as a discourse of multiple interactions, many audible, speaking voices, and common, unclear authorship than an individual formal text written on the page.

A process has begun in which John imagines Fanon's words in his *living* fictional text that is also part of the *living* book *Fanon*. After Fanon describes his text, he quotes his patient from the actual *The Wretched of the Earth*. He thus gives the patient voice and assumes the patient's voice in the fictional *The Wretched of the Earth* and also in *Fanon* (*Fanon* 191–92; *Wretched* 268–69). He implies the effort to create the *living/speaking* text of many voices whose authorship is uncertain. The fictional *The Wretched of the Earth* is inseparable from the life actions of Fanon the *living* man and from *Fanon*. *Fanon* has become the text of common, unclear authorship that Fanon describes as the fictional *The Wretched of the Earth*.

Two short sections follow that apparently question the creation of both Fanon's and John's texts. The first reference is to Rudyard Kipling's *Kim* and its apparently effortless mastering of voices and identities, which is the antithesis of the complex problems of representation of which Fanon and John are very much aware (192–93). The second section is in parentheses, and is the author John questioning himself about the false pretenses and shallow motives that the conventional forms of biography and autobiography hide. This is an easy subterfuge that does not attract him (193).

Significantly, the next section is a quotation from the actual text *The Wretched of the Earth* that moves beyond such potentially paralyzing questions about representation and form; it implies the need to attempt to create the *living* fictional text that is more than words: *"A permanent dialogue with oneself and an increasingly obscene narcissism never ceased to prepare the way for a half delirious state . . . where intellectual work became suffering and the reality was not at all that of a living man, working and creating himself, but rather words, different combinations of words and the tensions springing from the meanings contained in words. . . . Shatter this narcissism, break with this unreality'"* (*Fanon* 193–94; *Wretched* 313). What follows is a long section in which Fanon's "working and creating" is part of his *living* text *The Wretched of the Earth,* not a book featuring an intellectual engagement with words on the page.

The single word at the beginning of this long section is "Fanon" followed by a period, which has a different meaning than part 1's headings symbolizing the intellectual detachment of the writer; the word represents Fanon, *"a living man, working and creating"* in all the ways he did, including in his *living* writing as *Fanon* has now defined it. The single word "Fanon" previously appeared just before the section about Kipling's *Kim* (192). Immediately following the word, "Fanon shuts [Kipling's] famous book of empire," a "fake tale." In a sense, the second "Fanon," which is directly after a quotation from *The Wretched of the Earth* (194), opens the fictional form of this text which is the *living* book of Fanon's life that is positive, significant action that transcends writing. "Fanon" also clearly stands for John's *living* book *Fanon* portraying the *living* man. The writing process continues to bring together *Fanon* and the fictional *The Wretched of the Earth.*

Fanon is *living* in important ways in this *living* book that follows. It portrays him making his life with his new wife, Josie, in Lyon, working with the Algerian FLN revolutionary movement (196–97), and working at the psychiatric hospital in Blida, Algeria (197–200, 215–17). Part of John's imagination is bringing together Fanon and John's mother in the hospital as he lay dying. John creates the following device: "No. You tell *me* how my mother and Fanon wound up in the same place. You figure it out. . . . If an explanation's necessary. As if an explanation ever changes facts, the fact for instance that in this movie an old woman, my mother in a wheelchair, encounters Doctor Frantz Fanon as he lays dying in a hospital" (200).[19] John uses his mother further to imagine Fanon's relationship with his illegitimate daughter Murielle, who was born in Lyon (*Fanon* 203–07) and never knew him (Macey 133). Relying on his mother's voice that resonates with love, John portrays Fanon claiming his daughter by doing what he did best and fighting for her, thus bonding them in a relationship tantamount to love: "How long does it take to make a daughter. How long to name her. . . . Don't blame the years lost waiting for your father to claim you. He was busy in his way, intent on doing just that—

claiming you, my mother would say. Fighting a war for you. A claim's not in a name. He'll know you by your footsteps, your knock, my dear, not by your name, your country, your color, your fate. Just step toward him" (206–7). (A section follows that depicts the empathy and love expressed by John's mother and a woman worker in the hospital where Fanon is being treated (207–13). It further relates the mother to Fanon and Fanon's struggles against oppression with others in different places and times.)

Like the first, the second word "Fanon" followed by a period is printed by itself on a single line on the page, and a section with the heading "Lyon" followed by a period begins immediately below "Fanon." The first sentence after "Lyon" mentions the studio in Lyon of the Lumière brothers, pioneers in filmmaking. This reference is somewhat like the invocation of Jean-Luc Godard and his breakthrough cinematic techniques throughout part 2 as John tries to find a way to reproduce Fanon's life. Here, in the general context of his relationship of the Lumières' work to his writing of *Fanon*, John ironically asks, "Will I get lucky and unearth a definitive portrait of you. A view of you freeze-framed on the screen" (197). John cannot create a definitive portrait of Fanon in "Lyon" as the Lumières seemed to have captured reality definitively with their invention. However, "Lyon" parallels "Fanon"; in "Lyon," John is imaginatively "[u]npeeling Lyon" (197), not to tell a story of the Lumières or of the city's history, but to reveal Fanon's *living*, which ends in his human creation of his daughter Murielle.

In the final analysis, the *living* text beginning with "Fanon" is the imagination of Fanon's suffering/sacrificing, loving, and caring that consumed him and made him struggle for others and with them.[20] Fanon's life in two worlds, one the privileged life of the psychiatrist in which the "lady" "visitor" is always waiting outside the door (215, 217), and the other his life of revolutionary struggle against oppression, comes together in his identification with the oppressed. Fanon is "a doctor in charge, running the show, at least until fatigue and the weight of self-deception, the weight of lying to his patients brings him to his knees again and he hears the rattling of his chains, the moans and screams of the others locked in the hold with him" (216). Here, the description of the *living* text is reminiscent of the ambiguously authored bricolage (191) telling many stories of those commonly touched by oppression: "Allow the patients to declare themselves

Conclusion

Experimentation with the treatment of blackness is the most common feature of Wideman's writing. Central to both the later fiction and the later auto/biographies, which build on the first three novels, is Wideman's evolving use of experimental fictional techniques and themes to depict the writer/character's personal life and creative development as he deals with important black political, cultural, and social issues.

The three early novels represent an initial modernist phase in Wideman's career that differs from his later, postmodernist works, but an experimental focus in these early novels on the concerns of the black community clearly connects them to later works. Another connection between Wideman's early and later works is that the first novel portrays the same or similar characters and the same family relationships and community as do the works that follow the third novel, such as the Homewood Trilogy. In that fictional trilogy, a writer/character who is a surrogate for Wideman becomes central. This writer/character interacts with a family very similar to Wideman's, and returns to his childhood community, Homewood, which he had left to attend an elite white university. Each work of the Homewood Trilogy is more experimental than the last as the writer/character gets closer to his former community, develops artistically, and continues his treatment of black life. Both fiction and auto/biography after the early novels feature the writer/character's rapprochement with his home community, as well as similar structural and thematic experimentation; the exploration of artistic development; and social, cultural, and political portrayals. Developing from works that precede it, the novel *Fanon* (2008) takes experimentation to a striking new level, even for Wideman.

After the writer/character John has returned to the community and played a central role there in the Homewood Trilogy, *Reuben* takes the next step in the development that culminates in *Fanon*. This is particularly interesting because John is not a character in *Reuben*, and it does not depict his personal story. *Reuben* is one of Wideman's most experimental novels, however, and moves toward his recent emphasis on the construction of political fictions intended to help black people. The focal point of the fictions in *Reuben* is the words on the page, but the novel's fictions are also centered in the imagination and intellect or sometimes in magical ritual. It is hard to separate imaginative, intellectual, and even magically ritualistic creations from words, which are essential to interpreting or understanding most creations and narratives. This is largely beside the point, though, since what is important in the overall experimental development in *Reuben* is going beyond reliance on the formally *written* word. The character Reuben is not a writer, and the novel does not highlight its ideas about writing as clearly as the following works do. However, it prepares the way for John the writer/character to develop these ideas later. In the next two novels, the thematic emphasis is more clearly on politically effective stories or fictions written in imagination or by or through imagination that many people disseminate throughout the culture. Then, in *Fanon,* the writer/character attempts imaginatively and creatively to produce writing that engages *living* people beyond the page and that itself is *living.*

John is a character in the two novels that follow *Reuben, Philadelphia Fire* and *The Cattle Killing,* and through characteristically experimental writing, these novels thematically stress the political potential of writing in imagination or by or through imagination. In *Philadelphia Fire,* John is one among multiple formal writers of books and writers utilizing imagination who try to (re)write a positive myth of blackness. By the end, Cudjoe, a formal writer whose characterization is inseparable from John's, has evolved to the point where his text is a nonformal one written in imagination that has the ongoing potential to create political change, like the texts of other writers in the novel who write imaginatively. The highly experimental *The Cattle Killing* (1996), in which John is again part of a composite characterization of writers, extends the development of the theme of writing imaginatively by focusing on its practice in new, complex ways.

Writing imaginatively is a theme in the auto/biographies, too. Although both the novels and the auto/biographies utilize virtually indistinguishable experimental fictional strategies and deal with the writer/character John's personal life in the context of the political, cultural, and social, there is some difference. The auto/biographies focus more uniformly on the writer and his intimate relationships, without the intervening portrayals of characters who form a composite with the writer or are surrogates for him (parts of *The Island: Martinique* being an exception). However, in both *Hoop Roots* and *The Island: Martinique,* the writer deals almost solely with himself and emphasizes and practices creative, imaginative processes of writing/storytelling that are his life. Particularly in the exposé of creolized writing in *The Island: Martinique,* John specifies what he is doing in the imaginative writing process and then demonstrates the technique. Thus, he provides a clearer theory of his writing and makes his technical practice more explicit than in the novels. Although the auto/biographies may add a new dimension of theory and technical practice, these texts are not as radically innovative as *Fanon.*

In *Fanon,* the writer/character John clearly concedes that characters cannot actually *live* in his writing and that his writing cannot *live;* however, he attempts to push the narrative beyond the normal boundaries of writing to suggest the human *living* that it cannot represent, and to intimate that the novel itself is a *living* book. If nothing else, this has the value of forcing readers into new territory, making them aware of the false assumptions that often accompany reading, and that the easily consumable "reality" that books and other forms of narrative deliver as "truth" demands closer scrutiny. As the novel *Fanon* reminds us, the life of Fanon was real; however, the truth of that life now resides in an ongoing process of imagination that is never finished. Although we can never fully recover or know the truth, we can constantly engage in a critical process directed toward knowing. In trying to approach the *living* Fanon, the novel encourages us to do this. From this perspective, *Fanon* is much more valuable than a conventional story of the revolutionary that reaches a definitive conclusion. In revealing the limits of narrative and its superficial comforts, Wideman attempts to break those limits and to shake readers into examining previously unquestioned assumptions. While Wideman's effort in this direction is very interesting and worthwhile, it is unfortunate that most readers probably prefer the comfort of the familiar to the challenge his works offer.

Fanon also adds to the continuing story of the writer/character John. Looking back with perspective on Wideman's career, one wonders if this increasingly experimental interconnection of the writer/character's life and political quest with that of Fanon is where Wideman's work will conclude. Early in *Fanon*, John says he feels a "sense of urgency" (5) in writing the book, partly because "time's running out. I won't be writing many more books, if any." We do not know the extent to which the character is speaking for the real-life Wideman, but those who appreciate good, serious writing hope that he will continue to write. If *Fanon* were to be the last work, however, it would make a fitting end to this always experimental canon in which the writer has constantly struggled to authentically portray the political, cultural, and social realities of his black community.

NOTES

1. Brothers and Keepers, Fatheralong, Hoop Roots, and The Island: Martinique

1. Because of the greater structural difficulty and complexity of the last two auto/biographies, *Hoop Roots* and *The Island: Martinique*, the analyses of them in this chapter are significantly longer than those of the first two. Wideman's writing is never easy, but it does become more difficult and complex over time. Throughout this study, the length of the analyses of works varies based on their difficulty and complexity.

2. Critics agree that Wideman does not make a clear distinction between fiction and supposedly nonfictional genres. For example, Eugene Philip Page talks about Wideman "[blurring] the distinctions" (9) between "fiction and memoir" in *Brothers and Keepers*.

3. As stated, writing is the theme, and structure conflates with theme. In this context, John the writer is conscious that his entire book is a narrative device that features the figuration and symbolization of writing instead of the realistic description of the physical world. Writing is the main tool that he uses to connect with his brother. My analysis at places specifies narrative device, figuration, and symbolization, but writing as a conscious process is actually implied throughout this text, the other auto/biographies, and much of Wideman's writing in the postmodern phase of his career (after 1973). The self-consciousness about writing and emphasis on narrative process in *Brothers and Keepers* identifies it as postmodern. My later discussions of the evolution from modernism to postmodernism in Wideman's novels will deal much more with the postmodern.

4. Page concludes that, fictionally, Robby "actively collaborates with Wideman in developing the book; he too becomes a writer, as evidenced by his letters, his poems, and his graduation speech; he completes his associate's degree and is given the honor of delivering that speech" (12). Michael Feith makes the broadly similar point that the "final result is a truly dialogical book . . . [that] stages a dialogue between the two brothers" (672).

5. Great Time is briefly mentioned and also defined here in *Fatheralong*. I discuss Great Time in more depth later in the analysis of *Hoop Roots*.

6. Claude Julien points out the blank spaces as indicators of the narrative's "chronological disjointedness" and sometimes subtle movements back and forth (19–20).

7. Emphasizing that Wideman's auto/biography is fiction, Julien argues that the narrator in this story does not have "much in common with the considerate son/father in the other parts" (20). He is "not a person but a character in his own right, i.e., a functional cogwheel in a story."

8. Heather Andrade describes the connection between basketball and writing: "Basketball —namely, 'playground hoop'—becomes a metonym for the active storytelling enterprise suf-

fused with . . . emancipatory potential" ("Race, Representation, and Intersubjectivity" 53). Since the book is about liberating writing/storytelling, focuses significantly on basketball, and is entitled *Hoop Roots*, Andrade is correct. However, the book is also about love; the narrator/writer says and shows through his own characterization that love of writing, basketball, community, and family is a major impetus for writing.

Further, the narrator/writer says that music is very important. Music is seemingly another "metonym" for writing that he could not access or play, as he could basketball, to make a revolutionary statement about race: "[B]efore basketball and writing came music. All music but especially music performed by people who sounded like me, like the voices of Homewood. . . . Though I couldn't translate the lucid, shimmering counterpoint of quartet close harmony into words, part of the magic, the freedom of music meant that I didn't need to turn it into words" (14).

9. Conceptually and structurally, Great Time is prominent and obvious in Wideman's later works, but is not unique to them. Andrade argues that the concept of Great Time applies to earlier works by Wideman also. She states that in *Damballah* (1981), *Hiding Place* (1981), *Sent for You Yesterday* (1983), and *Brothers and Keepers* (1984), for example, "storytelling functions as a bridge between the past, present and future, and between myth, history and memory. Storytelling is born out of 'mosaic memory' and exists in 'Great Time'" ("Mosaic Memory" 344).

10. Jacqueline Berben-Masi says that the readers are implicitly among others listening to the narrator's story in *Hoop Roots* ("Of Basketball and Beads" 37–38).

11. See the discussion in chapter 5 of Great Time in *The Cattle Killing*, a work in which Great Time is akin to the postmodern. Katie Birat discusses the postmodern implications of writing in *The Cattle Killing*, concluding that "for Wideman the very power of storytelling lies in its capacity to embrace the endless movement of language itself, 'writing,' if not necessarily 'righting,' the wrongs of an 'upside-down' world" (641). The "endless movement of language" is like Great Time. As stated earlier, I discuss the postmodern later in discussions of Wideman's novels.

12. Basketball is played in Great Time just as stories are told there: "Playing the game is not counting time nor translating, reducing, calculating it in arbitrary material measures, not turning it into something else, possessing it or hoarding it or exchanging it for money. . . . [Playing the game is] riding Great Time, what you were and are and will be as long as you're in the air, the game" (57).

13. The writer may be invoking Fanon, a main focus in the later auto/biography *The Island: Martinique*, when he talks about the effect of speaking a language. Fanon's concepts of colonial language influence are congruent with the generally accepted postmodern idea that meaning is embedded in language by cultural power dynamics and not individually created by speakers. The writer thus becomes a postcolonial/postmodernist theorist in "Who Invented the Jump Shot." In the context of this study's focus, the self-consciousness about language and writing in *Hoop Roots* identify it, like *Brothers and Keepers* and *Fatheralong*, as postmodern. See the discussions of the postmodern in the later analyses of Wideman's fiction in this study.

14. Karen Jahn speaks to the way that readings of the stories in *Hoop Roots* are unique to each reader and thus in a sense arbitrary: "Like jazz performance, each reading of *Hoop Roots* is unique, for every reader brings different experiences and beliefs to the stories" (67). One

could add to this that readings of these stories, especially the fantastically improvised "Who Invented the Jump Shot (A Fable)," are also in a sense arbitrary because no two readings by the same individual would be the same. The writing in "Who Invented the Jump Shot (A Fable)" and other stories is random fabrication because, as Bonnie TuSmith explains, it is "improvisation—as in, 'I'm making it up as I go along'" (*Critical Essays* vii).

15. The improvisational play of the jazz musician is an equivalent to this. Describing the writing in *Hoop Roots,* Jahn states that "Wideman's writing performs musically like jazz" (59). "[F]or me Wideman's jazzing story in *Hoop Roots* plays the changes like [jazz musician Thelonious] Monk."

16. The narrator explains earlier that although he and Catherine see no women on the court, playground basketball in the present day does not exclude women. Thus, it transcends gender, too (166).

17. The Creole speech of the Africans on Martinique is a form of liberation like writing in *The Island: Martinique:* "How can captives forced to behave as slaves not become slaves. [Creole speech] is a positive response to this conundrum" (45). It is a "process of accultura-tion rooted in language" that extends to other cultural practices that symbolize resistance. It "depends on play" (46) and "challenges and contests the sounds and meaning of French, destabilizing the logic of privilege and discrimination that speaking 'proper' French autho-rizes." Through Creole speech and accompanying practices, "Africans disciplined themselves to gain some personal control in their dealing with their masters."

18. A significant part of the introduction is the largely factual and realistic beginning (ix–xiv) and the mostly straightforward description and explanation of chapters 2 through 4 (xxv–xxx). The introduction probably concedes to the expectation of accessibility because this is a book in the National Geographic Directions series, but the rest of the book is much more difficult creolized writing.

19. The text does not make it clear how victimization works in all instances of interac-tion. However, it seems implied that the enslaver/tourist, who is dehumanized by commit-ting oppressive acts, is also a victim.

20. In the surprising improvisational connections and turns of creolized writing, the reference to the boat carrying the unsuccessful fortunes of the child and of love come after a discussion of the successful fortunes of Christopher Columbus (17–19), whose voyages furthered New World oppression, although they were just as "blind . . . and blunder[ing]" (19) as John and Katrine's voyages in love. This incongruous comparison, similar to John's connection of himself to Thomas Jefferson, suggests that John cannot escape complicity in the oppressive legacy that his writing opposes.

Also, the image of lost children is a haunting one throughout Wideman's work, and some-times in earlier works—most notably in *Philadelphia Fire* (1990) and *Fatheralong: A Medita-tion on Fathers and Sons, Race and Society* (1994)—one of the lost children is Wideman's son Jacob. However, the Lawsons, a fictional version of Wideman's family, also suffer the pain of a lost child in the first novel, *A Glance Away* (1967). Eugene Lawson is born in the prologue, and his death in war years later is part of what clouds the rest of the book. In Wideman's second novel, *Hurry Home* (1970), the primary preoccupation of the main character, Cecil, is the death of his son, Simon. Almost three decades later, Kassima in *Two Cities* (1998), dedi-cated to Wideman's nephew (a lost child slain in gang warfare), has lost two sons to street violence.

21. When John focuses on the experience of love again at the end of the book, he talks about a "plentitude" in bodies tantamount to true human difference or diversity (165–67).

22. *The Island: Martinique* conflates with Fanon's *Black Skin, White Masks* (1967), which has chapters entitled "The Woman of Color and the White Man" and "The Man of Color and the White Woman," the former being the source of *Revenants*' epigraph, the latter providing critiques that intersect the characterizations of John and Katrine and Paul and Chantal. For example, the epigraph to one section of *The Island: Martinique* from the "The Man of Color and the White Woman" is, *"When my restless hands caress these white breasts, they grasp white civilization and dignity and make them mine."* The section focuses on a conversation between Paul and Chantal in which he interrogates her about her fascination with oppressed, colonized black men. It ends with Chantal saying that her proclivity represents rebellion against France's prohibition of black male/white female relations, which has generated so much hatred in her country and similarly in America. Chantal seems to long for love that goes beyond racial attraction, as does Paul, who cannot get beyond it, and as does the persona of *Black Skin, White Masks,* who references the same hard-to-break fascination with white skin. Possible interpretations of the intertextual relationship are endless, but both texts imply revolutionary potential.

Characterization generally shows the paradox and ambiguity of fiction in this auto/biography, and with regard to the documented lives of Fanon and Wideman, characterization blurs the line between fiction and the auto/biographical. Paul is another version of John, who in turn takes on the life of another character as Paul, similar to the way that John in *Fatheralong*'s "Father Stories" is a different character from John in the other stories. Further, the real-life people Fanon and Wideman are similar to John and Paul because they married white women.

23. The narrator says at the beginning of "25 December 2000," the beginning of chapter 1, "[t]his trip to an island begins—as if it's a story or a dream—on Christmas Day" (3). Reminiscent of Monroe's words, the story told through creolized writing is sometimes like a dream, one promising a better future in *"Revenants."* Also, Wideman's writing throughout his career, most notably in the early writing in *Hurry Home* (1970), is often inseparable from a dream state, usually one that reveals promise as well as peril.

24. Bergevin is right when he states that Wideman is a proponent of "[i]ndividual imagination *and* collective organizing—both are necessary to overcome slavery's legacy of victimization and self-hatred" (80). In "Journal," Wideman notes that "[i]ndividual insubordination, imagination, and collective social organizing are the basic ingredients of this resistance" (97). *The Island: Martinique* could certainly influence readers to organize collectively. However, it is still very much about the writing itself and how it can effectively change the minds and imaginations of the writer and readers. It is unclear what specific actions the writer and readers take as a result and unclear how and when change will affect the political order of society, but the primary goal of the book to affect minds and imaginations is a positive one.

2. *A Glance Away, Hurry Home,* and *The Lynchers*

1. See the discussion of Wideman's Homewood background and of his life and literary development in chapter 1.

2. See, for example, the interview by John O'Brien titled "John Wideman," in *Conversations with John Edgar Wideman*, ed. Bonnie TuSmith, 5–13 (Jackson: University Press of Mississippi, 1998).

3. In chapter 3, I present a larger analysis of the postmodern and how it applies to specific works.

4. The Irish modernist James Joyce was an influence on Wideman, and maybe Wideman was thinking about the beginning of *A Portrait of the Artist as a Young Man* when he wrote the prologue to *A Glance Away*. The "Fa la la, fa la, fa la" in Wideman's novel is reminiscent of the "Tralala lala" in Joyce's, where he uses song as part of the evocation of Stephen Dedalus's life.

5. Kermit Frazier describes the same quotation depicting the graveside in perhaps the first published essay on Wideman, which is one of the few that analyzes *A Glance Away*: "Wideman has lyrically created a painting through metaphor and repetition while delving into the sensibilities of several characters" (23). Frazier emphasizes Wideman's focus on imagination in this novel and the other two early ones.

Keith Byerman has written about the first two novels in "Queering Blackness: Race and Sexual Identity in *A Glance Away* and *Hurry Home*." Also, James W. Coleman, in *Blackness and Modernism: The Literary Career of John Edgar Wideman* (1989), and Doreatha Drummond Mbalia, in *John Edgar Wideman: Reclaiming the African Personality* (1995), have written about the early novels.

6. Byerman writes that the first two novels "have received relatively little critical attention, in large part . . . because the overt engagement with high modernism places them outside the conventional model of African American writing. Moreover, another aspect of these texts—the homoerotic—is even more troublesome for black critical discourse. Little room has been found for queer/gay studies in the analysis of black writing. Such presence in Wideman's early fiction is generally associated with the theme of modernist despair and sterility; in other words, the 'queer' is seen as the emblem of a failed modernity, intellectuality, and urban life" (93). It is not prominent in *Hurry Home*, but, as Byerman states, the relationship between Cecil Braithwaite and Charles Webb has homoerotic implications in the context of Webb's memories of sexual encounters with men. Byerman proposes an alternative reading in which both novels critique "racialized conceptions of gender."

7. The fascination with fire at the end particularly echoes the same motif in the first stream-of-consciousness section in Faulkner's *The Sound and the Fury*.

8. The O'Brien interview referenced is from 1972, when Wideman was making the evolution from modernism's influence to postmodernism's. The conception of history is postmodern in keeping with his published writing after 1981. The fact that his remarks relate to a modernist-influenced novel shows that one cannot always make clear distinctions between works published in the modernist and postmodern phases of his career. As with everything related to Wideman, there is always blending, conflation, and hybridization.

9. In describing himself, Cecil combines references to the Middle Passage with J. Alfred Prufrock's complaint about age: "I am tired of travel, weary of dancing once a day to whip music, nine-tailed cat songs. I grow old, I grow old" (66).

10. The clearest example of imagination's direct connection to actual oppression is the main conspirator Littleman, motivated by his constant imagination of past and present oppression, making a revolutionary speech, fighting the police, being beaten, and dying as a result. The portrayal of the close relationship between past and present oppression is part

of Wideman's writing throughout his career, as evidenced by the generally similar portrayal of oppression thirty years after *The Lynchers* in his auto/biography *The Island: Martinique* (2003), which is analyzed in chapter 1.

11. Ashraf H. A. Rushdy similarly describes the historical transformation of lynching from Littleman's perspective: "The plan of lynching in Littleman's mind . . . is meant to create conditions for African American self-definition; that is the primary transformation lynching undergoes, from a form of white terrorism to a site of black affirmation, from a destructive ritual to a unifying one" ("A Lynching in Blackface" 112). Rushdy argues that the novel is a critique of nationalism, which this act symbolizes: "Wideman's critique of black nationalism is not the kind of critique made by liberals in the sixties and seventies—that is, that black nationalism is racially divisive and that we should all gather under a less exclusive banner of a more integrated or multicultural America. His critique of black nationalism is ultimately a critique of nationalism itself" (119). According to Rushdy, Wideman gives no alternative to nationalism that will address oppression in this novel (123), but in later works suggests that family and community offer important benefits.

Also, see Trudier Harris's treatment of *The Lynchers* in *Exorcising Blackness: Historical and Literary Lynching and Burning Rituals* (1984).

12. Stream of consciousness still reveals the characters' thoughts and dreams in the novel. Writers use different forms of stream of consciousness, and Wideman utilizes several in different texts to reveal the intricate workings of characters' psyches. Frazier gives an example of one in *The Lynchers* in which the flow of thought in the mind of a character named Anthony moves between the contemplation of the body of his teacher and the uncomfortable feelings of the physical present where his coworkers are teasing him about his sexual innocence (*The Lynchers* 261; Frazier 25–26).

13. This move away from literary allusion and reference does not indicate a permanent trend in Wideman's writing. Later works present a large number of literary and critical allusions and references, but usually do not invoke modernism.

14. Sweetman is also the nickname of Wideman's father in the memoir *Fatheralong*, which characterizes the father and depicts a failed relationship between him and his wife in some of its stories. The broad similarities in *The Lynchers* and *Fatheralong* emphasize a point made earlier in this chapter: Wideman writes about the same characters and situations, a fictionalized version of the relationship between his father and mother in this case, in the early works that he writes about later. Another point, from chapter 1, is that the portrayals in both instances are fiction because both Wideman's fiction and auto/biographers are fictionalized.

15. Littleman recollects a prostitute who mocked his deformity during what turns out to be possibly the dream of Angela (127–28). The prostitute's actions sound too realistically cruel for Littleman to have dreamed the encounter; however, the incident could be a dream if it occurs in one.

16. Rushdy analyzes Saunders's feelings about the prostitute in the context of *The Lynchers*' negative critique of Black Nationalism ("A Lynching in Blackface" 117–19). According to the nationalist code, both black men and women who chose to have sexual relationships with whites were subject to violence.

17. Since all the characters' depictions and the text itself are so ensconced in dream/fantasy, it is hard to say if Littleman really dies at the end or if the ending is a manifestation

of Anthony's dream/fantasy (263–64). However, the narrative does seem to be describing the highly frustrated Anthony observing Littleman's death in the psychiatric ward where Littleman thought the hospital people would eventually put him.

3. *Hiding Place, Damballah,* and *Sent for You Yesterday*

1. The term "postmodern" also applies to the auto/biographies discussed in chapter 1.

2. "Poststructuralism" and "deconstruction" are virtually synonymous terms that refer to language systems, and critics include them under the rubric "postmodernism," which encompasses the entire range of artistic and human creation and interpretation of it.

3. See the definition and discussion of Great Time in chapter 1. See also Heather Andrade's "'Mosaic Memory': Auto/biographical Context(s) in John Edgar Wideman's *Brothers and Keepers,*" *Massachusetts Review* 40.3 (1999): 342–66. Andrade writes that "mosaic memory" is a fragmented collage of voices similar to the representation of stories in Great Time, and argues that the Homewood Trilogy, along with the auto/biography, "encapsulates, [and] simultaneously problematizes, [the] interfacing of 'mosaic memory' with the concept of 'Great Time,' a dynamic which fuels Wideman's philosophical ideals and underlies his literary vision" (343).

4. Both linear and circular figures of storytelling appear in Wideman's writing and are not contradictory. In *The Cattle Killing* (1996), for example, the circular figure represents endless oppressive narratives and the linear open-ended narrative creation that is potentially liberating. However, as with most things in Wideman's works, there are instances where the distinctions "bleed into each other," in Wideman's words, and are not clear.

5. A language with its biases embedded in words such as "black" and "African" in English is perhaps the most encompassing system. Prejudices are in the "system" that is the language and no less in the "systems" that are people speaking the language that are also its product because they cannot escape expressing reality through it. However, it is possible at least to attempt to subvert the embedded meaning of language as black people do on an everyday basis through language and as Wideman does by telling black stories that contest white ones.

6. The discussion here is similar to the one about Cecil's modernist dreaming in chapter 2. The emphasis on the actual storytelling that involves and engages others, as opposed to dreaming abstractly in isolation, makes the Homewood Trilogy and its stories postmodern.

7. The family tree at the beginning of *Hiding Place* names the surrogate character's father Edgar Lawson, making the surrogate's name John Lawson. In later works—*Fatheralong* for example—the father is still Edgar, but the family name is Wideman. The Homewood Trilogy's surrogate portrayals culminate in the characterization of Doot in *Sent for You Yesterday,* who is the same as John Lawson/John Edgar Wideman.

8. As Jacqueline Berben writes, this is a scene in which Bess symbolically births Tommy: "The image is so strong that his waking thoughts recreate the birth trauma" (527).

9. The discussion of *Damballah* will focus more on the role of song. In *Hiding Place,* song conveys elements of personal and communal spirituality in the characters' stories. Both Bess and Tommy re-create their stories and Homewood's partly through the memory of song. The singing of "Farther Along" at the Homewood A.M.E. Zion Church is at the core of Bess's positive story of her life with her husband and of the religious life of Homewood (22–23).

Similarly, one of the initial positive aspects of Tommy's story is the memory of him and the Homewood community being vivified and spiritualized through the singing of "My Lord, What a Morning" at the church (42).

10. John appears only briefly in *Hiding Place*. The intersubjective relationship is implied there, more strongly throughout *Damballah*, and even more in *Sent for You Yesterday*. The relationship is "uneasy" in *Sent for You Yesterday* because of the pain that he shares with the characters.

11. From the beginning of Wideman's career, point of view shifts fluidly. In the Homewood Trilogy, shifting point of view is most pronounced in the highly intersubjective *Sent for You Yesterday*.

12. Rushdy analyzes what the symbol of the letter writer means, writing that "the letter writer seems to be present, and therefore vulnerable, in a way that a narrator usually is not. The letter writer, we may say, gives the illusion of presence" ("Fraternal Blues" 322–23). For the purposes of my discussion, the "presence" of John Lawson along with everyone else in the past and present is important in John's concept of a participatory communal story.

13. This is the same incident portrayed at the beginning of *A Glance Away*.

14. The narration of the later work *Sent for You Yesterday* supports the implication that *Damballah* makes through its overall structure and the presence of John Lawson. In the later work, Doot, the surrogate narrator/writer, interacts with family and Homewood people, tells stories about what happened before he was born, sometimes speaks in the first person, and sometimes effaces himself in the third. He is always implicitly there, as is John Lawson in "Lizabeth: the Caterpillar Story" and the other pieces in *Damballah*.

15. John Bennion identifies the characters' connection: "Each character in *Sent for You Yesterday* is . . . linked through spirit and identity to every other" (143). The novel's epigraph suggests a similar connection: "Past lives live in us, through us. Each of us harbors the spirits of people who walked the earth before we did, and those spirits depend on us for continuing existence, just as we depend on their presence to live our lives to the fullest."

16. The description of Brother's skin is also Wideman's critique of race. Since Brother is supposedly black although he looks white, the fact that society calls him black shows that the racial designation is an arbitrary one made up for racist purposes. Wideman critiques the idea of race throughout his writing, most specifically in terms of an analysis of the paradigm of race in *Fatheralong* (1994) and *The Island: Martinique* (2003), discussed in chapter 1.

17. This is another version of the story told in *Damballah*'s "The Caterpillar Story."

18. The idea that Wilkes's piano songs are stories is similar to the idea that Reba Love Jackson's gospel songs are stories in *Damballah*'s "The Songs of Reba Love Jackson."

19. This image is reminiscent of a later one in *The Cattle Killing* (1996) in which the narrator is trapped by "[c]ircles within circles" of oppressive, nightmarish stories (149).

20. Brother's death on the railroad tracks has disparate associations with various parts of the novel. Brother's train nightmare in "In Heaven with Brother Tate" and playing on the tracks with Carl in part 1 (17–19) foreshadow his death by a train (or at least on the train tracks), and Carl's connection of his death to the ambiguous, mysterious "they" (120) relates to the train nightmare where some unknown force is propelling people, implicitly in Homewood, to horrible deaths (9–11). This is also a reminder of what John French says about Homewood "coming apart" after the departure of Albert Wilkes (67). Later in part 3,

in the story Doot tells about Brother, "In the [train] dream [Brother] had been Albert Wilkes, long dead Albert Wilkes coming back to Homewood again" (160), where "they" kill him like "they" kill Brother. The train dream prefigures much of the novel.

4. *Reuben* and *Philadelphia Fire*

1. See the analysis of postmodern stories in the Homewood Trilogy in chapter 3.

2. This figure associated with writing and storytelling also occurs specifically in *Sent for You Yesterday* and, later, in *The Cattle Killing*, and signifies the conception of stories in Wideman's writing after the early novels.

3. Philadelphia and Homewood are the novel's co-settings.

4. In "*Philadelphia Fire*, or the Shape of the City" (607–09), Jean-Pierre Richard provides a good analysis of the significance of Muybridge and his photography in *Reuben*.

5. Stephen Casmier says that "funk threatens to disrupt Wally's illusions and reconnect him to other bodies, displacing the disembodied, controllable memories and identities with inalienable bodies and their smells" ("The Funky Novels of John Edgar Wideman" 196).

6. Wideman has said that Cudjoe, also the name of Kwansa's son in *Reuben*, is a common name from the slavery past and West African tradition (Olander 167).

7. Zivanias is named for the alcoholic drink Zivania. Thinking of the accident, Cudjoe reflects on his name: "Maybe he couldn't resist the power in his name summoning him, *Zivanias, Zivanias*. Moonshine. Doomshine. Scattered on the water" (4).

8. Leslie W. Lewis talks about John being Cudjoe's "double": "In part 2, we are not only involved in Cudjoe's drama of consciousness . . . but are also involved in the drama of consciousness belonging to Cudjoe's double, Wideman" (154).

9. The writer John Wideman connects the two texts by describing his writing activities in *Philadelphia Fire*: "Arrived Maine Friday. Yesterday and today at old station on dock. Page proofs of *Ruben* to finish. Awake early. Try the old routines" (108).

10. The idea that Cudjoe and John are "brothers" writing the text is reminiscent of the auto/biography *Brothers and Keepers* (1984) in which the brothers John and Robby write the text in the fictional narrative that develops. This is another example of how fictional and auto/biographical works are similar in Wideman's writing.

11. In an interview, Wideman says the graffiti is produced by Simba the boy Cudjoe is looking for: "Simba Munto, the lion-man-boy, is out there in the street. It's his voice that energizes the raps. It's his voice that's in the background of Philadelphia. It's Simba and his friends who are putting graffiti on the walls. They're the ones who might be responsible for [James Baldwin's] fire next time unless all that negative energy and anger are somehow transformed to useful purposes—purposes that are useful to them" (Presson 110).

This seems to imply that iconic works like *The Tempest* have, in some instances at least, inscribed danger in children that is all too real, although it is not innately racial as white, Western texts would argue. Perhaps this is primarily true for Simba, and for black boys, but in part 3, interestingly, the danger has spread to white boys as well. Perhaps the "transform[ation] to useful purposes" implies the potential in the writing project that is *Philadelphia Fire*. Maybe this project is an attempt to change both the stereotypical illusion of race and the reality that language and story create. One should be aware of the illusion of race, but should concentrate on using stories in an ongoing process that attempts to move human life in a positive direction.

12. Cudjoe's words suggest multiple meanings. In the context of John's reference to an "airy other," Cudjoe is the "other" who can help John write by being the ubiquitous presence he initially strives to be who is "many places at once" (23), and in turn Cudjoe is John's "other" doing the same thing. On the other hand, in the context of Cudjoe's position in part 1, his words reference his need to escape the at least partly false vision of responsibility for his wife and sons that follows shortly.

13. John talks about staging The Tempest in the "late late 1960s" and not the mid-1980s, the time of the Philadelphia fire and the contemporary present of the novel. Most likely, he is intentionally conflating time to indicate how his rewriting must address a white myth that is pervasive in the 1960s, the 1980s, and essentially all times.

14. Cudjoe tries to tell many positive black stories, but a negative story about his character, generated from the white myth of blackness, is the clearest among all of them that emerge from everything he says. Along these same lines, he can present an analysis of the complex ways that the white story about Caliban works to affect black people, and thus ironically can relate the central part of the negative white story with authority and certainty, while he cannot do the same with a positive black one. He tells the white story in the context of the generally fragmented structure, but the authority and certainty of his voice when he tells it separates it from the diffident voice of the black stories.

15. Lewis says: "In the fragments of part two that represent the developing communication between Wideman and his son . . . it is not just difficulties but possibilities that are explored" (154). "In some ways . . . this story of Wideman's son extends Caliban into his 1980s self. And here, as in the reinterpreted Tempest, exactly who or what he remains to be seen" (156). Talking about the attempt of Cudjoe and his students to rewrite the play, Tracie Church Guzzio sees similar potential: "The act of writing their story and believing that it could be as true as the ones they are told . . . is the essence of Wideman's desire to create spaces in our narratives for new stories to be heard" (186).

16. Madhu Dubey says that "'The Book of Life' is Wideman's title for the MOVE text, called The Book or The Guidelines, which was disseminated in a variety of forms to an audience wider than the MOVE community" (587). She further says that Wideman models Richard Corey after a man named Donald Glassey who coauthored the Book with King the MOVE leader, and later became an informant against MOVE. In American poetry, Richard Corey is the subject of E. A. Robinson's poem "Richard Corey," in which Corey commits suicide as he does in Philadelphia Fire, which seems to be more than a coincidental parallel.

17. The story of vengeful children implies the story of Simba, the lost boy from the fire, and Wideman's son, and the account of children who take revenge strongly connects with the reference to the graffiti of the vengeful Kaliban's Kiddie Korps from part 1 (88–92). The Kiddy Korner in the quotation that follows from part 3 of the text (188) is a play on Kaliban's Kiddie Korps and a reference to the legacy of the oppression of Caliban, derived from the white story and particularly from The Tempest.

18. J. B.'s imagining of the palimpsestlike layering of his story in terms of "somebody else's dream in a book" is reminiscent of dreams and identities in Sent for You Yesterday that

are converging, conflated stories. The stories and emblems of stories in *Sent for You Yesterday* are layers of a palimpsest from the perspective of J. B.'s thoughts and in the context of part 3 of *Philadelphia Fire*. Perhaps the stories told by brothers, doubles, and twins in *Reuben* are layers of a palimpsest in this context also.

19. Society tries to solve its problems by taking action against the "bad guys" as defined in its mythic texts like *The Tempest*, but this does not work (189). Cudjoe's imaginative (re) writing in the concluding section of the novel opens up the entire society's possibilities as well as J. B.'s, other black imaginative and formal writers', and black people's generally.

20. Dubey concludes that "*Philadelphia Fire* strains to grasp the modernist solace of a distinctive stylistic signature, but the illegibility of this signature conveys its author's strong suspicion of a literary language that cannot render itself readable to the underprivileged urban audiences it wishes to address" (593). Instead of revealing Wideman's suspicion of his own language, I would say that the text's theme and formal structure are symbolic and representative.

5. *The Cattle Killing, Two Cities,* and *Fanon*

1. See the discussion in chapter 3 about defamiliarization in *Reuben* and *Philadelphia Fire*.

2. See the discussion of Great Time in chapter 1 and of postmodernism in chapter 3.

3. Tracie Church Guzzio analyzes *The Cattle Killing*'s complexity (180–82). She describes the young preacher's vision in the fit as a "[crossroads where] the past, present, and future intersect," and also talks about how his vision potentially makes various female characters different embodiments of the same person (183).

4. Accounts of Baartman and the Xhosa cattle killing are available from a wide range of sources, including easily accessible ones such as Google.com. Also, there are different spellings of Saartjie Baartman's first name. In some accounts her first name is given as Saarti.

5. See Gysin's discussion of the historical Xhosa cattle killing regarding Nongqawuse ("Do Not Fall Asleep in Your Enemy's Dream" 623–25).

6. Dr. Thrush's name suggests the act of rape, but there is no evidence from historical sources that Dr. Rush was a rapist.

7. The treatment of gangs relates to the death in gang warfare of Wideman's nephew Omar Wideman, the son of his incarcerated brother Robert, whom the memoir *Brothers and Keepers* portrays. *Two Cities* is dedicated to Omar; his death is an additional tragedy in Wideman's family along with the incarceration for murder of Robert and Wideman's son Jacob.

8. The book John is writing is more like an auto/biography than any other novel. It is broadly similar to the auto/biography *Brothers and Keepers* (1984) because, like the story of Wideman's incarcerated brother, Robert (also a character in *Fanon*), it is someone else's life story that is equally important to and inseparable from the writer/character John's.

9. The word "bricolage" comes from French anthropologist Claude Levi-Strauss. In broad, general usage and in the terms of Fanon's words in the novel, it means improvising and taking the materials that are available to create something.

10. "Bothers" and "doubles" are the terms used in *Reuben*.

11. The bloody, severed head relates *Fanon* to the contemporary times of global acts of

torture and terrorism. This is appropriate because, although Fanon died in 1961, he dealt with tortured and terrorized patients in his life, and torture and terrorism are more than contemporary threats that America and other "white" countries face.

12. This is from a manuscript of a journal that Fanon kept on a reconnaissance mission during the Algerian revolution (see Macey 438–40).

13. Wideman uses Macey's account on pages 438–45 of his book as the basis for the story about Fanon in "Africa."

14. The text continues to develop in the same patterns in the intervening sections before this last one in part 1. A memorable point at the end of "Pittsburgh—a Hospital" is John's imagination of his mother comforting the dying Fanon: "Fanon's mind skips off to other pastures, different sleeps, different islands. Mom mopping his brow like she used to mop mine when I had a fever" (76).

15. Reverend Frank Felder also appears briefly in the imaginary life of Mother Bess in *Hiding Place:* "Black Frank Felder, his big head like a bowling ball above the white collar, his tiny eyes squeezed shut, his mouth pained, busy at the corners like he's trying to talk to himself while he's singing the words of the hymn" (22).

16. Jean-Luc Godard is a French and Swiss filmmaker who was part of the French New Wave movement. His radical techniques challenged the conventions of mainstream filmmaking. Writer/characters often invoke other creative artists and their methods in Wideman's works.

17. Macey (294–95) also talks about and quotes from this part of *The Wretched of the Earth*.

18. Comparing Macey's accounts to Wideman's text, one cannot always be sure of the correspondence; however, clearly the "Africa" section of part 1 and much of part 3 utilize the "facts" from Macey in the imagination of Fanon.

19. The reference to a movie alludes back to part 2's central cinematic symbol and to the Lumière brothers' pioneer work in filmmaking.

20. Neither the novel *Fanon* nor biographies of Fanon state that his suffering and death from leukemia at age thirty-six were a direct consequence of his revolutionary life. However, both *Fanon* and the biographies portray a series of events that always leave open the possibility to speculate that his suffering and death were somehow linked to his lifelong revolutionary sacrifice for others.

21. The auto/biography *Fatheralong* (1994) also ends with "Love" followed by a period. At the end of this book, the narrator is trying to express the power of love that binds fathers and sons. In *Fanon,* John is talking about love in a broader context, but similarly the connection between John and the son Romeo is part of the context. Perhaps the period after "Love" also expresses similar possibilities and reservations in the two books.

22. Part 2 portrays the problems inherent in the idea that movie scripts that are acted necessarily cut through to the reality of human being better than writing can. In spite of the questions raised in part 2, *Fanon* suggests an ongoing, *living* script of life.

WORKS CITED AND OTHER SOURCES

Andrade, Heather Russell. "'Mosaic Memory': Auto/Biographical Context(s) in John Edgar Wideman's *Brothers and Keepers.*" *Massachusetts Review* 40.3 (1999): 342–66.

———. "Race, Representation, and Intersubjectivity in the Works of John Edgar Wideman." In *Critical Essays on John Edgar Wideman,* edited by Keith Byerman and Bonnie TuSmith, 43–56. Knoxville: University of Tennessee Press, 2006.

Bennion, John. "The Shape of the Memory in John Edgar Wideman's *Sent for You Yesterday.*" *Black American Literature Forum* 20.1–2 (1986): 143–50.

Berben, Jacqueline. "Beyond Discourse: The Unspoken Versus Words in the Fiction of John Edgar Wideman." *Callaloo* 8.3 (1985): 525–34.

Berben-Masi, Jacqueline. "From *Brothers and Keepers* to *Two Cities:* Social and Cultural Consciousness, Art and Imagination: An Interview with John Edgar Wideman." *Callaloo* 22.3 (1999): 568–84.

———. "Mother Goose and Brother Loon: The Fairy-Tale-in-the-Tale as Vehicle of Displacement." *Callaloo* 22.3 (1999): 594–602.

———. "Of Basketball and Beads: Following the Threads of One's Origins." In *Critical Essays on John Edgar Wideman,* edited by Keith Byerman and Bonnie TuSmith, 31–41. Knoxville: University of Tennessee Press, 2006.

———. "Prodigal and Prodigy: Fathers and Sons in Wideman's Work." *Callaloo* 22.3 (1999): 677–84.

Bergevin, Gerald W. "'Traveling Here Below': John Edgar Wideman's *The Island: Martinique* and the Strategy of Melancholy." In *Critical Essays on John Edgar Wideman,* edited by Keith Byerman and Bonnie TuSmith, 71–89. Knoxville: University of Tennessee Press, 2006.

Berry, Stacey L. "The Individual and the Collective: Threatening Blackness in Wideman's *Philadelphia Fire.*" In *Critical Essays on John Edgar Wideman,* edited by Keith Byerman and Bonnie TuSmith, 161–73. Knoxville: University of Tennessee Press, 2006.

Birat, Kathie. "'All Stories Are True': Prophecy, History, and Story in *The Cattle Killing.*" *Callaloo* 22.3 (1999): 629–43.

Byerman, Keith. "Introduction: Wideman's Career and Critical Reception." In *Critical Essays on John Edgar Wideman*, edited by Byerman and Bonnie TuSmith, x–xii. Knoxville: University of Tennessee Press, 2006.

———. *John Edgar Wideman: A Study of the Short Fiction*. New York: Twayne, 1998.

———. "Queering Blackness: Race and Sexual Identity in *A Glance Away* and *Hurry Home*." In *Critical Essays on John Edgar Wideman*, edited by Byerman and Bonnie TuSmith, 93–105. Knoxville: University of Tennessee Press, 2006.

Carden, Mary Paniccia. "'If the City Is a Man': Founders and Fathers, Cities and Sons in John Edgar Wideman's *Philadelphia Fire*." *Contemporary Literature* 44.3 (2003): 472–500.

Casmier, Stephen. "The Funky Novels of John Edgar Wideman: Odor and Ideology in *Reuben, Philadelphia Fire*, and *The Cattle Killing*." In *Critical Essays on John Edgar Wideman*, edited by Keith Byerman and Bonnie TuSmith, 191–204. Knoxville: University of Tennessee Press, 2006.

———. "Resisting the Frame Up: *Philadelphia Fire* and the Liberated Voices of Ramona Africa and Margaret Jones." *Cycnos* 19.2 (2002): 225–40.

Cherki, Alice. *Frantz Fanon: A Portrait*. Ithaca: Cornell University Press, 2006.

Coleman, James W. *Black Male Fiction and the Legacy of Caliban*. Lexington: University of Kentucky Press, 2001.

———. *Blackness and Modernism: The Literary Career of John Edgar Wideman*. Jackson: University Press of Mississippi, 1989.

———. *Faithful Vision: Treatments of the Sacred, Spiritual, and Supernatural in Twentieth-Century African American Fiction*. Baton Rouge: Louisiana State University Press, 2006.

Douglas, Jennifer D. "'Ill Seen Ill Said': Tropes of Vision and the Articulation of Race Relations in *The Cattle Killing*." In *Critical Essays on John Edgar Wideman*, edited by Keith Byerman and Bonnie TuSmith, 205–20. Knoxville: University of Tennessee Press, 2006.

Dreiser, Petra. "Black, Not Blank: Photography's (Invisible) Archives in John Edgar Wideman's *Two Cities*." *Mosaic* 37.4 (2004): 185–201.

Dubey, Madhu. "Literature and Urban Crisis: John Edgar Wideman's *Philadelphia Fire*." *African American Review* 32.4 (1998): 579–95.

Ehlen, Patrick. *Frantz Fanon: A Spiritual Biography*. New York: Crossroad, 2000.

Fanon, Frantz. *Black Skin, White Masks*. New York: Grove Press, 1967.

———. *A Dying Colonialism*. 1965. New York: Grove Press, 1967.

———. *Toward the African Revolution: Political Essays*. New York: Grove Press, 1967.

———. *The Wretched of the Earth*. 1963. New York: Grove Press, 1968.

Feith, Michel. "'The Benefit of the Doubt': Openness and Closure in *Brothers and Keepers*." *Callaloo* 22.3 (1999): 665–75.

Frazier, Kermit. "The Novels of John Edgar Wideman." *Black World* 24 (1975): 18–35.

Gibson, Nigel C. *Fanon: The Postcolonial Imagination*. Cambridge, Mass.: Polity Press, 2003.

Grandjeat, Yves-Charles. "Brother Figures: The Rift and Riff in John E. Wideman's Fiction." *Callaloo* 22.3 (1999): 615–22.

———. "'These Strange Dizzy Pauses': Silence as Common Ground in J. E. Wideman's Texts." *Callaloo* 22.3 (1999): 685–94.

Guzzio, Tracie Church. "'All My Father's Texts': John Edgar Wideman's Historical Vision in *Philadelphia Fire, The Cattle Killing,* and *Fatheralong*." In *Critical Essays on John Edgar Wideman*, edited by Keith Byerman and Bonnie TuSmith, 175–89. Knoxville: University of Tennessee Press, 2006.

Gysin, Fritz. "'Do Not Fall Asleep in Your Enemy's Dream': John Edgar Wideman and the Predicaments of Prophecy." *Callaloo* 22.3 (1999): 623–38.

———. "John Edgar Wideman's 'Fever.'" *Callaloo* 22.3 (1999): 715–26.

Harris, Trudier. "An Aborted Attempt at Reversing the Ritual: John Wideman." *Exorcising Blackness: Historical and Literary Lynching and Burning Rituals*, 129–47. Bloomington: Indiana University Press, 1984.

Hennessy, C. Margot. "Listening to the Secret Mother: Reading John Edgar Wideman's *Brothers and Keepers*." In *American Women's Autobiography: Fea(s)ts of Memory*, edited by Margo Culley, 295–321. Madison: University of Wisconsin Press, 1992.

Howley, Colin. "'Ball and Chain': The Basketball Court and the Trope of the Prison Yard in Contemporary American Narratives." *Aethlon* 21.1 (2003): 79–91.

Hutcheon, Linda. *A Poetics of Postmodernism*. 1992. London: Routledge, 1988.

———. *The Politics of Postmodernism*. 1989. London: Routledge, 1989.

Jahn, Karen F. "Will the Circle Be Unbroken? Jazzing Story in *Hoop Roots*." In *Critical Essays on John Edgar Wideman*, edited by Keith Byerman and Bonnie TuSmith, 57–70. Knoxville: University of Tennessee Press, 2006.

Janifer, Raymond E. "Looking Homewood: The Evolution of John Edgar Wideman's Folk Imagination." In *Contemporary Black Men's Fiction and Drama*, edited by Keith Clark, 54–70. Urbana: University of Illinois Press, 2001.

Julien, Claude Fernand Yvon. "Figures of Life in *Fatheralong*." In *Critical Essays on John Edgar Wideman*, edited by Keith Byerman and Bonnie TuSmith, 17–29. Knoxville: University of Tennessee Press, 2006.

Lee, James Kyung-Jin. "Where the Talented Tenth Meets the Model Minority: The Price of Privilege in Wideman's *Philadelphia Fire* and Lee's *Native Speaker*." *Novel* 35.2–3 (2002): 231–57.

Lewis, Leslie W. "*Philadelphia Fire* and *The Fire Next Time*: Wideman Responds to Baldwin." In *Critical Essays on John Edgar Wideman*, edited by Keith Byerman and Bonnie TuSmith, 145–59. Knoxville: University of Tennessee Press, 2006.

Lynch, Lisa. "The Fever Next Time: The Race of Disease and the Disease of Racism in John Edgar Wideman." *American Literary History* 14.4 (2002): 776–804.

Macey, David. *Frantz Fanon: A Biography.* New York: Picador USA, 2001.

Mbalia, Doreatha Drummond. *John Edgar Wideman: Reclaiming the African Personality.* Selinsgrove, Pa.: Susquehanna University Press, 1995.

Morace, Robert A. "The Facts in Black and White: Cheever's *Falconer,* Wideman's *Philadelphia Fire.*" In *Powerless Fictions? Ethics, Cultural Critique, and American Fiction in the Age of Postmodernism,* edited by Ricardo Miguel Alfonso, 85–112. Amsterdam: Rodopi, 1996.

Moreno, Michael P. "The Last Iron Gate: Negotiating the Incarceral Spaces of John Edgar Wideman's *Brothers and Keepers.*" *Journal X* 9.1 (2004) 53–70.

O'Brien, John. "John Wideman." In *Conversations with John Edgar Wideman,* edited by Bonnie TuSmith, 5–13. Jackson: University Press of Mississippi, 1998.

Olander, Renée. "An Interview with John Edgar Wideman." In *Conversations with John Edgar Wideman,* edited by Bonnie TuSmith, 165–79. Jackson: University Press of Mississippi, 1998.

Page, Eugene Philip. "'Familiar Strangers': The Quest for Connection and Self-Knowledge in *Brothers and Keepers.*" In *Critical Essays on John Edgar Wideman,* edited by Keith Byerman and Bonnie TuSmith, 3–15. Knoxville: University of Tennessee Press, 2006.

Pearsall, Susan. "'Narratives of Self' and the Abdication of Authority in John Edgar Wideman's *Philadelphia Fire.*" *Melus* 26.2 (2001): 15–46.

Presson, Rebekah. "John Edgar Wideman." In *Conversations with John Edgar Wideman,* edited by Bonnie TuSmith, 105–12. Jackson: University Press of Mississippi, 1998.

Ramsey, Priscilla R. "John Edgar Wideman's First Fiction: Voice and the Modernist Narrative." *CLA Journal* 41.1 (1997): 1–23.

Raynaud, Claudine. "'Mask to Mask. The "Real" Joke': Surfiction/Autofiction, or the Tale of the Purloined Watermelon." *Callaloo* 22.3 (1999): 695–712.

Richard, Jean-Pierre. "From Slavers to Drunken Boats: A Thirty-Year Palimpsest in John Edgar Wideman's Fiction." *Callaloo* 22.3 (1999): 656–64.

———. "*Philadelphia Fire,* or the Shape of a City." *Callaloo* 22.3 (1999): 603–13.

Rodriguez, Denise. "Homewood's 'Music of Invisibility': John Edgar Wideman's *Sent for You Yesterday* and the Black Urban Tradition." In *Critical Essays on John Edgar Wideman,* edited by Keith Byerman and Bonnie TuSmith, 127–44. Knoxville: University of Tennessee Press, 2006.

Rowell, Charles H. "An Interview with John Edgar Wideman." In *Conversations with John Edgar Wideman,* edited by Bonnie TuSmith, 86–104. Jackson: University Press of Mississippi, 1998.

Ruffin, Kimberly N. "Mourning in the 'Second Middle Passage': Visual and Verbal Praxis in John Edgar Wideman's *Two Cities*." *CLA Journal* 48.4 (2005): 415–39.

Rushdy, Ashraf H. A. "Fraternal Blues: John Edgar Wideman's Homewood Trilogy." *Contemporary Literature* 32.3 (1991): 312–45.

———. "'A Lynching in Blackface': John Edgar Wideman's Reflections on the Nation Question." In *Critical Essays on John Edgar Wideman*, edited by Keith Byerman and Bonnie TuSmith, 107–26. Knoxville: University of Tennessee Press, 2006.

Samuels, Wilfred. "Going Home: A Conversation with John Edgar Wideman." In *Conversations with John Edgar Wideman*, edited by Bonnie TuSmith, 14–31. Jackson: University Press of Mississippi, 1998.

Schmidt, Klaus H. "Reading Black Postmodernism: John Edgar Wideman's *Reuben*." In *Flip Sides: New Critical Essays in American Literature*, edited by Klaus H. Schmidt, 81–102. New York: Peter Lang, 1995.

Silverblatt, Michael. "Interview with John Edgar Wideman about *Fatheralong*." In *Conversations with John Edgar Wideman*, edited by Bonnie TuSmith, 158–64. Jackson: University Press of Mississippi, 1998.

Simpson, Tyrone R., II. "'And the Arc of His Witness Explained Nothing': Black Flanerie and Traumatic Photorealism in Wideman's *Two Cities*." In *Critical Essays on John Edgar Wideman*, edited by Keith Byerman and Bonnie TuSmith, 221–39. Knoxville: University of Tennessee Press, 2006.

TuSmith, Bonnie. "Benefit of the Doubt: A Conversation with John Edgar Wideman." In *Conversations with John Edgar Wideman*, edited by TuSmith, 195–219. Jackson: University Press of Mississippi, 1998.

———. "Introduction: The Value of Reading Wideman." In *Critical Essays on John Edgar Wideman*, edited by Keith Byerman andTuSmith, vii–x. Knoxville: University of Tennessee Press, 2006.

———. "John Edgar Wideman." In *Conversations with John Edgar Wideman*, edited by TuSmith, 119–25. Jackson: University Press of Mississippi, 1998.

———. "'One More Time': John Edgar Wideman's *Sent for You Yesterday*." *All My Relatives: Community in Contemporary Ethnic American Literature,* 84–94. Ann Arbor: University of Michigan Press, 1993.

———. "Optical Trickerism: Dissolving and Shapeshifting in the Works of John Edgar Wideman." In *Critical Essays on John Edgar Wideman*, edited by Keith Byerman and Bonnie TuSmith, 243–58. Knoxville: University of Tennessee Press, 2006.

Varsava, Jerry. "'Woven of Many Strands': Multiple Subjectivity in John Edgar Wideman's *Philadelphia Fire*." *Critique* 41.1 (2000): 425–44.

Waligora-Davis, Nicole A. "The Ghetto: Illness and the Formation of the 'Suspect' in American Polity." *Forum for Modern Language Studies* 40.2 (2004): 182–203.